S0-BDO-640

RAISING
WINNERS

RAISING WINNERS

A Parent's Guide to Helping Kids Succeed On and Off the Playing Field

SHARI YOUNG KUCHENBECKER, Ph.D.

TIMES BOOKS

RANDOM HOUSE

Copyright © 2000 by Raising Winners, Inc.

All rights reserved under International and Pan-American Copyright Conventions. Published in the United States by Times Books, a division of Random House, Inc., New York, and simultaneously in Canada by Random House of Canada Limited, Toronto.

Library of Congress Cataloging-in-Publication Data
Kuchenbecker, Shari Young.
    Raising winners : a parent's guide to helping kids succeed on and off the playing field /
Shari Young Kuchenbecker.—1st ed.
        p.   cm.
    Includes index.
    ISBN 0-8129-3167-X (alk. paper)
    1. Sports for children—Psychological aspects.   2. Parenting—Psychological aspects.
3. Self-esteem in children.   I. Title.
GV709.2.K83   2000

                                                                                    99-45023

Random House website address: www.randomhouse.com

Printed in the United States of America on acid-free paper

98765432

First Edition

This book is dedicated to
all parents investing love and time
into their children
(for you are all true winners)

and to my family
for sharing growing . . . together

What Makes Winners?

A winner is . . .

☆ **W**illing (wants to learn, coachable, is motivated)

Win or lose, rain or shine, good day or bad, the real winner is the kid who is always there. Whether they are in the starting lineup or not, they are willing to do what they can do for the team.

—Coach Dick Held, AYSO soccer, Pacific Palisades

☆ **I**nvested (dedicated, loves competition, is a team player)

Intelligent, unselfish team players—hard-working, exceptionally quick and maneuverable for their height, and far more interested in team results than in individual statistics.

—Coach John Wooden, UCLA basketball, ten national championships in twelve years; first individual to be inducted into the Basketball Hall of Fame as a player and a coach

☆ **N**egative—

☆ **N**OT! (has a positive attitude, has good sportsmanship, handles losing well)

A winner is a kid who hates to lose, but it is more than just that. I remember Danny Farmer after a big loss. He never said a word. He took off running at incredible speed around the gym and made a CIRCLE OF FIRE. He made it around the second time and stopped at the back line. He put his hands out in front of him, flat palmed, sort of like he was pushing on a huge glass wall and he blew out as he pushed. His face was bright red, but as he pulled his hands down to his sides, he was calm again. It was his way of getting re-focused for the next game. It was pretty clear he was going to lead the team on to winning . . . and he did.

—Coach Bill Ferguson, Los Angeles Athletic Club director, seven-time Junior Olympic gold medalist coach

☆ **E**nthusiastic (loves to play)

Kids need to be genuinely coachable, learn to cope with the ups, and especially the downs, of competition, and work hard to maintain that enthusiasm and pure love of the game that they had as novices. Winners are kids who are enthusiastic and *love to play*.

—Coach Jeff Porter, Brentwood High School two-time girls' volleyball state champion coach

☆ **R**einforcing (listens, gives best effort always, encourages/praises others)

When someone really gives it their all, puts their best effort out there during practices and in games, listens when you talk, those are the kids who see the court. It's great when you see a player revving the team up, making a difference not only in their play but their teammates, as well, and it makes a difference in how you feel about being a coach, too.

    —Coach Jesse Quiroz, Harvard-Westlake High School, California state champion coach; Santa Monica Beach Club director

☆ **S**elf-Efficacious (tries hard every time, strives to improve)

Winners say, "Give me the chance—I'll get the job done." Real Winners take personal responsibility, never blame other players, and just do what they know how to do.

    —Coach Chris McGee, teacher, two-time national championship coach

Contents

AUTHOR'S NOTE   xi

ACKNOWLEDGMENTS   xvii

INTRODUCTION Why Play Sports?   3

1. What's the Right Sport for Your Child?   15

2. Self-Efficacy = Lifelong Success   35

3. Balance in the Young Athlete's Life   62

4. All-Star Athlete Parents   76

5. "I Love to Play!": Motivation and the Young Athlete   88

6. Coaches Need Strokes, Too   105

7. Eating and Sleeping Right to Play Well   121

8. Feelings: Competition Brews a Thick Hormone Soup   140

9. The Growing Athlete: Injuries, Prevention, and Time   164

10. Self-Efficacy, the Mental Game, and Learning   188

11. Role Models: Just Do It!   201

12. Athlete Spurts, Stalls, and Burnout: Parents' Job As
     Jock Supporters   217

13. Turning Girls and Boys into Great People Through Athletics 241

14. College Scholarships: Academic Success +
     Athletic Excellence + Balance   263

15. Fun, Perspective, and Other Mysteries   286

EPILOGUE   The Van   297

APPENDIX A   Youth Athletic Organization Harassment Policy   299

APPENDIX B   Sports Proactive Information Formative Feedback
     Inventory   305

APPENDIX C   National Sports Organizations:
     Resources for Parents   307

APPENDIX D   Four-Finger Whistling   309

REFERENCES   311

INDEX   313

Author's Note

I am the parent of three young athletes. I've earned the title of Soccer Mom and_____Mom (fill in the blank with a sport) honestly—on plank-hard bleachers in competition arenas from dawn to dusk and on mud-slick sidelines in a downpour. In the process, I've learned some fundamental truths about kids, competition, and success. Oh yes, and I also happen to have a lifelong athlete for a husband, a doctorate in child development and education, as well as help from coaches, kids in sports, professionals, all-star athletes, parents, and professional athletes who generously shared their secrets.

This book is not about my children's athletic success nor my success as a parent. In fact, my mistakes and regulation goofs in parenting young athletes make for better reading. In my worst moments, I once coaxed a coach to put my child on a team, hollered at a referee, and pushed my child to play on a sprained ankle. In better moments, I have hosted team cookouts, collected money for coaches' gifts, devised a positive system for encouraging volunteer coaches to praise young athletes, typed sideline cheering sheets, kept my mouth shut, and given out 1,673 soccer participation trophies in one year. From the worst to the best, this book was written with the hope that you might do better and avoid some of my well-meant but nonetheless real mistakes, so that the new generation of young athletes might have a better psychological world in which to develop.

The title *Raising Winners* came from such a mistake. I wanted to grab those parents who, like myself early on, naïvely connect *winning a game* with *being a winner.* I titled this book *Raising Winners* to reach parents who want to help their child win more games while learning to raise their children to be real winners as people. If they are winners as people, some of our children will go on to win a lot of games, but all will go on to become better individuals. Sports have a lot of lessons to teach—some of them tough, some of them fun—but all of them valuable, if we as parents can manage to facilitate the learning process.

SPORTS PSYCHOLOGY TRAINING

My window into competitive sports opened in 1971 when I married a terrific athlete and ex-center of Stanford University's basketball team. My then-new spouse was using his competitive athletic skills dissecting cadavers at UCLA medical school, and we were a pair of poor graduate students. While I worked three part-time jobs and pursued a Ph.D., we entertained ourselves with the fruits our UCLA student IDs could provide. These included student seats at football, baseball, tennis, and basketball games. (Lew Alcindor, aka Kareem, had graduated, but UCLA was on top with Bill Walton and Sven Nater.) The student IDs also gave us access to tennis courts, swimming pools, the bowling alley, and pool tables at Ackerman Union.

My first practical lesson in sports psychology was in the student stands of Pauley Pavilion. Here we were, sitting in the nosebleed section at a 1972 UCLA basketball game. Sorting out whose basket was whose and zone defense versus double-teaming all seemed fairly logical, but fouls were a puzzle. If a player fouled and the referee didn't see it, this was good. If a player fouled and the referee saw, sometimes it was good and sometimes bad. Odd system. Taking time from his binocular-assisted observations, my spouse explained that the knocking around under the basket of a low-percentage free-thrower was a good maneuver if it stopped the shooter from scoring. I got it! Sports have absolute (algorithmic) and conditional (heuristic) rules of logic. I wanted to explain this interesting insight, but my spouse, hereafter called XXLT, watched every play through 10X magnification, reverent silence, and acuity only an ex–basketball center can claim. Tutorials were reserved for time-outs, halftimes, and an occasional spontaneous explanation.

At the first basketball halftime, as all the young players grabbed their warm-up jackets and headed for the locker room, I asked XXLT, "What do they all do during the break? Drink juice? Lie on tables and get massages from pretty girls?" I was right out of the power-of-positive-reinforcement bachelor's program at Stanford, and it was pretty obvious these boys needed a bit of nurturing and praise for their excellent work.

"Ha!" said XXLT, "the coach yells and screams and tells them the stupid stuff they did in the first half." He was not into tact nor praise, having been raised in the rigors of the old school traditional sports-training programs. He was a master of "constructive criticism," calling spades spades, and I was dumbfounded. What? No praise? No special recognition for trying hard? Where did the players get their motivation? I thought games were supposed to be fun. Obviously, I had never been a competitive athlete from the old school.

While XXLT continued his regular tutorials in sports education, we both progressed in our degree programs. In the early seventies I took an assistant professorship at Chapman College. As fate would have it, I was assigned to teach the psychological and sociological foundations of education to two large sections of would-be teachers. A memorable proportion of those students came from the very successful Chapman baseball teams (1975–1976; 1976–1977).

POWER OF A ROLE MODEL

Everyone learns by watching. In multiple opportunities to observe coaches in the seventies and eighties, I saw only one truly exceptional coach. Coach John Wooden of the UCLA basketball team was an on-court gentleman with clear compassion for his players. I *knew* he was on the right track, and recent research on coaching has supported my early assessment. With intuitive confidence, I sent my Chapman baseball players to watch Coach Wooden as a powerful positive role model, and I thanked XXLT for giving me the opportunity to start those athlete-teachers-to-be on the road toward success.

I continued teaching at Chapman for many years, receiving my doctorate in 1976 and tenure in 1978. Those were treasured years as XXLT (a resident in surgery and later faculty at UCLA) and I persisted in the ad hoc sports development program. My tennis game improved slowly, but my sports stories quickly became a source of terrific university lecture material. My students taught me much when they pushed me to explain hard-to-get concepts. Sport stories ruled! Terms like "intermittent reinforcement" sounded fuzzy, but made perfect sense when rephrased as success in stealing bases. When John Wooden's book, *They Call Me Coach,* was published, it became assigned reading for all my teacher-education athletes.

Our children were born in 1978, 1980, and 1984, and I continued teaching at Mount St. Mary's College, UCLA, Pepperdine, and Loyola Marymount University while holding a lot of team mom jobs. Three seemingly divergent forces wove my life—teaching psychology, raising children, and attending sporting events. My first goal in life has been to simply raise the children well. (Graham and Susan Nash—you have been on the right track about kids for a long time.) I've learned a lot about raising kids in the thick soup of competitive sports.

KIDS IN SPORTS

As our children moved into competitive athletics, not only did they outgrow me, but the challenges they faced were big—height, injuries, coordination, motivation, competition for spots, coaches, team chemistry, wins and losses. We wanted to raise winners in every sense of the word. Hundreds of halftimes, time-outs, and smelly socks later, the picture of the Real Winner among kids in sports began to emerge.

Our two girls and one boy have participated in volleyball, basketball, soccer, baseball, football, tennis, Ping-Pong, archery, badminton, surfing, in-line skating, archery, paintball, darts, horseshoes, snorkeling, horseback riding, bodyboarding, boogieboarding, skiing, surfing, biking, golf, gymnastics, dance, beach and grass volleyball, wallyball, swimming, and a few more I've probably forgotten for now. Ironically, the oldest didn't enter sports until the age of twelve (her university team won the 1996 and 1997 NCAA volleyball championship), and the youngest started sports by hanging from the trees in front of the house at fourteen months and began self-styled skating lessons on her sister's skates in the kitchen at two years old.

GIRLS AND BOYS IN SPORTS

By 1990, the substantial mosaic of sports had changed. Our family went to see the high school homecoming game. It was a traditional football afternoon right down to the hotdogs, ketchup, brisk wind, pompoms, and cheerleaders. (The only truly uncommon aspect of the game was getting to see Fred Savage make a homecoming touchdown. Where was my Nikon for *that* priceless photo op—no flash needed. His joy lit up the end zone!)

Following the celebrated touchdowns and doleful off-key singing of the alma mater, fans were encouraged to go into the gym for eighth-grade, junior varsity, and varsity girls' volleyball games. We moved with the crowd, herd-style, to the school gymnasium. We paused in the door of the gym, as the game was already in progress.

Rows of high school students—boys, girls, men, and women filled the bleachers. I stopped. Women on the court and men in the stands! Boys and MEN were cheering with gusto for a GIRL. Pass, set, and the outside hitter made a great spike. The ball shanked off the opponent's forearms and the crowd jumped up with a booming cheer. MEN cheering for WOMEN! Guys were shouting and whistling in appreciation of a woman's *talent* with a volleyball. Amazing. Moreover, the girls wore comfortable shoes and sports bras, not the push-up bras of the cheerleaders I grew up with.

The girls on the volleyball court were learning things women of my era never learned. These young women were learning to compete openly. They were learning to win. More important, they were learning to lose. They were learning to make mistakes in the middle of the court . . . and keep on playing. Generations of solo dishwashers and diaper changers afraid to make a public mistake faded before my eyes as I saw winners on both sides of the net who were willing to enter the competitive athletic arena.

In 1971, one in seventeen women played a sport. Now, 55 million—one in three women—call themselves athletically active. Two new magazines recently came out on women's athletics—*Sports Illustrated for Women* and *Condé Nast Sports for Women,* now *Women's Sports & Fitness.* The primary audience for these magazines is the twenty- to thirty-year-old woman who grew up under Title IX, the 1972 Supreme Court rule mandating that schools spend equally for men's and women's sports programs. While few programs came close to equal spending, the essential concept of the 1972 mandate has been identified as facilitating the entry of women into the potentially rewarding world of competitive sports. The controversial 1997 Supreme Court ruling mandating equality of collegiate men's and women's sports funding in proportion to the college population independent of student interest promises to keep the momentum moving forward.

I will be the first to point out that competition is not new for women. Women have a long history of daily competition in nebulous social arenas and also have enjoyed forays into popular athletics including skating, skiing, tennis, and even a women's baseball league, but the major advances have been recent. Women's indoor and beach volleyball enjoyed national interest in the 1996 Olympics, and the Women's National Basketball Association (WNBA) and the American Basketball League (ABL) for women formed in 1997. In July 1999, more than ninety thousand fans crowded the Rose Bowl to cheer the U.S. women's soccer team to victory in the World Cup and we celebrated together—men and women, boys and girls—as Brandi Chastain's last shot cleanly slammed by China's goalie. Now, sports belong to both men and women. Dads and moms alike have a range of athletic opportunities with sons *and* daughters, but don't start sending pink footballs to newborn girls. Women have come a long way baby, but men and women must make wise choices together to nurture a better tomorrow.

For more information about these and other issues raised in this book, see www.raisingwinners.com.

Acknowledgments

Much of *Raising Winners* was written before, during, and after my children's athletic events. The ideas presented are a compilation of many hours of observation, substantial literature review, and generous help from coaches, parents, professors, and longtime athletes. First, thank you to the National Institute of Mental Health and Norma Feshbach—terrific mom and professional—for guiding the research on empathy. Special thanks also go to Stephen L. Kuchenbecker, M.D. (aka XXLT); my mom and dad, Janet Young Kelly (aka Equestrian Mom, Ice Hockey Mom); my children Katherine, Kris, and Karalyn; Ed, Cece, Edward, Stephanie, and Luke; Marietta and Robert Wedell. My first two professional thank-yous go to coach John Wooden for providing the vision and the role model of a great coach, and to Dr. Albert Bandura for providing the academic vision and perspective to understand the rich self-efficacy-building experiences available for youth through sports participation. In addition, I would like to thank Dr. Eleanor Maccoby for her suggestions and support; Dr. John Santrock; Dr. Renee Harrangue; Dr. Michael O'Sullivan; Dr. Dorothea Ross; Dr. Seymour Feshbach; Dr. Bert Mandelbaum; Dr. Kevin Ehrhart; Dr. Eileen Yager; Dr. Martin Seligman; Dr. William Tamborlane; Dr. and Mrs. Norman Mirman; Dr. William Dement; Dr. Fred Rivara; Dr. Abe Bergman; Dr. Eleanore Meyer; Dr. Suparna Jain; Dr. Richard Baker; Dr. Michela Gunn; Dr. Daniel Wann; Dr. Burton White; Dr. Jay Rosenberg; Kathy Smith; Charlie Jones; Coach Payton Jordan; Garry Trudeau; Barbara Bauer; Kristin Folkl; Jani, Mike, Corinn, Kjersi, and Cailin Nomad;

Jack Blatherwick; Headmaster Thomas Hudnut; Darin David; Coach Lee Maes; Brian Baise; David Tashima; Haldis and Kurt Toppel; Cary and Sue Spaulding; Sheldon, Cassandra, and Arianna Chernove; Gene Asselta; Ken and Pat Anderson; Nina Yribe and Jack Schneider; Adam Strom; Jim Thompson with the Positive Coaching Alliance; Aunt Winnie Day Liebman, Evelyn Westmoreland, Tammy Kuchenbecker, David Kuchenbecker, John and JoAnn Kuchenbecker; Dr. Philip Zimbardo; Dr. Merlin Wittrock; Dr. Ruby Takanishi; Dr. Leland Swenson, Dr. Nan Krakow; Dr. Ed Zigler; Dr. Stan Califf; Dr. Larry Ryan; Dr. Patricia Walsh; Dr. Ron Barrett; Dr. Larry Bernard; Don Shaw; Denise Corlette; Dick Held; Debbie Held; Jeff Porter; Jimmy Blackman; Turhan Douglas, Greg Albright; Nabil Mardini; M. J. Deutschman; Jesse Quiroz; Jennifer Weiss; Danny Burk; Nigel Duokhov; Garrett Maxwell; Jeannie Lane; Bill Ferguson; Chris McGee; Eric Wells; Craig Forsyth; Stefanie Knutson; Cathy Ferguson; Gerry and Sally Gregory; Kareem Abdul-Jabbar; Suzy Spitz; Mark Spitz; Kent Steffes; John Kessel; Sam Lagana; Eileen Hiss; Jerritt Elliot; Rick Citron; Tim Jensen; Eric Dahlstrom; Luis Rodriguez; Anthony Brown; Lynn Murphy; Janice Meichtry; Coach Gary Bradison; Gladys Aranda; Elsa Kircher; Cole; Mitchell Waters; Coach Michael Boehle; Coach Eric Wells; Coach Grebenow; Lucy Leonardi; Patrick Brown; Kim Krull; Jim Praeger; Evelyn Hooker; Ellie Novaess; Jeaney DuPras; Jennifer Ruud; Kathleen and Joe Gentile; Karlene Bradley Von Szeliziski; Joan Carmen Heffner and Van Heffner; Jane and Ed Feldman; Haicha and Vic Lambert; Dale and Crystal Neal; Park and Erin Liu; Maggie Haves; Carol Tracy; Mary Jean Schaffer; Valerie Woodard; Sally Thompson; Dee Stark; Jennie McDonald; AYSO Region 69; my friends at National Charity League; kids, parents, coaches, and assistant coaches from my children's teams; all my Loyola Marymount students, Christy M. Rigg, Cindy M. Weglarz, Erin E. Alvarez, Kevin J. Fleming, Sandy Ribera, Courtney Ball, Kristen M. Rockenbach, Nicole R. Pohlot, Anna Wisda, Stacie Stern, Elizabeth Fraines, Daniella Sahagun. Jenny Lyn Waltermeyer, Chrystal Maher, Carla Workman, Daryn Beauchesne, Beth Goss, A'Neiko Webb, Ann Marie Froysaa, David Sanchez, Courtney Scott, and Monica French, Adriana Shoji, Jim Kahng, Cara Schindler; and Jeff Schnell from Pepperdine University, for their hard work and time collecting data; and to the many coaches who participated in the interviews and Coaches' Survey of Real Winners. My hat is off to all of you and I thank you for letting me into your academic and athletic worlds and for sharing your insights. Finally, I want to thank my editor, Betsy Rapoport, mother of two and Yale soccer athlete, and her team: Mindy Schultz, Stephanie Higgs, Laura Moreland, Mary Beth Roche, and Nancy Inglis. Taking my too-academic words and helping me create a book that speaks from a parent's heart required true insight and gifted editing; thank you for both.

RAISING
WINNERS

INTRODUCTION

Why Play Sports?

"I want my kid to be a winner! A champ. The best!"

Sound like you? Parents just like us fill baseball, soccer, football, and track fields, basketball and volleyball bleachers, ice rinks, gymnasiums, and tennis stands around the world. We all want the most for our children. We want them to be happy, successful, and, if they are in sports, we want them to be winners.

In reality, no one starts out as a winner in sports. Big doses of quality parenting and balanced development create winners. These things *plus* athletic potential, years of practice, lots of sweat, good coaching, and motivation nurture athletic success stories. How should you guide a young athlete? What are the important underpinnings of becoming a winner? How can you help your young child grow to fulfill his or her true potential?

Tough questions? Not really. Many parents may be surprised to learn that they already have the knowledge it takes to raise a child in athletics because quality parenting and quality athletic training have the same fundamental rules. Amazingly, some truly terrific parents leave their common sense at home when they walk out the door to drive their child to a game or practice. Some rationalize that harsh treatment is a necessary evil in sports. Others defer expertise by acknowledging that they were not athletes themselves. The fact of the matter is, harsh treatment is never necessary, and parents should have confidence in their common-sense knowledge and intuitive insight to their child's needs. Supporting a child in sports simply extends our ongoing quality parenting at home.

I've offered some common-sense guideposts for parents in the dynamic process of raising young athletes in boxed sections entitled Tips. Most are simply reminders of what you already know; use these rules to help you in your day-to-day decision making. Of course, application of a rule takes your love, dynamic judgment, balance, and care.

TIP   Trust what you know.
Quality athletic training and quality parenting have the same fundamental rules.

SPORTS HAVE CHANGED

I loved the uncomplicated way sports used to fill out our lives. About 4:00 P.M. in the afternoon, after walking home from school, having our snacks (Twinkies were fine in those days), doing our homework (we had a lot less then), and ten minutes of being underfoot, whoever was looking out for us would say, "Why don't you go outdoors and play?" The rest of the family wouldn't be home for a couple of hours and dinner wasn't until sunset, so the afternoon was ours for the taking.

We would trundle out into the streets from our various apartments and houses as if a silent whistle—heard only by the kids of the neighborhood—had convened our impromptu afternoon sports practice. Without much fanfare, the practice of the day was determined by the mood and equipment of our ragtag team. If someone had remembered to bring a bat and someone else had a ball, there you go, we played baseball. If a prized red rubber ball appeared, we played kickball or four square, but an open wall often made handball our afternoon choice. If someone brought skates—the old kind you strapped onto your not-so-good shoes and tightened with a key—we would all take a group temperature and trot back to get our skates, too. If no special sports gear appeared, no problem, we could play kick-the-Campbell's-Soup-can between gutter-to-gutter goals. A few kids with a creek or lake nearby had enviable afternoon practices skipping stones to leaf and twig targets across the water.

In the old days, the great athletes rose to the top of our catch-as-catch-can teams through talent, leadership, and regular four o'clock appearances. Some of the great stone skippers became pitchers. Some of the top swingers and climbers became gymnasts. Now, it takes a full-fledged support system for a kid to participate in even one after-school activity—whether it be Little League, park recreation, or an elite club team. First, someone has to find out about it and sign the kid up in advance. Enrollment fees vary, ranging from $5 up to $3,500 per year for some club sports. Parents are lucky if they live within walking distance of practice and game sites. Most don't. Someone needs to drive the kid back and forth—five minutes or as much as three hours each way. Special equipment can be as simple as a pair of athletic shoes for blacktop basketball or as expensive as an entire ice hockey goalie getup costing $1,500 or more. Games themselves are another chauffeuring event, with game watching a major workout for some parents. In addition, parents are on call for snacks and water duty, not to mention the now-traditional season-end party celebrating the close of this often herculean family undertaking. With parents' busy work schedules and driving requirements, it comes as no surprise that many parents recoil and quit after only a season or two.

Sports Are No Longer Safe, Cheap After-School Baby-Sitting

Harboring well-founded reluctance to leave our children unsupervised, organized sports seem a blessing to those of us who loved the freedom of our after-school ragtag teams. On the surface, sports continue to offer many benefits, but currently serve up a mixed bag parents need to monitor. On the positive side, kids get to play. On the negative side, haphazard facilities, equipment, and supervision can open the door to injuries. And for better and for worse, organized sports for young athletes have become a heavily adult-invaded process, with coaches, assistants, kids, and parents of other kids exhibiting various levels of maturity. Try visiting a tournament where several coaches are working with their teams. Listen as parents and coaches talk to the kids on and off the field. Some of the stuff going on is great, but you'll also hear, "Just hit the damn ball, Ginger. What's the matter with you today?" "Steve, get out of the midfield. What are you, some kind of idiot? I told you to stay back on this play." "Dammit, Kasey, get off your butt and play defense for a change!"

This verbal roughing-up is alarmingly commonplace for school-age children—on soccer, T-ball, and football fields and in gymnasiums across

America. It's a typical by-product when well-meaning parents and coaches are thrust into youth sports with no training and unclear guidelines of how to create a quality athletic learning experience. In a top-down phenomenon, we often see the best-quality training offered at the highest ages and levels, leaving the youngest, lower-level kids at greater risk.

Parents with even one year of sports under their belts know that the psychological support demands more energy than the obvious driving and equipment obligations. In the past, the athlete who managed to stay in sports was by necessity one tough character, developing thick skin to survive a multitude of coaches' criticisms and eke out a living with infrequent praise. Resilience was a well-earned bonus for the surviving young athlete, but most youngsters just dropped out of organized sports, often leaving with bad memories and a personal sense of failure. Now, kids not only need to survive the competition and the occasional rough coach, but sometimes their own parents and parents of other kids as well as their teammates.

Some Things Have Changed for the Better

Here is one place where things have happily changed for the better. The last twenty years mark a watershed transition period in our understanding of the athletic training process. We now know more about quality coaching, and through education, coaches from all sports are improving. Increasingly, many organizations now sponsor coach training programs.

How can you best help your child? How can you become an asset to their personal and athletic development? You may be relieved to learn that you already have a crucial ingredient in place: a desire to do a good job with your kid. Your motivation to do well, for your child's sake, forgives many mistakes. Through it all, your child feels your sincere effort to do the best you can. Of course, there are limits, but your desire to do well will help you stay attuned to your child's changing needs as he or she grows with and through sports. This book will help you with both a general approach to sports and more specific advice on how to tailor activities to your child's needs.

GROWING THROUGH SPORTS

All parents know that good experiences nourish excited participation in anything, including sports. Athletics provide opportunities for learning life's lessons, gaining real self-esteem, and experiencing a healthy, physically active lifestyle. Professionals, researchers, and especially savvy grandparents will tell you that participation in sports leads to balanced development and forms the foundations of success.

Personal Development

Some of life's most important lessons can be learned in the safe, supervised environment of sports. Shy four-year-old Caitlin learned to stretch and curl (like the legs on a spider) with her gym classmates and discovered she had made seven new friends at the same time. Fourteen-year-old Trevor was having trouble focusing in school. Then he became inspired by a new basketball coach, worked hard, excelled, then transferred his new work ethic to academics and made honor roll the next quarter. Ten-year-old Angela had always been overshadowed by her older brothers' academic prowess, but joined an American Youth Soccer Organization (AYSO) soccer team on which her quick running at forward brought in goal after goal. The joy of victory was made especially sweet through the newly earned respect of her big brothers. Matthew's first loss in an important ice hockey competition at age nine was the ideal opportunity for this natural athlete to begin to understand that quality of play is more important than the score on the board.

Sports are practice for real life. There are things to be learned. Rules to play by. Goals. Setbacks. Progress. Nurtured through adult guidance, sports provide many rich early learning opportunities for developing maturity.

Development of Skills and Real Self-Esteem

Participation in sports also develops real self-esteem. Watch a young athlete's genuine joy after mastering a tricky new shot on goal in soccer. Notice the radiant grin of the skater who lands a double axel or the kid making the three-point shot for the first time. And does anyone ever forget that first home run? Solid self-esteem earned through hard work grows by meeting challenges on the playing field. Mastery empowers and cannot be artificially duplicated, taken away, or forgotten.

Involvement in Healthy Physical Activities

Playing sports also gets kids off the couch and into exercising. Physical activity is fun and promotes lifelong health. Research shows that the more time a kid (or adult) watches TV, the more likely he or she is to be overweight and underachieve academically. Lifespan specialists say, "Live longer—stay active" and "Use it or lose it!" All sports provide opportunities to learn and improve no matter where or when you begin.

PLAYING FOR FUN

Ideally, our kids play sports because they want to. Involvement in athletic activities is natural for kids and the rewards are many, but in the process of having fun, they also have wonderful opportunities to discover who they are.

Mark Spitz, winner of nine Olympic gold medals, believes the best part of sports comes through the process of discovering who you are and what you can do. Your children deserve the opportunity to explore what they enjoy most. Some kids are lukewarm to baseball but love skateboarding; some thrive on competition, others dread it. Sports let kids disover their own uncharted path. When asked what makes someone a winner, Spitz, the most successful athlete in the history of the Olympic Games, said simply, "It's the mystery, magic, wonder, and the innocence of it all; the wonder in never having done it before, that is the motivation." Would he have swum the twenty-six thousand miles it took to become successful if someone had given him a book on how to do it, page after page spelling out exactly what came next? He says, "No way!" According to many athletes, curiosity about who you can become creates the motivation to persevere.

GETTING STARTED

Kids come into sports for a lot of different reasons. Whether you have a child who already plays a sport or is considering signing up for the first time, you might recognize him or her among the following:

KINETIC KRISTIN: Kristin seemed to cry more often than other preschoolers. She sobbed continuously when placed down for a nap and shrieked as bedtime approached. Long after other children would fall asleep exhausted, she was still wailing. Her worried parents consulted a pediatrician, who recognized her boundless energy and prescribed more physical activities. As she grew, gymnastics classes, volleyball, basketball, softball, and swimming all helped absorb this energetic child's get-up-and-go.

INTENSE DOUG: Doug seemed to take everything very seriously. At five, a dead butterfly on the porch brought a week's worth of worried questions. At seven, the board game won and lost by chance rolls of the dice stirred up three trips to the library to learn if anyone really could perform psychokinesis. Some early success on skis at age ten seemed to be just the opening his parents needed to bring sports in to balance out his life. Saturdays on the preteen and later teen ski school bus were wonderful breaks from his usual mentally intense routines and seemed to truly lift his spirits.

CALAMITY JANE: Leave her alone for ten minutes and there was trouble. Jane had more coordination than common sense. Doing headstands on the couch at age one was cute. Hanging from trees and climbing to the top of the jungle gym at three were fine, but when she decided to climb to the top of the piano, nab the sewing shears, and do an Acapulco cliff dive, her parents knew she needed some formal training. Gymnastics and swimming lessons fit the bill.

COUCH POTATO JEFF: After school, Jeff's first preference was to watch TV, play video games, or sleep. The school classes were easy and homework took less than an hour total, even in his toughest classes. By the time Jeff was ten, he had become a star on the home game of Super Mario Brothers, but his sedentary activities coupled with prepubertal hormones had packed on the pounds. He needed to get off the couch and get some of his excess weight off, too. AYSO soccer had open enrollment, and with much protest, Jeff joined a team. Two seasons later, not only was he a top goalie, but his height and weight had gotten back into proportion.

A TEAM OF HIS OWN—RICHARD: Richard was the youngest of four children whose parents both worked and then spent their few precious hours after work running errands and chauffeuring his older brothers and sister to their various activities. Richard was a good sport, shy by nature and slow to make friends; he came along for the ride to everyone else's activities. When he was nine years old, it was a sharp coach who noticed him hanging out in the bleachers during his brother's practice and asked if he would like to join a team of his own—and that helped Richard come into his own.

ANNA AND LISA, HOME ALONE: Carly, a single mom, worked two jobs and never got back to the apartment before 7:00 P.M. Enrolling her daughters, Anna and Lisa, in park league basketball and YMCA swimming seemed inspired until her daughters started telling how the basketball coach called them "Butterfingers" and "Miss Barbie." Neither got much playing time, but the coach's daughter always seemed to be on the court. Parents know kids home alone after school spell trouble. Latchkey children have higher incidences of risky behavior, including drinking and smoking, and dropping out of school. In an effort to avoid problems, many parents like Carly look to organized sports programs for after-school relief baby-sitting, but find with the hours of activities come additional parental obligations. On advice from a friend, Carly began attending practices and games. Not only did her daughters' playing time increase, but the derogatory name-calling disappeared.

"My best friend is playing Pop Warner. Can I?" and "We jumped on the trampoline in gym class today. It was fun, can I take a class?" Dozens of stories bring kids into sports. The crying three-year-old's story is Kristin Folkl's, currently recognized as the best female two-sport athlete in the country, WNBA player, four-time All-American, three-time national Division I volleyball champion, and Player of the Year (1997) in the Pacific-10 Conference. The intense five-year-old became a two-specialty physician who took up flying airplanes as a second hobby. Couch Potato Jeff went on to play soccer throughout high school but switched over to recreational running during college because his emergency medical technician training kept him too busy. Richard, who wanted a team of his own, became a high school champion quarterback who earned a scholarship to the community college. Calamity Jane is still in progress ... but with far fewer calamities.

With monitoring, kids can grow through whatever sports activities they enter.

Caution, Parents!

When the reasons to join sports come from your kid, they are usually great reasons. Their benefit and development should always be your first goal. A word of caution to parents: Don't dump your needs onto your child. Check yourself when you talk about your child's activities. Do you find yourself saying, "I always wanted to have a career in the major league, but ..." or "I just want to tell you about what we did with Sonny this weekend. We went to the junior national competition and *we* got first in the eastern states." Or "Mrs. Flotbottom, Dahlia lives to play and *we* would just love to join your country club's peewee elite tennis team."

Warning: Parents, if you look to fulfill your own athletic dreams, one-up your neighbors, or climb the social ladder, do your child a favor and stop where you are. This is your child's path, not yours. Work on separating your needs from the healthy development of your young athlete. Unselfish parenting is essential, and untended parental egos can be a significant handicap to your child's development. Your own maturity will be crucial for guiding your young athlete.

PLAYING SPORTS: A DOUBLE-EDGED SWORD

As athletes and their parents quickly learn, competitive sports can bring significant personal gain. Talented kids earn the respect of teammates, coaches, and parents alike. Not only do they get picked first in gym class when teams are being chosen, but their status transfers. Success on the playground often translates to leadership status. Peer respect, coach support, local recognition, and growing self-efficacy are but a few of the benefits to be gained through athletic achievement.

Parents need to know that benefits of success are more than counterbalanced by potentially very damaging forces. To see these polar forces in action, watch what happens at the end of many games. The winning team celebrates vigorously—shouting, slapping hands, and mugging to the crowd, catching everyone's attention. But take a moment to watch the faces on the losing team. For every smile on the winning side, often an equally sad face sags just a few feet away. For every winning congratulation, a criticism or blaming finger seems to be pointing silently at an unlucky player for losing. Even the parents from the winning team have a jauntier pace as they walk onto the field to greet their child, while the parents on the other side move more slowly, more deliberately, deflated. In some game and post-game situations, players, coaches, and even parents have been known to exchange verbal and physical attacks—name-calling, punching, and shoving. It seems that high emotional investment in sports escalated by the pressures of competition pushes some folks over the edge into inappropriate behavior—kids and parents alike who left their common sense at home.

Many parents confess that they are more stressed while watching their young athletes play than when doing anything themselves. The body language of invested spectating parents speaks volumes. There they are on the sidelines, kicking ghost balls, blocking invisible attackers, and getting mighty worked up over a kids' game. Often, parents' faces mirror their players' reactions in intense vicarious agony and ecstasy. Can a parent be too involved? What are the correct boundaries between parent and child?

Ideally, parents provide perspective and emotional balance for their young athlete. Occasionally, they forget common sense and go over the edge. A 1997 Garden Grove Little League meeting brought five dads to a fist-swinging, pile-on-the-floor brawl over a hotshot pitcher's age eligibility in the eleven- to twelve-year-old division. Moms shielded their children, shrieking for their husbands to stop until the police were able to break it up. Injuries included key gouges, bruises, minor abrasions, wounded egos, and damaged parental role models. One news reporter said the preteens were the best-behaved folks there. Regrettably, explosive emotional arguments between parents of opposing teams and even parents on the same team are increasing, with reports of parental mayhem on the rise.

EMPATHY FOR YOUR CHILD

You don't need a textbook to tell you how to recognize your child's emotional needs. If you care about how your child feels, your foundation is already in place. Your empathy is the key. Remember how you felt when you first looked at your baby? Remember when she took her first steps? Remember how your heart broke when he told you no one wanted to eat lunch with him? Remember how you felt the first time he put on his jersey with your family name in red block letters on the back? Remember the day she cut her leg playing and had to be rushed to the emergency room? Those feelings were all based on empathy, the caring bond that lets you feel as your child feels.

When your son serves the ball out in tennis, a quick glance and you know he feels miserable . . . and so do you. When your daughter slams the puck toward the goal and misses, your heart sinks only half a heartbeat after hers. As a parent, your empathic insight provides a valuable wealth of information about your child's developmental needs. Empathy with your child enhances your motivation to watch and listen and makes you a powerful force in his or her development.

However, the same empathy that gives you added insight into your child's needs may severely hamper your ability to be objective. Most parents quickly respond that they are the exception. *They* are objective, they'll swear. Please know that very few parents maintain objectivity for more than a split second. Necessarily, you need to be very cautious and monitor your empathic emotional responses, separating empathy from projection, particularly when intense feelings may guide you to make choices that serve your needs, not your child's, or get in the way of letting your child grow independently.

How many times have you seen an enraged parent storm up to the coach over something that happened to his child? Often the young athlete was okay, but the excessively involved parent lost perspective and projected his feelings onto the child. Being taken out or left on the bench are all part of the process of learning to play sports. Some emotionally invested parents watching their child play become overwhelmed by their child's experiences. When something painful happens to their child, these parents lash out at the people seen as inflicting pain on their child (and, vicariously, on themselves). Misguided emotion can lead them to make impetuous choices and immature emotional displays that ultimately undermine their child's development and ability to cope independently.

Too little empathy for the young athlete allows parents to lose emotional touch with how the young athlete feels. Unaware, unempathic parents may push too hard and ignore signs of a child's emotional needs. The skater who is near tears at the edge of the ice rink as the scores are posted doesn't need to be berated for missing the double axel. She knows she missed it. The quivering-lipped pitcher who walked the last nine batters doesn't need a lecture on winding up better. The young golfer who misses the putt doesn't need to be told to "try harder next time." With empathy, you can see the player's misery and know support is needed, not "constructive criticism."

TIP   Empathize with your child.
Empathy will provide needed insight into your child's emotional experiences and keep the lines of communication open.

Parents need enough empathy to have compassion and insight into their child's experiences, but not unbridled emotions compromising their mature perspective. The gift of balanced empathy with your child will help you make complicated judgments and provide appropriate emotional support as long as you keep your child's best interests at the forefront. Furthermore, you will provide an invaluable role model of empathic caregiving while teaching your child the art of empathizing with others.

1

What's the Right Sport for Your Child?

YOU ARE YOUR CHILD'S FIRST COACH

Some parents may be surprised to realize they supply their young athlete's entrance into sports and as such are their child's first coach. While you may never have thought of yourself that way, you are. Chapter 6 looks at coaches in the traditional sense, pointing out qualities to look for and things to avoid, but it is important that you understand that as your child watched you play or watch sports, he or she learned from you fundamental attitudes about being an athlete. Your child has seen the physical activities you select, the games you play, your sportsmanship, and acquired indelible memories of your favorite sports moments. From the presence of a helmet when you ride a bicycle to the pile of peanut shells between your brand-label cross-trainer athletic shoes at the baseball game, your child saw it all. Like it or not, whether spectator or player, the behaviors and attitudes of you and your spouse have formed the foundation for your young athlete's development.

Do you love to be active? Do sports arouse your passion? Is your spouse athletic? Does your family do sports activities? Do you have one sport you are truly excited about? Do you decorate your living room with sports equipment? Do you focus free time on chances to do athletic activities? Do you love to win? Do bad referee calls make you furious? Do you play armchair coach for every Monday Night

Football game? Even before your young athlete could walk, the answers to these questions—your active role-modeling—taught your young athlete some of the most powerful lessons in sports.

If you are a sports spectator rather than a participant, consider becoming physically active. Sharing time with your child in recreational activities you enjoy encourages him or her to be active and benefits everyone's health as well.

THE RIGHT POSITIVE ATHLETIC EXPERIENCE AT THE RIGHT TIME

Young athletes develop best when they have the right athletic experience at the right time. You know your child is on track when he or she loves the sport and can't wait to go to practices.

What makes an athletic experience the right one at the right time? To answer that question, parents can look three places: the young athlete (as a developing individual); the team (ages, skills, players, friendships, and the coach as a dynamic educator); and last, the real-world constraints.

Focus on Your Young Athlete

Focus first on your child. Ask your child what he or she wants to play, where, and how often. A great athletic experience means a great match for the individual at that time. Supplement your child's ideas with objective information you've gathered from watching your youngster. Who is he or she? What does he or she need physically, emotionally, and intellectually at this point in his or her development?

Listen to what your child tells you. Watch his or her movements, effort, and emotional experiences. Look for clues to emotional processes. Gather ideas from current teachers and coaches. By seeing and understanding where your child is, you will be better prepared to find and support the best experiences to match his or her needs.

Younger athletes and their parents often place high priority on enjoyment alone, while more experienced players seem to seek enjoyment as well as excellence in training specific skills and advanced strategies. You and your young athlete will need to reassess regularly and be flexible to a growing child's changing needs. Parents should keep overall personal balance in mind (see chapter 3).

Now it's time to check out the available sports. Go with the sport or sports your child seems most eager to play. In the long run, his or her interest and motivation will dissolve differences in skills and experience. Be flexible with switching around, too. The kid who wants to play a new sport every season has many sports-medicine doctors' backing. Pitcher's shoulder and tennis elbow (both often the result of young joint overuse) can be avoided while still allowing the child to stay in shape by cross-training in a number of different athletic activities.

Of course, common sense tells parents there should be a limit on sport-to-sport hopping. Two or three years down the road, when investing in costly new equipment is the bottom line or the reasons to switch seem half-baked, most parents rightfully worry that their daughter or son is not giving any sport an adequate chance. Watching, listening, plus using the information in chapter 12 on supporting your child to stay or leave while keeping your child's overall development in mind will help you provide the dynamic guidance needed.

Check Out the Team

Obviously, the coach makes a big difference in the quality of the athletic experience. Coaches who make practices fun as well as facilitate positive learning tend to have team members who love to play. Chapter 6 delves into what to look for in a coach and how to recognize quality coaching. Chapters 8, 10, and 11 explore the thinking, feeling, and acting components in the young athlete's performance. Keep your eyes open for the coach who is generous with praise, who has an analytical eye for seeing and teaching the right skill at the right time, and who truly appreciates the young athlete as a developing individual.

Next, check out the teammates. Just as your kid has learned by watching you, he or she will also learn by watching teammates. Social psychologists say, "It is a rare cucumber that comes out of a pickle jar as anything but a pickle." Simply stated, the people your child hangs out with powerfully influence his or her development. If some of the kids on a team are bad news, the situation can't be fixed, and there is an alternative team, spend time before the season begins to find the right team. Teams are more than pickle jars and kids are more complicated than cucumbers, but the social aspects of a team need to be considered carefully. A lot more than athletic skills are being learned on sports teams.

Real World and Family Considerations

The final place to look when deciding on an athletic experience for your child is at the real-world constraints of your family. This is where ideals are balanced with reality—what you realistically as a family can do at that time. Included here would be:

- Travel time for practices and games
- Carpool availability
- Friends on the team
- Safety of the facility
- Uniform and equipment fees and other costs
- Other family members' needs
- Parents' work schedules
- School schedule and homework demands
- Family activity goals
- Other special considerations

What is right for the individual child must be considered within the family structure. When too many family compromises are made to benefit one child, your family's balance suffers and thus ultimately the child's balance will suffer. If money is tight and all the family resources are needed to put the child on the hockey traveling team, you need to keep your balanced perspective and say no. If joining a certain team means regularly missing family activities or religious services, again say no. If travel time for games cuts excessively into work or professional obligations, again, the opportunity is not worth the family cost, so say no. (How families work out support and training of an advanced athlete with realistic athletic scholarship potential or the Olympic-caliber athlete poses only a modestly different question. Chapter 14 provides some guidelines for exploring alternatives and making decisions in these somewhat more complicated situations.)

TIP   **Find the right athletic experience at the right time.**
Balance the young athlete, team, and family considerations.

WHAT SPORT IS BEST FOR YOUR CHILD?

Let your young athlete's interests lead the selection of athletic activity. Different sports present different types of learning experiences. Given enough time, most kids find a sport or sports matching their special learning talents.

Support your child's interests. Never pick or push a specific sport simply because you like it. The child shoved into baseball may come to hate it if your shadow falls over his every game. You need to let the young athlete do the picking. Some individuals are physical learners or "Just do it!" kinds of kids (see chapter 11). Some kids have powerful feelings that handicap them in some sports but serve as tremendous assets for other sports (see chapter 8). Hot emotionality can be an blessing to an ice hockey player but a major hindrance for a golfer. Some young athletes discover the strategic mental aspects of sports to be intriguing and gravitate toward setting in volleyball or pitching in baseball (see chapter 10). Let your child discover who he or she is through picking their own sport and position.

By keeping the goals of athletic participation in mind, you will probably agree with many professionals who feel that offering a wide range of athletic opportunities early is best. Entering sports late and specializing too early both have several drawbacks. Three things should be kept in mind:

FIRST, goals for young athletes should focus on personal development, true self-esteem based on self-efficacy (see chapter 2), and participation in a healthy, active lifestyle. Learning to love the process of playing should be the young athlete's primary objective.

SECOND, good athletic experiences are preferable to bad experiences. If you let a child pick his or her own athletic activities, the experience is more likely to be successful simply because you let your kid make the selection. No experience may be better than a bad experience, which is a sure quick killer of youthful enthusiasm. Early talent with a sport does not necessarily mean the motivation will endure. Appropriate guidance and support work wonders here.

THIRD, let your young athlete make athletic choices based on his or her physical development at the time in relation to peers and his or her interests. Some kids get their size early and some get it late. The giant of the fifth-grade soccer team may turn out to be average in height by tenth grade when later-developing kids hit puberty. The short geek of the ninth-grade class with size 15 feet may suddenly hit adolescent hormone heyday and become the dream of the varsity basketball coach.

In sum, skip crystal ball predictions. Let your kids pick the sport appropriate for their ages, maturation, and interest. Don't put unrealistic pressure on children toward what they may or may not develop by age eighteen. Naturally, at more advanced levels of a sport, certain physical characteristics have certain advantages, but athletic training for young athletes does not guarantee a magic ticket to a college scholarship or career in any professional athletic association. A five-foot adult will have a tougher challenge in football than as a jockey, and a six-foot, ten-inch adult may find quicker success on the basketball court than a gymnastic mat. Your job is to support and encourage your child's development through athletics, not predict the future by forcing choices. Keep the focus on having fun and learning through sports.

Parents should skip hormone manipulation for the sake of athletic potential and avoid doctors who recommend it. It is not advisable physically or psychologically. Physically, research suggests that many children receiving growth hormone supplements only get the height they would have gotten a little earlier, and the long-term side effects remain unknown. Psychologically, whether the goal is to increase or decrease height, the message a child gets when you schlep them to doctors about their size is that the way they are made naturally is not good enough. This is a terrible message for anyone. Kids need to know they are just right, just the way they are. They are and will be the height they are meant to be.

Should You Push Your Child into a Sport You "Know" Will Be Ideal?

Chapter 5 has some ideas for you to consider, but briefly, the more you elect to push a child, the more you risk robbing your child of the best reason to play: internal motivation. You should be a resource for your child. Learning the balance between encouraging positive athletic development and pushing your child is one of the biggest but most important challenges to raising a young athlete.

Individual vs. Team Sports; Eye-Hand Coordination vs. Leg Sports

There are many alternatives for parents and their kids to consider: individual sports (gymnastics, track, swimming) versus team sports (basketball, football, soccer, hockey) and eye-hand coordination sports (tennis, basketball, Ping-Pong) versus leg sports (soccer, skiing, in-line skating). With so many sports to choose from, sampling a wide variety of experiences will help your child discover just what he or she enjoys most.

One very athletic family confessed that their daughter, a very athletic and social girl, left tennis for volleyball because she got too lonesome practicing on the tennis court alone with a ball machine. Another young man was consistently frustrated with the mistakes of his basketball teammates so went into competitive swimming to let his individual efforts shine. There are many alternatives, each with strengths and weaknesses for individual kids. Enjoy the process of exploring alternatives as a family. Family biking, snorkeling, hiking, skiing, and snowboarding trips are fun, and many young athletes will tell you they got started on "their" sport after a family trip.

What to Expect—Ages and Stages

When should you start your child in a sport?

Start athletics when your child shows an interest, not when you decide it's time.

How you stimulate an interest in athletics and how you support the interest without pushing is a lot tougher call. We know kids develop natural curiosity in things they positively experience, so try including them when you do things—go snowmobiling, go to a baseball game, or play around in a swimming pool. Even simple things like tossing the ball around in the living room can develop eye-hand coordination, positive attitude, and self-efficacy. While few athletes begin at one year old as Tiger Woods did, early learning helps hardwire physical skills. Remember to keep things positive and the enjoyable process of learning will help foster a love of athletic activities. Chapters 5 and 12 look at the many sides of starting and supporting a child in sports.

Through the brouhaha about one-year-old Tiger Woods starting with a tiny golf club, some parents may be tempted to begin their little tots very early on a sport's path expected to bring fame and fortune. Is preschool training necessary to create an athletic success story? Aristotle first observed that early training may squander talent. Moreover, as sports physicians observe, extensive training using focused muscle groups and joints may lead to overuse syndrome long before the athlete reaches physical maturity. Currently, physicians recommend that young athletes use a balanced approach and cross-train while their bodies grow. Chapter 9 focuses on what parents should know in order to guide their children through athletic training and how to reduce the likelihood of injuries and lifelong damage.

For every early-start story, there are many more stories of athletes who came to a sport much later. Progress in a sport is like a road, with ups and downs, but a road you can start on at any age. Generally, younger players move forward at a slow pace as they compensate for physical immaturity. The older, more athletically fit player who has been cross-training in other activities will join a new sport and show a rapidly rising learning curve, regularly surpassing other players who have been training longer (chapter 12 looks at burnout, a common concern for the athlete and his or her parents). Parents should have some peace of mind in knowing that it is never too late to start. Not uncommonly, winners of 10K races, senior division, explain that they didn't start running until they were well past fifty.

Parents need to relax about the ages and stages. Questions like "Is ten too late to start in gymnastics?" and "My child is eight and the worst on the team. Should I get him a soccer tutor?" can be answered by simply giving your child the opportunity and time to play. There are few specific ages that absolutely make or break a young athlete's career. Moreover, the lessons sports have to teach are ready and waiting whenever kids start the process of competing. Whether your child is five or fifteen, learning to try hard, take wins and losses with equanimity, and enjoy the process of physical activity are all wonderful lessons to be learned.

Physical, emotional, and cognitive development do not necessarily proceed hand in hand. The young, physically coordinated child may be ready to handle complex ball dribbling but be emotionally unprepared to learn to lose graciously or win without arrogance. The decision of when a child should start in sports is one of the dynamic questions requiring love and understanding to answer.

The psychological ramifications of starting sports are many and powerful, with the lessons to be learned of varying difficulties for different kids. While few choices are absolutely irreparable, a parent's good judgment helps here. Some kids do better to start young and proceed with extra help in the needed areas, while others may be better off simply waiting. Some parents shop around the available sports and discover an athletic activity suitable to their child's current mixed physical and emotional needs. Sometimes, it may be useful to give a sport a trial run, see how it goes, then reassess based on what unfolds.

PORTRAIT OF A SUCCESSFUL PARENT

Researcher Diana Baumrind at the University of California at Berkeley observes four common parenting styles, each associated with different outcomes. While few parents exactly follow one or the other, authoritative parenting is generally associated with the most successful outcomes.

Authoritative parenting encourages children to be independent but still places limits and controls on their actions. Extensive verbal give-and-take is allowed, and parents are warm and nurturant toward the child. An authoritative parent might put his arm around the child in a comforting way and say, "You know you should not have done that; let's talk about how you can handle the situation better next time." Children whose parents are authoritative are socially competent, self-reliant, and socially responsible.

Authoritarian parenting is a restrictive, punitive style in which the parents exhort the child to follow their directions and to respect work and effort. The authoritarian parent places firm limits and controls on the child and allows little verbal exchange. For example, an authoritarian parent might say, "You do it my way or else. There will be no discussion!" Children of authoritarian parents are often anxious about social comparison, fail to initiate activity, and have poor communication skills. And in one study, early harsh discipline was associated with aggressiveness in the child.

Permissive-neglectful parenting is a style in which the parents are very uninvolved in the child's life; it is associated with children's social incompetence, especially a lack of self-control. Children have a strong need for their parents to care about them; children whose parents are neglectful develop the sense that other aspects of these parents' lives are more important than they are. Children whose parents are neglectful are socially incompetent—they show poor self-control and do not handle independence well.

Permissive-indulgent parenting is a style of parenting in which the parents are highly involved with their children but place few demands or controls on them. Indulgent parenting is associated with children's social incompetence, especially a lack of self-control. Such parents let their children do what they want, and the result is that the children never learn to control their behavior and always expect to get their way.

—John Santrock, *Life Span Development,* 1997, p. 247

PORTRAIT OF A SUCCESSFUL YOUNG ATHLETE

Entranced parents watch their five-year-old squarely kick a soccer ball and see another Pelé or Mia Hamm. Parents of the ten-year-old catching the pop fly see another Mark McGwire or Mickey Mantle. The local ice rink features a budding six-year-old in a camel spin, and her parents fast-forward to Michelle Kwan or Tara Lipinski.

Many parents are quick to see their own child's success as a harbinger of fame to come, but what truly creates success in the long run? During 1997 and 1998, I tapped four resources—coaches, parents, athletes, and youth athletic associations—to compile the portrait of a successful young athlete. With the help of my students, my information-gathering included field observations, checklists completed by coaches, free written responses, anecdotal stories, and participant observer data, as well as individual interviews with coaches, parents, and athletes.

COACHES' DESCRIPTIONS OF A REAL WINNER

Professional, collegiate, American Youth Soccer Organization (AYSO), Pop Warner Football, Little League, USA Youth Volleyball Association (USAYVA), club, park league, elementary, junior and senior high coaches across the nation and across youth sports participated in the initial study of "real winners."

When 658 coaches were asked to "describe in your own words a young athlete who is a real winner," the picture coaches painted focused squarely on psychological attributes, not physical skills:

> Winners are coachable—willing to accept what the coach says and assume responsibility to work. Winners are good listeners. Winners analyze mental errors. Winners follow directions as best as they can. Last, winners love competition! Winners see a direction! Winners have a focus! Winners make a commitment to doing well!
> —Mark Spitz, swimmer, youth athletic coach, winner of nine
>   Olympic gold medals

> Winners have real shiny trophy cases, but they lost a lot of games along the way! They know how to lose, but they really hate it.
> —Bill Ferguson, LAAC club volleyball director, seven-time Junior
>   Olympic gold medalist coach

> A winner has a look in his eyes like "Give me the ball—I'll get the job done!"
> —Chris McGee, LAAC 16s Junior Olympic gold medalist coach

> The winner can be at any level—first, third, fifth, or very last—providing he or she sets a goal, works hard, participates to the best of his or her ability, and achieves a new pinnacle in life. This is a winner. To just worship at the shrine of number one is a mistake because everyone is a part of the process. If there weren't a lot of people involved, there couldn't be a winner. You've got to have other people. So everyone plays a part in making the winner a winner. We all do something and we all contribute and share—coaches, parents, other participants—everyone involved in the process of sports makes it happen.
> —Payton Jordan, record-breaking runner—youth and senior—
>   Stanford University coach, teacher, U.S. Olympic Team head
>   coach, International Teams coach, and World Games coach

Is Athletic Skill Genetically Determined?

Experts tell us genes make a big difference, but not as big a difference in the long run as motivation and practice.

While you cannot coach genes, you can coach skills. Our research with coaches tells us that attitude and motivation powerfully affect observable talent. Coachability creates the key to learning. Damage coachability and you damage potential. Damage sportsmanship and you damage personal growth. Damage love of play and the young athlete quits.

Bottom line: don't waste your time counting on, crediting, hassling, or blaming genes. You can't change genetics anyway (yet). Work on the things you can affect: coachability, sportsmanship, motivation, and practice opportunities. Chapters 4, 8, and 9 give ideas for parents to consider.

Specific Qualities Coaches Value Most in Players

To learn the specific qualities coaches value most in a young athlete, coaches were asked to check 5 items from a 128-item checklist of words they thought "most described a winner." Half of the words described physical characteristics and half were psychological. Across the board, 4.2 out of 5 attributes chosen were psychological, highlighting the value of positive mental and emotional qualities. When asked themselves to think of three words describing winners, coaches generated an average of 2.9 out of 3 psychological attributes as the most important qualities for a winner.

Coaches' Words Describing Young Athletes Who Are Real Winners
(Percent of coaches selecting each word)

Loves to play	43.0%
Has a positive attitude	32.7
Is coachable	29.8
Is self-motivated	27.4
Is a team player	25.7
Strives to improve	21.1
Is dedicated	20.8
Gives best effort always	18.5
Practices good sportsmanship	16.3
Encourages and praises others	14.6
Tries hard every time	12.9
Loves competition	12.3
Is mentally tough	12.2
Has supportive parents	12.2
Is self-assured	11.9
Mentally pushes self	10.9
Is enthusiastic	10.6
Is a good listener, follows directions	10.5

Is a natural physical athlete	10.2
Physically pushes self	9.7
Has good eye-hand coordination	8.8

There were no significant differences between the 46 college coaches and 408 youth athletic coaches who completed the survey. Whether comparing the words chosen from a list (average 4.26 versus 4.13) or words they thought up themselves (average 2.89 versus 2.80), college and youth coaches alike indicate the importance of positive psychological underpinnings for success.

From the top down, across all ages and sports, the bottom line for parents is consistent—athletic success largely grows through positive psychological attributes. Notably, only one in ten coaches selected natural physical abilities as important, with the rest of the physical characteristics diminishing from there.

Most coaches can tell stories about physically gifted athletes they have known who left the sport because they simply lost their love of the game or didn't have the mental or emotional foundations needed to stay with it.

When the coaches were asked, "What damages a young athlete's potential the most?" 95.5 percent of the damaging factors coaches perceived were psychological and only 4.5 percent were physical limitations (injuries 1.2 percent and drugs 3.3 percent).

Coaches' Views of What Damages a Young Athlete's Potential Most
(Percent of coaches selecting each factor)

Criticism, negative feedback	13.7%
(general 9.7%; coaches 1.7%; parents 2.3%)	
Pressure, pushing	9.3
(general 5.9%; coaches 0.2%; parents 3.2%)	
Bad attitude (hostile, hard on self)	7.4
Negativity (poor self-esteem, self-doubt)	7.3
Cocky (allowing athlete to believe he or she is better)	6.8
Parents	6.7
Poor coaching	5.2
Low motivation, indifference	3.6
Lack of positive guidance, positive feedback	2.1
Lack of support	2.0
Winning overemphasized	1.8

Other damaging factors a few coaches mentioned included psychologically undermining of the youth, irresponsibility, blaming others, poor sportmanship, too much freedom, public ridicule, peer pressure, bad role models, anger, lack of balance, and "too much, too soon."

You Know One When You See One

Coaches tell us that real winners stand out. Coaches recruit them and teams fight to get them. Other players jockey for positions on their team because it's fun to play with a winner. Whether by adjectives or descriptions, the positive personal qualities winners bring to each team create athletic success stories even when a game is lost:

> The soccer game was between two rival schools. At the end, the score was tied with a shoot-out to follow. The goalies took their positions and the two teams lined up. Energy was high and the two lines of players looked like nervous colts heading for the glue factory. Nine kicks and five blocks later, the victory rested on the shoulders of one fifth-grade goalie. The other team kicked a great shot high and into the corner of the goal. The kicking team won and the defeated goalie got up out of the dirt, clapped her hands together, and ran to wrap her team members in a big group hug. "We'll beat them next year, you'll see!" No tears. A hope for the future. This young athlete is a real winner!
>
> —Fifth grade teacher, coach

> It had been a long day in the El Camino gym. Five volleyball matches later, the team had the bad luck to draw a game against the number-one-ranked team. They needed to win to stay in the competition. Shoulders sagged as the opposing team was announced. Faces drooped and eyes dropped . . . with one exception. Eyes dancing up and down the row of her teammates, she caught the gaze of the setter and gave a lopsided grin. A wink to the next team member she could see. The lopsided grin and the wink were infectious. Shoulders came up a bit as this ray of positive energy reflected from player to player. A skip and a hop down the row of players, she slapped all their hands then bounced, Tigger-style, into the middle of the court.
>
> "Great job! Let's get this ball! Come on! We can do it! Good pass! YES!" She was a constant stream of positive encouragement to her teammates and a tireless competitor, giving her best on every play, every

time. The team went on to play their best game ever, and it was not in small part because they had the grinning, winking player.

—High school teacher, club volleyball coach

DO WINNERS WIN EVERY GAME?

When coaches, parents, and athletes were asked to describe the young athlete they thought was a real winner, not one respondent said "a real winner never loses a game." Every player loses games! The real winner transcends winning a game or two, a championship season, or even a national tournament. All players lose some games, but the real winners are young people who keep playing long enough to learn the skills of the game and simultaneously the important lessons competitive athletics have to teach. The real winners love the process of playing, win or lose.

TIP   Real winners love to play, win or lose.

A winner learns to put game wins and losses in perspective. No one likes to lose, but a lot can be learned from losing. Good winners outnumber good losers at most levels of competition, but ironically, you find the best losers at the highest levels of competition. It makes sense. Since most people take to winning easily, losing challenges players and screens out the poor losers. Many players, coaches, and parents struggle after a loss and learn to deal. Not surprisingly, it is the young athlete who keeps playing—win or lose—who emerges as the real winner in the long run. By staying with the game, the persistent athlete gets the opportunity to develop the techniques and skills that eventually earn consistent game wins. Losses are a part of every athlete's past and future. It is the gifted parent, friend, or coach who can use the loss to help the player or team grow from disappointment.

KEEPING WINS AND LOSSES IN PERSPECTIVE

Coaches, parents, even a Good Samaritan stranger can provide perspective and help turn a loss into a learning experience for the young athlete:

My son was about eight years old and playing in Division 5 (U10) soccer. We had just gone to the sectional playoffs, and they played their hearts out . . . and they lost. And they were so disappointed.

Curt came off the field . . . and he was crying. The more I said, the worse he got . . . So he was storming off, tears streaming down his face, and he was saying horrible things about the ref and about things that happened, and I finally decided I had better just be very quiet and just accompany him as he was storming around the field, walking, talking, and crying. It was maybe a five- or six-minute walk around this very large complex, and he was still not feeling better. I was helpless. I didn't know how to deal with him or how to make him feel better. We walked by this man sitting at a picnic bench. The man seemed to watch us for a while, then he got up and walked over to us. He looked at Curt and he looked at me. Then, sort of with his eyes, he asked permission to speak to my son and I nodded.

This unknown man walked up to my son, then squatted down to his height and he looked at him and said, "Did you just lose a game?" Curt, through his tears said, "Yes!" Then he said, "Were you a good player? One of the best players on the team?" Curt said, "Yes!" and he started to cry again. And the man said, "Tell me one thing, did you give it all you had? Did you play the best that you knew how to play?" Curt looked at him and he said, "Yes! I did! I did! And we still lost!" And the man said, "Well, if you can tell yourself that you gave it your all, then you should be smiling. No one that gave their all should ever walk off a field crying." Curt stopped and he looked at him and he said, "But I gave it my all and we still lost." "Yes, you did, didn't you." And then the man said to Curt, "Put into perspective what just happened. You lost and you feel terrible. You lost a game." Curt said, "Yes!" "But you didn't lose your parents. Just look at what would happen if you'd lost your parents." It was kind of scary to me as a mom because I felt this was a conversation far beyond an eight-year-old, but it wasn't. Curt said, enthusiasm growing in his voice, "Yeah, you're right! Yes, I still have my parents." And then the man said, "You go to school, right? You still have your teachers." Curt said, "Yes, I do! I do!" And then they entered into some small talk and the man said good-bye and I said good-bye and I added, "Thank you, very, very much!" and he walked away. My son felt very, very good.

That conversation allowed my son to accept the loss that day along with the many wins before and after. It helped make my son a competitive athlete who could learn from losing and enjoy the winning."

—Haldis Toppel, mother of Curt Toppel, long-distance
runner/basketball/soccer/volleyball player, Loyola High School,
Los Angeles, Volleyball Junior Olympics MVP, 16s and 18s gold

medalist, member of the 1997, 1998, and 1999 U.S. Junior National
Volleyball team and named 1999 top college recruit

Recognition and the glory of winning a game may keep some kids
going for a while, but real winners keep playing no matter what the
win/loss record. The great parent or coach helps the players learn from
any experience. The missed hit, the unblocked goal, the bad call, the biased ref—all are valuable experiences. In this way, each experience becomes an opportunity to learn.

Quantity Time Yields Quality Moments

The lessons in sports are not timed to fit into a sequence or curriculum, and frequently there are limited ways to prepare a player for the real
emotional impact of an important loss. The greatest opportunities to
teach and nurture growth often come unplanned, at unpredictable times.
Coaches and parents need to be alert for those teaching moments and respond appropriately. Forget the notion that you can drop by at your convenience and bestow your pearls of wisdom on your child. Large
quantities of time go into finding those quality moments when your
young athlete has the real-life motivation to learn the important lessons
available through sports.

DO WINNERS SHOW UNUSUAL SUCCESS EARLY?

Some winners show success early, but many don't. Their early physical
skills are often indistinguishable from everyone else's, but one thing successful athletes consistently show is *coachability*. A consistent theme
running through the descriptions by coaches, professionals, athletes, and
parents emphasized the young player's eagerness to learn and his or her
receptivity to coaching. All coaches, from volunteer coaches of five-year-
olds to professional coaches, emphasized loving to play, a positive attitude, and coachability over innate talent or genetic gifts. Coaches know
they cannot change genes. Whatever genetic potential a kid has is set at
conception. From conception on, it's up to you to find resources to nurture and develop the individual.

> **TIP   Winners are coachable!**
> Coachable = Loves to play, has a positive attitude, is a team player, is self-motivated, strives to improve.

Every team a real winner joins benefits in the richest sense of what athletics can be through his or her enthusiasm, sportsmanship, and true love of the process of playing, but many successful athletes don't start out that way. A glimpse of unusual success or a moment of remarkable sportsmanship may be recalled, but often, early on, the real winners look like every other kid on the team. Some even play far worse, but motivation and time transform initial differences.

> I was so bad when I started. They would only bring me in when our team was waaay ahead. I had no idea what I was doing. I'd go up to shoot it and airball . . . it wouldn't even hit the backboard. Since I had been playing football and done pretty well, I think I spent half of the first season deciding to quit. I'm sure glad I didn't.
> —twenty-one-year-old two-sport college athlete

> Everybody expected me to do really well because I was tall and my dad was this great basketball player. I didn't. It was pretty bad. I remember even in seventh grade feeling like I was never going to get it together.
> —twenty-year-old NCAA college athlete

> I remember my first baseball game. They put me out in left field. I guess I needed glasses, 'cause I never even saw the ball coming. The next season, I got contacts and it went a whole lot better.
> —thirty-eight-year-old attorney, who played college
> ball on a full athletic scholarship

SELF-FULFILLING PROPHECY

In the late 1960s, Harvard psychologist Robert Rosenthal and co-researcher Leonore Jacobson went into grade-school classrooms with an elaborate academic assessment program and identified handfuls of children from each class as "intellectual bloomers who will show unusual gains during the academic year." Teachers learned that the "Spurters" had been identified by the testing procedures and were certain to experience a tremendous academic growth this particular year. In fact, the Spurters had been selected randomly, and the researchers did nothing more than make the spurting prognosis. When researchers returned in the spring of the same year and repeated the academic assessment, they indeed found substantial achievement had occurred among the Spurters.

Robert Rosenthal believes that at least four processes were activated to bring about the positive performances. First, the teachers were warmer and friendlier to the "late bloomers," providing a socially approving climate. Second, teachers translated their positive hopes into greater demands—the quality and quantity of material to be tackled. Third, teachers paid extra attention to the late bloomers, giving clear and immediate feedback (praise and criticism). Finally, more response opportunities were created for the Spurters, with greater rewards when they met teachers' expectations.

Self-fulfilling prophecy works in classrooms and certainly applies to athletic playing fields as well. While no formal studies have been done, many parents recognize the importance of coaches' expectations. When a coach notices a child, the notice alone probably works the first level of magic, with positive expectations adding crowning opportunities in numerous ways. Expect skill growth and you will see the growth. Parents, kids, and coaches share self-fulfilling prophecies, and when everyone's positive expectations agree, the momentum in the upward spiral can be phenomenal.

If a coach sees your child's tremendous potential and supports his or her growth, congratulations, but if the coach doesn't see him or her in this same rosy light, have patience, the next coach might. A coach's appreciation of a player has dynamic aspects parents can only modestly affect. "But my child really is talented" rings hollowly to the coach who has decided otherwise. Hang in there, Mom and Dad; if your child loves the sport, one coach shouldn't daunt the process.

TIP   Winners are made, not born.

To sum it up, most young athletes start out slowly. Sometimes they have some underpinnings of coachability, athleticism, or good sportsmanship, but not always. Sometimes they have some extra pizzazz, sometimes not. Almost always, their parents become their balanced supporters and advocates because winners are nurtured to succeed, not born stars. And remember, being a star isn't the goal. It's a nice bonus, but not the measure of success in sports.

Each parent, coach, and sports enthusiast has the opportunity to contribute to the professionalization of sports. Contact your national sports organization and ask about their youth development program (numbers for major current programs are listed in the back of the book). If your region doesn't have a program, look into the possibility of building a youth support organization in your area. For example, by calling the AYSO national office (800-872-2976), you can receive information on how to set up a region, as well as obtain programs on coach and referee training. Since AYSO is run by volunteers, you get some professional benefits for smaller fees.

Most folks recognize a fundamental truth about raising kids. Quoting Professor Dumbledore from J. K. Rowling's *Harry Potter and the Chamber of Secrets,* "It's our choices . . . that show what we truly are, far more than our abilities." And it is our job as parents to guide our children toward wise choices; choices with more options ahead than less; choices with hope for the future. Some kids will win some games. Some won't. Some kids will stay in sports. Some won't. But our children and we will all be winners in the truest sense if we wholeheartedly invest ourselves in the process.

The purpose of *Raising Winners* is to help you raise a real winner—both in life and on the athletic field. A real winner plays happy, plays hard, and develops through the process. While many parents intuitively understand quality parenting, most are reluctant to believe that their knowledge applies to athletics. Have confidence in what you know. The good news about raising winners in all senses of the word is that all our kids are winners, whether they win or lose any athletic competition. Our children are winners whether they play sports or not. The truth is, some kids will win some games, some won't. Some will stay with sports, some won't. Our children are winners because we believe in them and sincerely strive to help them become successful, happy, whole people in a challenging, changing world.

2

Self-Efficacy = Lifelong Success

Moms and dads want their children to have good self-esteem, but what is it? Ask a dozen parents and a dozen professionals and you'll get as many answers. Is it something that has to be built—like a building from the foundation up—or is it something everyone starts with and bad experiences destroy? Moreover, how can parents help their children develop this important quality?

Garry Trudeau recapped one truth from self-esteem research in *Doonesbury,* August 10, 1997.

As Trudeau highlights, *real* achievement means meeting a *real* challenge. Showing up at camp, finishing a lanyard, and remembering a computer password may challenge some kids, but obviously not Jeff. Loose definitions of self-esteem have created a mixed bag of popular developmental programs that yield mixed outcomes. Parents are wise to be wary of yet another promise for "better self-esteem" or a panacea for "good self-concept."

Self-esteem is a judgment of self-worth derived from many sources. Research psychologist Seymour Coopersmith of New York finds children exhibiting high self-esteem often have parents who are accepting, set explicit standards for attainable behaviors, and provide generous support and latitude during the process of acquiring a range of potentially valuable competencies.

BY G.B. TRUDEAU

DOONESBURY © 1997 G. B. Trudeau. Reprinted with permission of UNIVERSAL PRESS SYNDICATE. All rights reserved.

SELF-EFFICACY

Personal competence in a specific area such as athletic skill can contribute to building a robust sense of self-worth. Stanford psychologist Albert Bandura, author of *Self-Efficacy: The Exercise of Control* (1997), defines self-efficacy as the can-do attitude that says "I can do something that makes a difference." Great research supports the importance of a can-do attitude; it also makes sense to most kids and their parents. Interestingly, self-efficacy is not based upon skills per se, but on personal judgment of one's skills.

Self-efficacy is specific to each skill, not a global state of being. Unlike the catchall basket of "self-esteem," individuals seem to develop a specific sense of self-efficacy for each different activity they try. In this way, your son could have a good sense of self-efficacy about basketball free throws (which he has done often at home in the hoop over the garage), but have a limited sense of self-efficacy when asked to play forward in a game on a park league team with older kids (which he has never tried before).

A can-do attitude in sports can become a way of life. While each sport trains specific skills and gives kids confidence in their ability in each skill area, can-do competence gives kids "go power" to try similar new things. It lets kids walk up and open new doors for themselves. A kid with positive experiences increasing self-efficacy takes on challenges, embraces new opportunities, and forges ahead. Parents can support kids' understanding of themselves using the self-efficacy model and watch their child's personal growth build.

According to Bandura, our judgment of self-efficacy comes from four things: role models, past success, verbal encouragement, and physiological state at the time. So the kid who has watched a parent or older sibling play a sport such as volleyball, seen TV or live games, been successful in the past, receives verbal encouragement, and is in a good physiological state (positive attitude, good stamina, no pain, no injuries, no illness, etc.), is likely to have a very strong can-do attitude and be successful at volleyball. Interestingly, kids and adults alike typically expect their next performance to be slightly better than their past performance level. The can-do attitude of positive self-efficacy makes young kids and seasoned athletes alike anticipate improvement on the very next performance and work toward it.

Has your young softball player ever bragged to you, "I'm going to do great in the game today. In practice, I didn't miss a ball!" only to find herself falling short of her own expectations? Commonly, ebullient young athletes will tell their parents how great they are going to play, but come away disappointed. Bandura's self-efficacy phenomenon explains both the source of their improvement (rising performance based on increased experience) and their own dissatisfied critical assessment of their achievements (expectations always rise faster than actual accomplishments). It is similar to the carrot and the horse, except athletes—young and old—generate their own carrots through rising hopes. Many lifelong athletes will tell you they are their own worst critics and often feel they could have done better, but they manage to keep the carrot in sight and redouble their efforts when their performance falls short. By understanding this process, you can help.

The concept of self-efficacy has a very valuable core for parents. Help your young athletes, especially at younger ages, learn that something they do makes a difference. Let them know it is normal to expect a lot of themselves. Teach pride in trying—no matter what the outcome—and help your children understand that their expectations rise as fast if not faster than their skills. That's a good thing. They need to understand that effort spent learning something is effort well spent. They need to know their positive attitude is essential because it builds opportunities for physical fitness and lifelong health.

TIP   **Help your child learn self-efficacy: support the can-do attitude.**

Should I Encourage My Daughter in Athletics?

Learning life's lessons, building self-efficacy and real self-esteem, and beginning an active healthy lifestyle benefit young boys and girls alike. Parents may recognize their own sexist background when it is Dad who boasts stories of past athletic teams and Mom has little or nothing to compare. One in three women now participates in sports. Quality research summarized by the Women's Sports Foundation tells us that girls who play sports

- like themselves more,
- have more self-confidence,

- suffer less depression,
- have a 60 percent lower likelihood of breast cancer,
- have fewer unwanted pregnancies,
- have a later age for first intercourse,
- have fewer sex partners (among those who are sexually active),
- are more likely to use a condom,
- are more likely to use birth control,
- learn what it means to be strong.

This may be some of the best-publicized research in gender equality history, with highlights featured in Nike's ad campaign. The message is clear. The traditional cultural route to female identity once focused primarily on social popularity and physical attractiveness. While there are and long have been other avenues for women to build self-efficacy, including theater, music, art, design, philanthropy and more, sports uniquely teach some of the gender-specific tactics of competition once unavailable to women.

Parents who play sports may have an easier time encouraging their daughters to pursue athletics, but school programs seem to be giving our young girls early exposure and thus preparing them to make better choices for themselves. Giving your daughter the chance to observe women's games at the local high school or university may spark her interest. Check out the women's soccer or volleyball schedule and plan a family night. You may be pleasantly surprised to watch your daughter enjoy new successful female role models, while you all have a special window into new learning and cultural change in progress.

Developing Self-Efficacy

For parents, the flip side of the empowerment coin instructs you, "Teach your child to do things for herself or himself." It is up to your child to do it, not you. Your child's sense of competence is undermined whenever you do something for him or her that he or she can do alone. Remember when your child first learned to feed herself? No matter how messy, most kids want to do it on their own. If you did it for them, it would have undermined their developing self-efficacy. Of course, you as an adult could do it more quickly and neatly, but that is not the point. Applied to athletics, once your child learns how to put on her hockey skates and pads herself, your well-meaning but unneeded intrusions undermine her own efforts. A major point of being a parent is to help kids learn independence and acquire skills so they can take care of themselves when you aren't there.

Encouraging Self-Efficacy

In the world of athletics, parents need to value and encourage self-efficacy wherever the sport permits. Keep your eyes open. If your kids pack their own lunch for school, have them pack their own snack for practice. Given that preschoolers are capable of making and packing their own lunches with guidance, if your child doesn't pack his or her lunch by age nine, consider putting this excellent efficacy opportunity in place, that is, of course, unless cafeteria lunches are mandatory. For sports, get an appropriately sized duffel bag and encourage your youngster to be in charge of the stuff he or she needs for sports, including snacks, shoes, equipment, safety gear, uniform, and, of course, water. Kids as young as five can be in charge of their soccer cleats and shin guards. Six-year-old ice skaters can carry their own blades with a safety handle. Nine-year-old skiers can handle skis, poles, goggles, hat, gloves, and boots. It is up to you to help them know how capable they are by simply having them do it!

Listening and Watching

The words "I can do it by myself!" ring richly to the ears of parents encouraging their kids' independence and growth. It takes nothing more than heartfelt motivation and time to become an accurate listener and watcher. Parents always need to keep the lines of communication open with their child by listening willingly.

Many parents have gotten into such a habit of correcting their child that they believe they can and should correct their child's feelings as well. Feelings are not correctable, like mistakes on a page. If your child expresses a feeling you don't like, it's futile to say, "No, you don't feel that way." *They know they do.* Many times, what a kid says on the surface may not mean what parents originally think. There are lots of things a kid can mean when he says, "I feel awful" or "I feel like dying." That is where really accurate listening comes in. Say, "Tell me what you mean when you say . . ." Ask about a time that made that feeling come up. Reflect what you heard in your own words and see if that is what your child was trying to say.

Accept, Reflect, and Clarify

Imagine your fifteen-year-old daughter coming home from a park league basketball game. She throws her bag on the floor, gets some milk, and slams the refrigerator door. "I hate basketball." Bite your tongue if your immediate response is "No, you can't possibly! Look at all the trophies in the bookcase." She just told you she hates basketball, right now, right this minute. Things may change, but for right now, she does hate it. Accept it. Okay. Reflect what you heard to make sure you got it correctly. (Besides, you want to hear more.) Keep the tone of your voice nonjudgmental. "You hate basketball?" Clarify. "What happened that made you hate basketball today?"

Now that you are engaged in a conversation with your daughter, she will probably—but not always—tell you what happened ("I was open all day for a pass, and Carie never gave me the ball—plus the coach did absolutely nothing!"). You can listen. Say "Hmmmmm" and "Ohhhhhh" and make other listening noises. By just listening, your important job as monitor, supporter, and mentor will have been fulfilled and you may have learned something more about who your child is and how she feels.

Parents are wise to seize those moments when they can really communicate with their kids. Feelings are often raw right before and after a game or practice, and children slip you openings because they want your perspective. Parents who become open sounding boards are in an ideal position to use their children's eyes and ears to screen and support experiences.

Sometimes, the golden moment for communication can come up in the car on the way to practice or in the backyard tossing the ball around. Be ready for it. You can say, "I was wondering what you're feeling about . . ." Then listen. Don't interrupt or interject your ideas. Let your child explain, in his or her own words, exactly what he or she perceives. As you listen, make mental notes about things that seem unclear. Again, don't interrupt. Nod your head. Make listening noises ("Hmmm"). Encourage explanation ("Tell me more"). When your child is done talking, try saying back what you think you heard. Ask if you got it right. Accept and tell your child that you may make mistakes in what you thought you heard. Ask questions about things that seemed unclear and help your child clarify what he or she means so you can understand better. Be very cautious about hearing what you want to hear or trying to put words into your child's mouth. The purpose of this process is to understand your child—not necessarily to take any action. By simply listening, you are validating your child's individual perspective. In the process of clarification, you can sort out misunderstandings and come to better appreciate your child.

"TELL ME MORE . . . HMMMMM, OHHHHHH, AND UH-HUH"

Cory stormed into the kitchen, threw his ice hockey gear into the corner, then pulled the kitchen chair around to seat himself with a loud *thwump*. I turned just in time to see his eyes glistening as he swiped his sleeve over his face. Clutching the chair frame so hard his knuckles were white, he clenched his teeth as he growled in his changing thirteen-year-old voice, "I HATE my team!" His voice cracked once in the middle as he repeated his diatribe again. "I HATE MY TEAM. They are a bunch of losers!"

I started to dry my hands and took a deep breath. "Oh, what happened at practice today to make you decide you hate your team?"

That was all I had to say. He was off and running. As the story unfolded, my son explained that his teammates took what he did for granted. When he does super, well that is just expected, but "I make one bad pass and they act like it was a big deal. They screw up passes all the time, especially Todd, and he is the first one to scream he can't get to something." I poured a glass of orange juice and handed it to him.

"What did Todd say that upset you?" Blind alley. It wasn't what Todd had said exactly. He and three other guys always had an excuse for everything they did wrong. "He should suck it up and get over it!" Cory explained as he waved his arms animatedly. There was a pause. I tried to get the conversation going again. "Hmmmm." Cory's face flashed a grimace but he charged again. I listened, making several "Ohhh" and "Really" comments as I peeled carrots. The other guys hardly played and when they came in, they felt like they were going to get yanked at the first mistake—which they often did—so during practice, they really whined. "Ohhhh."

Funny thing was, by the end of our session—I don't know if you could call it a conversation—Cory had figured out that this was his second year on the team and that this was the way it worked. These other kids would either learn or leave. He just had to do what he knew how to do: play hockey!

He said, "Thanks, Mom!" as he put the glass on the counter and left after wiping and stacking his stick and helmet onto the shelf behind the pantry. I wasn't sure what I had said, but it seemed to have worked.

—Mother, of fifteen-year-old Bantam ice hockey player

Scaffold Support

Helping your child develop self-efficacy means watching over your young athlete with the goal of creating and appropriately supporting his or her development. Simply put, it's usually inadvisable to just toss your kid into the emotional pool of sports and watch to see if he sinks or swims. Parents need to offer scaffold psychological support. Trampoline coaches use ceiling-rigged harnesses to let athletes try difficult new jumps; the coach eases up on the harness tension as the child's skills increase. Similarly, you need to provide just enough psychological assistance to let your child learn that she can devise and carry out plans, but not so much as to intrude and rob her of the chance to do what she can for herself. When your child is very young, the scaffolding may need to be heavy-duty psychological girders. When seven-year-old baton-twirling Tamara gets a sudden case of nerves and decides she cannot possibly go on stage although she has practiced for three months, her mom reads pure terror on her face as she looks through the curtains at the audience. Here is when a good dose of supportive talking can help. Tamara's mom can restate the obvious: The twirling is for fun. Tamara has practiced for three months. The routine has been rehearsed again and again. Doing what she knows how to do is all she has to do. Everyone wants her to do well. Her mom might even clue her in on the mental trick of seeing everyone in the audience as a cabbage head . . . or better yet, let her pick a vegetable and giggle at the mental image she creates.

As your child's self-efficacy increases, the girders must fade into lighter and lighter parental assists. The same extensive verbal support that helped the seven-year-old twirler would be quite out of place for a fourteen-year-old with three years of competition under her belt. In this case, her mom might say, "I understand how you feel. What do you usually do when you start feeling this way?" Or "The last portion of your routine looks really sharp." It always works to share honest compliments and boost sagging confidence, no matter how long someone has been playing.

FOUR TYPES OF PROBLEMS FOR YOUNG ATHLETES

Observant parents may see and anticipate problems long before their child does, but the best advice to parents is to respect your child's growth process. When you think you see a problem, unless it's a question of safety, do nothing. Say nothing. Let your children see and solve their own problems as they emerge. A missed starting lineup, disappointment in personal performance, even social squabbles often will work themselves out as your child matures in the process. Keep the lines of communication open, however, to monitor your child's experiences. I've found typical problems for your athletes fit into four categories: "buy, drive, supply, and monitor" problems; "tough it out" problems; "take care of it yourself" problems; and "parent intervention mandatory" problems.

TIP **There are four types of young athletes' problems:**
1. Buy, drive, supply, and monitor
2. Tough it out
3. Take care of it yourself (player opportunity to grow)
4. Parent intervention mandatory

---

1. "Buy, Drive, Supply, and Monitor" Problems: Parent Support Required

There are a number of supportive activities parents should anticipate when they have a child in sports. Buying shoes and equipment, driving to and from games and practices, supplying water, snacks, pre-game meals, and caring for injuries all take fair amounts of parental time and involvement. "Buy, drive, supply, and monitor" problems are the most frequent ones during sports participation. Luckily, most parents are already well trained in these areas.

Problems requiring ongoing day-to-day parental support include

1. Buying shoes
   "My shoes hurt. I think they're too small."

Make sure the sports shoes, uniforms, safety devices, etc. are the correct sizes. Kids grow and appropriate footwear is your job.

SOLUTION: Buy new shoes that fit.

2. Buying equipment

"My shin guards are too short. They rubbed a blister."

Make sure the sports equipment, safety pads, and paraphernalia are the correct size. Kids grow and appropriate equipment is a parent's job.

SOLUTION: Buy new equipment to fit.

3. Driving

"Practices are Thursdays from four to six. How am I going to get there?"

Arrange to take your child and pick him or her up on time. Arranging car pools of parents for practices and games is an excellent way to share driving and encourage team spirit.

SOLUTION: Drive or arrange car pools for games and practices.

"Coach says our away game needs drivers. Can you drive?"

Help when you can. Again, setting up a roster of parents to carpool will help share the responsibility and encourages appropriate parental involvement.

SOLUTION: Drive or participate in a car pool.

4. Water

"During practice, I didn't have any water. I took a drink from the water fountain, but the water tasted old."

You can purchase a commercial plastic water bottle with a sport top and encourage your child to refill it before each practice and put it in their sport bag.

SOLUTION: Get a sport water bottle and have your young athlete bring it to practice.

"I can't find my water bottle. I think I left it on the field after the last practice."

Care for equipment, uniforms, even water bottles presents excellent opportunities for building self-efficacy.

SOLUTION: Have your child write her name on her water bottle or decorate it with waterproof markers. If you child loses one bottle, she will feel bad enough and you can be gracious. Buy a new bottle and simply repeat the name writing/decoration process. One or two lost bottles is all it usually takes. Having kids pay for a bottle out of their allowance or birthday money is one way to go, but most kids learn the lesson quickest when they have invested their time and creative energy. This goes for making them responsible for writing their name or initials on each part of their uniform and equipment. It makes it truly theirs and their connection to it a well-placed investment of time. (As testament to this simple fact, you'll find that most folks who spent hours as youths rubbing oil into their baseball gloves still proudly have that glove.)

5. Food

"Halfway through the game, I started shaking. I was so hungry."

Make sure that the foods you supply for breakfast, lunch, dinner, pre-practices, and pre-games are adequate. Young athletes are growing and need extra calories and nutrition to support their activities. Read chapter 7 on nutrition and get your young athlete involved in making his or her own healthy food choices. Know the foods to have on hand for snacks and remind your child to pack healthy choices.

SOLUTION: Make sure you have healthy snacks on hand. Your child should be responsible for bringing his or her own favorite treats to games and practices. Or supply a snack or offer to set up a team snack roster with each family taking a turn.

6. Screening injuries

"My knee really hurts every time I run."

Growing young athletes are expected to experience some minor aches and pains. Sorting out what is normal from true medical problems requiring attention may mean a visit to an expert. The athletic trainer, pediatrician, family practice doctor, internal medicine specialist, orthopedist, podiatrist, or other specialist can help you make these judgments. Carrying medical insurance that covers athletic injuries and physical therapy is a good idea for families with an active young athlete.

SOLUTION: Watch. Consult a professional. Consult a physician.

2. "Tough It Out" Problems: Standard Sports Operating Procedure

The second kind of problem that all kids encounter in sports activities comes with the athletic training territory. Preschoolers to senior citizens get tired, they have time conflicts, their muscles get sore, and minor injuries happen. Learning to tough it out is just another valuable lesson in sports.

Help your child understand these "that's-just-the-way-it-is" problems, including

1. Sports take work
    "They made us run around the field three times."
    "I get tired during practice."
    There is work that goes into developing a skill. This may come as a surprise to some kids, but that's just the way it is. Learning to put effort toward a goal is one of the best lessons sports have to teach. The more a child complains here, the more you need to encourage sticking with the challenge. As long as the effort is appropriate to the age and developmental level of the child, your job is to serve as a sounding board and to encourage your child to stick to it.
    YOUR RESPONSE: "Yes, sports take work. Yes, you will get tired from exerting yourself. But the process is good and the learning is good. Go for it." Explain the value of the learning and other reasons why the experience is valuable.

2. Sports take time
    "Practice after school every day cuts into my social life."
    "Practice takes a lot of time. I missed my favorite TV show again."
    Weekly practices and games are hours spent in beneficial physical activities. Sports build cardiovascular function and social skills, plus it reduces the time spent watching TV. Parents need to help youngsters use their time in positive ways, whether in games, homework, community service, school activities, or helping around the house. Large vacuums of unallocated time provide opportunities for risky behaviors and often prove harmful for individual development.

YOUR RESPONSE: "Yes, sports take time. What a great way to spend it!" Explain the positive value of physical exercise. Support choices that bring a positive benefit back into the community, school, or the individual.

3. Physical activity sometimes makes kids sore
   "My legs hurt."
   "I fall down."
   "I think I pulled my muscle. I can't turn without it hurting."
   Developing athletic skill means developing muscles and coordination. When done gradually, the building process is slow and incurs only small aches and pains. Rest and occasionally a bag of ice after exertion are all that are required to get ready for the next round. However, overtraining or pushing too fast will cause moderate pain, and kids need to know when to stop. A well-trained coach is alert to individual differences in endurance and gives options to let players meter their own training.
   Pain is the body's signal that something might be getting used excessively. The old dictum "No pain, no gain" is simply wrong. Too much pain and you damage the tissue and burn out the young athlete. Teach your child to respect pain signs, monitor the intensity of the workout, and balance his or her development toward gradual increases in skill and stamina. Self-efficacy in monitoring your own body's signals is crucial for healthy growth.
   YOUR RESPONSE: "Yes, developing muscles for [the sport] may make you a little sore. Watch you don't push too hard or give up too easily." Explain balance and self-monitoring.

4. Your kid isn't as good as a friend, sibling, older player, or star athlete
   "Jeff can kick the soccer ball from one end of the field to the other."
   "So-and-so thinks she's better at basketball than I am."
   Skills develop over time. Some young athletes in a sport start at age two and some don't start until high school. On every team, in every city, there will be players ahead of or behind your child. Help your child value his or her own developmental process and focus on his or her improvement over time.

Don't fall into the trap of making comparisons. The parents who say "Oh, you are so much better than John and Tim" put their child in competition with a straw foe. The real competition for any athlete comes from within. The goal is to develop individual potential to its fullest, not to beat some other young athlete.

YOUR RESPONSE: "You are [be specific here] hitting the ball so much farther than you were last season. Remember when you hit one to the outfield last game? I see you improving every game. What else do you think you are doing better this season?" Explain why it's important to work toward individual goals, not to beat others.

5. Young athletes are not as good as they want to be
   "I'm trying as hard as I can and I can't kick the ball any better."
   "I keep thinking 'Hit the ball,' but I keep missing it."

   Often, the young athlete with the best potential has a VIVID picture in mind of what he or she wants to do. The visual image of an older peer role model, favorite professional player, or star athlete guides his or her every effort. Your child wants to be Wayne Gretzky when he steals the puck, or Tony Gwinn or Ty Cobb when he hits the ball, or John Smoltz when he pitches, but the maneuver often falls short, and in your child's mind so does he or she. The young hockey player heads for her goal and remembers seeing Cammi Granato's shot in the Winter Olympics or the basketball post recalls Rebecca Lobo's slam dunk in the last quarter of the first WNBA game, and each girl comes away disappointed in her own performance.

   YOUR RESPONSE: "Give yourself time. You're on the way." Explain about self-efficacy and rising expectations as he or she improves. Let your child know that the mental image of what he or she wants to do is wonderful and even Wayne, Tony, Ty, Cammi, and Rebecca work the same way: they always expect more of themselves than they are able to do, but they keep trying—and they keep improving. Help your child understand the importance of practice in developing a talent. All sport superstars have invested long hours perfecting skills, and trying to improve is a worthy goal in itself.

3. "Take Care of It Yourself" Problems: Opportunities for Players to Grow

This third category of typical problems kids encounter are challenging, but provide developing athletes with opportunities to learn to take care of themselves.

Interestingly, kids rarely see problems that are bigger than they can solve. With the exception of abuse, if a child sees a problem, she often has the resources to figure out the solution. (Nature rigs most learning this way.) If you listen to the problems of the five-year-old on a gymnastics team, they are five-year-old insights. They aren't worried about the technical quality of the coach's instruction; they're worried about their itchy leotard or whether the tallest girl in the class is going to push her way to the front of the line again. If the twelve-year-old quarterback on Pop Warner tells you he knows he needs to throw the ball differently to make it forty yards but this particular coach isn't helping, then ask what he thinks he needs to do to fix it. Practicing with Dad in the park or having his friend over "to do some passing" both work to build strength and hone skills. The best solution to the problem the young athlete encounters often is the one he or she generates, not only gradually building athletic skill but problem-solving efficacy as well.

Once in a while, your kid will come up with a solution that means buying better equipment, changing teams, getting a couple of private lessons, or adding a summer specialty camp. Use your mature perspective, evaluate, and consider your child's solutions when possible. For parents, that means back to "Buy, Drive, Supply, and Monitor," but remember to teach your children that honest effort, time, and hard work—not expensive equipment—make up for most differences between players.

Problems where a player can be encouraged to take action for himself or herself include

1. Playing time

"I don't get enough playing time."

"I can hit the ball as well as John can, but he plays all the time."

"Why does Taylor always get to start? I have as good a hit as she does."

"I deserve to be on the court all the time. When I'm in there, we win."

2. Coach-player communication

"Coach doesn't like me."

"I never get to do a throw-in."

"I don't know what I'm supposed to do. The coach never tells me."

3. Player-player communication

"The setter never sets me. She only sets Jasmine."

"So-and-so bosses me around on the field."

"So-and-so takes my balls."

"So-and-so cuts me off."

"Mason is always bragging about every time he scores. He forgets I'm the one passing the ball to him. Without me, there would be no score."

4. Self-evaluation of skills and potential

"I've been playing longer than she has, but she gets all the breaks."

"Coach makes me feel stupid when I make a mistake." (This might require your intervention if you suspect verbal abuse, particularly with younger players.)

5. Handling difficult situations

"Coach yelled at us for a half hour after we lost the game." (This might require your intervention if you suspect verbal abuse, particularly with younger players.)

The solution to all these problems:

1. Listen

2. Let your child know you understand how he or she feels

3. Ask your young athlete to think of possible solutions to the problem:

"What are two things you might try?"

"What could you do to change things?"

4. Support good decision making:

"What are the pros and cons of your idea?"

(Support critical thinking—don't do the thinking for your child.)

5. Encourage your kid to go to the source of the problem:
   a. Speak to another player who bothers her
   b. Speak to the coach to learn what she can do to sort out the problem
   c. Let the coach know you support your child's suggestions
6. Check back and monitor how the situation is progressing

You are your child's resource, and your child's long-term development is your primary goal. Having the child resolve the situation for himself or herself is ideal, so be willing to repeat steps one to four to nudge progress along. You may need to step in if resolution is stalled too long or is truly beyond the young athlete's capability.

TIP   **Let young athletes learn for themselves through solving common problems.**

4. "Parent Intervention Mandatory" Problems

The fourth type of problem young athletes may encounter poses serious threats to their safety and well-being. As a parent, you must step in if you see inadequate playing field safety, potential risk of injury, possibility of maltreatment, abuse (psychological, physical, sexual), or sexual harassment.

a. Field Safety

Each sport has regulation court and playing field safety guidelines. Learn the safety information for your child's sport and keep a lookout. You might also consider obtaining Red Cross certification and/or having trained professionals at the site as well. Handy parent skills include First Aid and CPR.

All accidents cannot be prevented, but the numbers can be reduced with alert personnel and a community consciousness of safety. A loose goalpost, poorly positioned mats, spectators straying into the line of fire, or bent protective wiring can be tragic oversights. Simple safety principles and double-checking are required. One site director and coaches may not be enough. Players, parents, and spectators need to share in the responsibility of assuring that sports are safe for our youth.

Check your child's equipment regularly to be sure it fits properly and check during practices to make sure he or she is wearing it. Make sure the coach monitors equipment too. Increasing safety is often as easy as checking equipment for secure attachments, ensuring appropriate safety nets are tightly fastened, or reminding young athletes to pull back from potentially dangerous activities. In open fields, this may include halting an impromptu game of slide tackle in the mud or discouraging kids from leaping across abandoned beams. In gymnasiums, parents can help by reminding kids not to hang on basketball hoop rims, particularly older glass-backed rims, which are prone to shatter. Even keeping an eye out for younger kids climbing on closed bleachers or playing too near the batting cage can reduce site injuries. Gather information, keep your eyes and ears open, and help when appropriate. All parents working together can make an ounce of prevention worth many pounds of cure.

b. Injuries

Each year, out of an estimated population of 100 million U.S. children ages five to fourteen, 775,000 are treated in hospital emergency rooms for sports injuries, according to the National Electronic Injury Surveillance System of the U.S. Consumer Product Safety Commission.

U.S. 1998 Athletic Sports Injuries
(Birth to twenty-four years of age)*

Football	314,038
Basketball	495,481
Baseball and Softball	141,215
	+ 65,182
	= 206,997
Cheerleading	9,937
Soccer	142,237
Hockey	20,695
(Ice, Field, and Street)	
Gymnastics	30,534
Volleyball	45,407

*National estimate of injuries based on emergency room visits (1998) reported by the National Electronic Injury Surveillance System, U.S. Consumer Product Safety Commission. Sampling error range from .12 to .07.

The estimates are based on emergency room visits in specific sports, but parents should know all sports and recreational activities carry some risks. Of the 210 categories listed, over half qualify as sports or recreational activities, apparel- or equipment-related. Even bleachers have their hazards. In 1998, there were 19,161 bleacher-related emergency room visits. Of course, these numbers miss the minor injuries, but should serve as a sobering reminder to be safety-conscious.

Injuries to young athletes fall into two broad categories: acute injuries and use-overuse injuries. Both require parental support and intervention. Injuries are discussed in chapter 9.

Families need good resources to handle ongoing care and give advice when questions arise. A pediatrician, family medicine physician, orthopedist, athletic trainer, sports medicine specialist, chiropractor, nurse practitioner, school nurse, community health worker, or other health-care expert can serve here. Annual checkups are important, giving parents and young athletes a chance to ask questions relating to athletic activities, but it's important to have your doctor's number on hand should a problem arise. Know how to get to your neighborhood emergency room and be sure that your coach and caregiver both have emergency phone numbers and authorizations in hand to treat your child, should an emergency arise when you are not present.

c. Harassment and Abuse: Verbal, Physical, or Sexual

All youth athletic organizations are bound by the federal government guidelines protecting civil rights of participants. Parents should become familiar with the contents of Appendix A, a sample of a rigorous youth athletic organization harassment policy defining the limits of appropriate behavior. Participation in any sports activities should be free from all types of harassment, including verbal, physical, and sexual. Discrimination on the basis of any individual characteristic is forbidden, and procedures for pursuing incidences of harassment are mandatory in every youth athletic organization. Recent legislation mandating a school's legal responsibility for harassment occurring within its confines has clear implications for all institutions caring for children. Schools and youth athletic organizations alike are responsible for assuring an individual's civil rights are upheld.

It is common sense that kids deserve a positive learning environment. While laws can mandate responsibility, no one but a child's parent has a greater vested interest in that child. Keep the lines of communication open and listen for hurts your child may experience or complaints your child may make. Watch games and practices. Conversations here can help your child develop personally. This is one area, however, where the victim of maltreatment often feels responsible for incurring the wrath or abusive behavior and is afraid to complain. By knowing your child's maturity level, you can judge his or her vulnerability in new situations. There are no hard and fast standards for which ages are most vulnerable. While problems are rare, watch your child's coach, assistant coach, and other personnel. Be alert for changes in your child's behavior.

HARASSMENT OR MALTREATMENT: VERBAL, PHYSICAL, AND SEXUAL ABUSE

1. Verbal Abuse

"Coach told me I was an idiot."

"Coach said all of us who missed the block were 'pussies.' "

Coaches who demean or belittle players (purposefully or inadvertently).

Derogatory treatment of an individual.

PROFESSIONAL STANDARD: Expect all people speaking to your child to use positive language. Psychological growth flourishes with positive treatment and is severely hampered by insults and frequent criticism. By direct words or indirect actions, the demeaning treatment of a child is unacceptable and you must take a strong stand in opposition to verbal maltreatment of your child.

HOW TO RESPOND: You can insist that older children respectfully but appropriately tell the offending individual (possibly a teammate or coach) that negativity and degrading comments undermine their play. Speaking to the coach and team captains, as well as calling a team meeting, may help. Younger players and older players who have been unsuccessful in changing an offending individual's negative behaviors may need your help.

Speak to the coach. If the coach is the offending individual, the approach remains the same. Calmly discuss the alleged verbal comments and your child's emotional response. Clarify any misunderstandings and establish clear boundaries as to the treatment you find acceptable. You may want to show a copy of our organization's harassment policy or the sample policy in Appendix A. Be prepared to contact organizational and state authorities if necessary.

YOU BETTER NOT CALL MY SON "MIZZ JESSIE" NO MORE

Jessie was never what you would call a loud kind of kid. When other boys would whoop it up, Jessie usually sort of stood back. He wasn't a sissy, mind you. He had two really good friends through grade school and knew how to speak up for himself. That's why I was so surprised when he was on this high school baseball team in ninth grade and got miserable. At first I didn't catch on. He just came in from practice every day, real quiet like, but one night I saw him bending over his open schoolbooks and his back was shaking. He was crying his eyes out and not making a sound.

I tell you it nearly broke my heart to watch his little back heaving like it was. Well, I went over and put my hand on his shoulder and he got still. I knelt down and said, "Jessie, what's the matter?" At first he couldn't get the words out, but eventually, he explained that the coach on the team had been "bagging on him." I wasn't sure what "bagging" meant so I asked. Jessie said the coach called him "Mizz Jessie" and pretended to sashay across the locker room or even when he headed for the outfield. My son's thin, but his brother Brian was nearly nineteen before he got a whisper of peach fuzz. Well, I took a gulp and just wanted to murder that insensitive coach for hurting Jessie's feelings.

"Why, Jessie," I said, "that twerpy coach isn't worth the time of day. What did you say to him?" He explained he walked as fast as he could to just get out of his way. He told me there was no way he could tell the coach to stop without getting the coach mad at him and teasing him more. Well, I let it go on a whole week, asking Jessie what had happened and what he could do about it. Nothing was changing; in fact, it seemed to be getting worse.

So Monday morning, I put on my Sunday dress and hat and I went over to the school. I marched right in and spoke first to the football coach. He had been really good to Brian, who had been his placekicker for three years on varsity. I told him what that baseball coach was doing. He understood right away. Next, I went down the hallway and found the baseball coach. I told him what he was doing to my son and why it was wrong and I did just so happen to mention I had also told the football coach—who was also the school's official athletic director. Well, I guess I don't have to tell you. That was the last time my son was teased. He went on to get better and better that year. He had been in a terrible slump. By his junior year, he earned MVP, and I don't think he had a bit of peach fuzz even yet, but no one ever dared to call him Mizz Jessie after that day again.

—Mother of two sons who both played ball in college, Georgia

WITH THE VERY YOUNG ATHLETE: Have open conversations with your child and within your family regarding appropriate ways to communicate and respect others. Be clear in your mind about appropriate behaviors and live up to your own ideals. Model respectful treatment for all people and help your children learn through your example.

2. Physical Abuse

"Coach grabbed my shoulder and shoved me off the court."

"The assistant coach grabbed the net and threw me into the closet."

"The kids on the team started to punch me, then the coach just looked the other way."

PROFESSIONAL STANDARD: Expect all people working with your child to show physical respect. Grabbing, shoving, hitting, restraining, spanking, slapping, strangling, and other forms of physical contact meant to coerce or force an individual are wrong. While some states permit corporal punishment in the schools, no teammate, coach, or youth athletic personnel should ever strike a child, nor should parents give their permission for such behavior to occur.

HOW TO RESPOND: Parents of older players need to evaluate the severity of the problem. If the problem is within your youngster's range to face, encourage him or her to speak to the offending individual directly. Try role-playing what needs to be said, and monitor your child's ability to explain the problem and arrive at a suitable solution.

CHARLIE ROLE-PLAYS SPEAKING UP WITH HIS DAD

There was an old tradition at the school of hazing the freshmen who made it on to the baseball team. My son Charlie's first year, there were only three freshmen, and hazing lasted a whole week long. On the first day of the indoctrination, Charlie came in looking a little riled. He is a medium-sized kid, but really strong. I watched him all during dinner and he was withdrawn and wouldn't look me in the eyes. Finally, I went into his room after the dishes were done and I asked him straight away what was wrong. He avoided answering for a while, but I just kept poking. Finally, he let out that the guys on the team had done an almost bare-butt spanking of the three freshmen as a hazing. The first day, each member of the team got one spank. Tomorrow it would be two, the next day three, and so on up to seven. He said it wasn't the pain. Something about it seemed wrong.

Well, my husband had played baseball in high school too, so I asked Charlie if we could get Dad in on this. He was embarrassed at first, but then seemed relieved and said it was okay. My husband listened, then asked Charlie what he felt like saying to the guys on the team. Charlie pulled himself up really straight and said, "Dammit. This is a pretty stupid tradition. This is immature and I don't like it. Why do you guys want to keep this up?" I just clapped my hands, and his dad said, "There you go, Charles. *That* is what you say to the team captain *and* to the coach if he doesn't listen tomorrow before school." They talked awhile longer and his dad had him repeat some stuff while his dad pretended to be the team captain. I could hear him all the way in the kitchen. Later, Charlie got on the phone with the other two freshmen and they all agreed to meet with the team captain and coach together. You know what? It worked. That was the end of our high school baseball team's hazing tradition. Three years later, Charlie was team captain and I didn't have to remind him of his freshman year. We all remembered, and were glad to have it behind us.

—Mother and Father of four children, Texas

Younger players and older players who have been unsuccessful in changing an offending individual's behavior need your help.

First, speak to the coach. If the coach is the offending individual, the principles remain the same. Discuss the alleged physical behavior and your child's emotional response. Clarify any misunderstandings and establish clear boundaries as to the treatment you find acceptable. You may want to show a copy of your organization's harassment policy or the sample policy in Appendix A. Be prepared to contact organizational and state authorities.

WITH ALL ATHLETES: Have open conversations with your child and within your family regarding appropriate limits to physical behavior by adults, peers, and others.

3. Sexual Abuse

"Assistant Coach patted my tush and it was weird."

"Coach says he will give me a special lesson at his house. I don't want to go. Last time I was alone there and it wasn't fun."

PROFESSIONAL STANDARD: Expect all people to care for children as children without molestation or violation. Intimate touching and/or sexual contact with developing children, illegal in all states, constitutes a breach of trust and violation of the developing child's rights. Victims of childhood sexual abuse tell of lifelong trauma and decades of recovery from the violation of their childhood. Be especially watchful for signs of trouble. Sudden changes in behavior should put parents on the lookout. When the young boy suddenly starts showing unusual embarrassment over his body, hiding behind the shower curtain, or the young girl becomes very withdrawn from her peers and shies from contact with certain people, ask questions. While some of this may be normal modesty, sometimes a traumatic event can trigger the sudden change.

Children and teens typically are threatened by abusers and feel responsible, thus are afraid to talk. Open lines of communication are especially important here to catch problems.

HOW TO RESPOND: Speak to the alleged offending individual directly. Enlist the coach's assistance. If the coach is the person accused, the principles remain the same. Discuss the alleged sexual behavior and your child's emotional response. Clarify any misunderstandings and establish clear boundaries as to the treatment you find acceptable. You may want to show a copy of your organization's harassment policy or the sample policy in Appendix A. As you listen and watch the individual respond to your statements, be prepared to contact appropriate organization and state authorities.

When you speak to the individual, listen carefully. He or she is an "alleged" perpetrator until such time as they are convicted in a court of law. An accusation is not a conviction. Once your child has intimated inappropriate behavior, as a parent I would be sure to attend every single event from then on and watch like a hawk. Your child's perspective is valuable information and must be validated. In many instances, the organization needs to be alerted about verified occurrences and a complaint submitted for their files.

The organization will be responsible for follow-up, but you are responsible for your child's well-being, so monitor and support your child appropriately.

Misunderstandings can happen and children can misconstrue actions, but parents must be prepared to call the police should the evidence point to sexual abuse. Physical evidence will be helpful to document allegations, and counseling support is available to victims and their families at the Victims of Crime Resource Center (800-842-8467).

WITH THE YOUNG ATHLETE: Have open conversations with your child and within your family regarding appropriate ways for adults to behave with children. Children as young as two can feel reassured to learn that their bodies deserve respect. Remind your kids that they are very special and they only get one body and it is theirs to care for. No one has the right to hurt them or invade their private body space. Knowledge empowers kids and encourages respect for themselves, their physical space, and their right to say "No!" even to adults and others in positions of power. Keep the lines of communication open and let kids know you are there to help them if anyone ever threatens to violate their safety or well-being. There are several good age-appropriate books on the market now such as Cornelia Spelman's *Your Body Belongs to You* for the preschooler and grade-school child; Chaiet and Russell's *The Safe Zone: A Kids' Guide to Personal Safety* for the junior-high age; and *Dr. Ruth Talks to Kids* for high-school age. Be sure to give your children the information they need *before* they need it.

Because of the potential for harassment and maltreatment, parents and coaches need to know that prosecutable definitions of child maltreatment include physical and sexual abuse; fostering delinquency; lack of supervision; medical, educational, and nutritional neglect; and permitting drug or alcohol abuse among minors.

TIP   Quality Child Development = No Harassment, Endangerment, or Maltreatment

Bullying and teasing have long been social problems, but experts agree there has been a tremendous increase in the last fifteen years. School reports of verbal harassment document unprecedented cruelty, physical injuries are becoming increasingly severe, and notable perpetrators of school violence often pinpoint social ostracism and teasing as their motivation.

Sports activities offer children chances to build social as well as physical skills. Run amok, sports can engender an elitist attitude where bullying and teasing may seem sanctioned by administrators, thus perpetuating the harassment. The lines between coach and athlete, athlete and nonathlete, even between athletes of different sports can create artificial boundaries. What is good-natured teasing versus verbal harassment? What is personally developing versus individually undermining?

Competitive sports can stir complicated emotions, which may result in undesirable behaviors, not only on the part of the player, but on the part of parents and coaches as well. All individuals working with kids in sports need to be reminded of the goals of athletic training: individual development within our society first, physical development second, and winning, a distant last on any list.

Dorothea Ross offers an excellent book entitled *Childhood Bullying and Teasing: What School Personnel, Other Professionals, and Parents Can Do*. In a culture where the opportunities to learn face-to-face social skills are increasingly limited, quality social learning in athletic situations becomes all the more important. Ross's book gives guidance on spotting children who are at risk for being harassed and harassing others and provides point-by-point programs on how to stop kids from teasing and how to reduce bullying behaviors. In a culture that permits a media diet of gratuitous violence, sports events can get out of hand. You as the parent must monitor the youth athletic program and individual team experiences to be sure civil rights and appropriate treatment are consistently maintained.

PHYSICAL FITNESS AND LIFELONG HEALTH THROUGH SELF-EFFICACY

Self-efficacy and real self-esteem grow in an environment of close monitoring and support. Albert Bandura's book *Self-Efficacy: The Exercise of Control* (1997) has great suggestions in his chapters 3 and 9 on how to build your child's resilient sense of athletic efficacy. Your interventions should fade as your young athlete's capacity for self-direction increases. Isn't it ironic? The ideal goal for parenting your child is putting yourself out of a job. The young athlete's independence is your medallion of success.

3

Balance in the Young Athlete's Life

I see it everywhere. When adults and children are together, the gentle job of guiding, encouraging, and balancing the next generation fills the time and space completely. At a hotel swimming pool, I watch a giggling daughter held in the palm of her dad's hand. Cannonball style, legs and arms pulled into a tight tuck, the child listens to Dad's calm words as she gets wound up to become a human projectile, shooting across eight feet of air into the pool with an impressive splash. Cooing softly nearby, a swollen-bellied pregnant mom whispers to her clinging eighteen-month-old son as she slowly, step-by-step, immerses them both in the water. As the water tickles his knees, his fearful face relaxes momentarily and a fleeting, timid smile flashes up at Mom. The wet-faced eight-year-old close by bursts above the water's surface after independently swimming from the steps to the middle of the pool into her mom's outstretched arms. They smile matched goofy smiles. Who is happier? I can't tell. Both faces radiate as they grin proudly at each other.

Without much fanfare—no trumpets, no brass bands to celebrate the powerful work in progress—parents around the world are guiding the next generation toward adulthood. We as parents naturally surround our children with environmental experiences helping them grow up well—sometimes directly teaching and often simply setting an example.

MOST PARENTS DO A PRETTY GOOD JOB MOST OF THE TIME

Reassuringly, Harvard researcher Jerome Kagan finds that many parents intuitively balance their child's development. Without special training programs or advanced degrees, the cooing pregnant mom helped her frightened toddler become accustomed to the water; she also balanced his emotional needs for reassurance. By providing balancing experiences, parents naturally prepare their child for emotional resilience.

From the young person's point of view, the family is their first resource for personal balance. When the family focuses large proportions of energy onto their youth sports activities, most kids conclude they and their sports are very important. When the family ignores these things, many children conclude those things don't matter. Unless you maintain your role as a balancing influence in your young athlete's life, your child's performance, as well as winning and losing, may quickly assume disproportionate value.

Many youngsters get lost in sports when their parents disappear in the psychological sense and quit monitoring them. Why send your daughter off at fourteen to the varsity swim team tryout without preparing her, watching, understanding, and balancing? The cannonball, torpedo-tossing dad wouldn't pitch his daughter off into the deep end without making sure she landed and returned safely. Why should he drop her off at a soccer tournament seven years later and not make sure she safely traversed the psychological space during the potentially stress-ridden day?

The role of monitoring and providing balance doesn't end when your child begins puberty. Genetics don't suddenly take over and peers don't become an unconquerable force (though both may be used as convenient excuses). In fact, during the adolescent juncture between eleven and fifteen, your best efforts may be crucial to support balance and nurture your child's lifelong health, since research has shown that this is the time when many children investigate risky behaviors. Sports activities can be the positive alternative.

TOO MUCH, TOO LITTLE

Some parents do too much, try too hard, fill in too many blanks. Some parents do and try too little. I have erred in both directions at times and both have problems.

Quality parenting means helping your child balance thinking, feeling, and actions. The successful young athlete knows what he or she needs to do (thinking), feels good about doing it (feeling), and does it (acting).

TIP   **Real winners have balanced thinking, feelings, and actions.**

Researchers find that as children mature, they develop increasing potential to separate how they think, feel, and act. Mature behavior often relies on an individual's capacity to overcome immediate feelings and behave appropriately in the situation, an art you must teach your child. Kids at funerals, weddings, mealtime, experiencing disappointing failures, big game losses, even waiting in the endless line at the grocery store must learn they cannot act out everything they feel at the moment they feel it. The balancing and rebalancing lessons we parents teach our children are crucial to helping them smoothly join the social world, and athletics provide many chances for them to practice what we preach.

I often overhear parents providing wonderful balancing and rebalancing to their kids in gyms and on playing fields. "You know, even though the scoreboard says you're a winner, you still have to carry your own gym bag," said one dad with a lopsided grin when a winning streak inflated his son's ego. Apparently, carrying his bag to the car and taking out the family trash were now both beneath him. Sharp parents make it clear that the star jock still has duties just like everyone else. When the young softball pitcher showed increasing distress over her team's loss, I heard her parents provide the perfect counterbalance by reassuring their daughter that she was doing fine. "Losing games is okay! It's all a part of learning, and you and your team look better every week." The kinds of conversations often fall into place while the families are leaving the playing field, driving to and from games and practices, sitting over dinner, or getting ready for bed. Parents should never underestimate the importance of these ongoing tune-ups to stabilize children's experiences.

It isn't easy to teach our kids to balance their thoughts, feelings, and actions because we often have the same problems in our adult lives. In the following six sports scenarios, each describes too much or too little emphasis on behavior, feelings, or thinking, and each shows common ways young athletes can get out of balance.

Too Little Emphasis on Action

School-age children's obesity rate bulged from 10 percent in 1980 to 22 percent a decade later. Many kids today are quick to fall into a passive pattern of sitting—watching TV, playing video and computer games, or just surfing the Internet. Even biking to the library, a bookworm's modest exercise of the past, has been eliminated. The online encyclopedia and a Net of information are just a click away.

> Jeff was always an easy child. He was the second of four, and his mother had welcomed his sweet temperament and reveled in his ability to amuse himself. Lately, however, he mostly loved watching TV and using the family computer for Net surfing. The doctor noticed that Jeff's weight seemed to have been increasing faster than expected for the past two years, while his height remained steady. Embarrassed by recent weight gain, Jeff usually opted for oversized clothes and XXX sweatshirts to hide his rolly tummy. Sore knees slowed down his walk home, and recently, he had been inquiring about bus service to take the load off his ankles as well. Jeff liked the idea of a bus because it would get him home a half hour earlier and he would be able to play on the computer longer and catch a new TV show before dinner.
> —from S. Kuchenbecker, case stories, Loyola Marymount University, 1997

Jeff's parents need to recognize the problem, but not go overboard. No big rush to the "fat-kid summer camp" or whipping out and lashing the latest "obese teen diet" to the refrigerator. Simply, Jeff's family needs to make a commitment to daily physical activity in overall balance. Jeff's mom and dad could take him to the park, play catch, or shoot some baskets. They could plan a family outing to the local college's football game or track meet, providing models of enjoyable ways to get exercise. Joining an after-school YMCA activity is another alternative. In time, TV and sedentary, passive activities will be replaced by more rewarding healthy activities, and in the process, Jeff's height will catch up to his weight gain.

Too Much Emphasis on Behavior

Regularly, children place large portions of their identity into areas of athletic success—particularly when their actions receive inordinate attention. On occasion, parents also come to see their child only as a "gymnast" or "hockey goalie" and the young athlete becomes vulnerable to ignoring other vital aspects of herself.

Jana had been in gymnastics since she was three and a half. She was a naturally energetic and coordinated toddler, and her parents found a gym program to focus some of her ebullient energies. Described as a good-natured child, she eagerly took to the program and soon rose to the top of every class. Coaches loved her. By junior high, she was well known in the region, having swept several competitions. Her routine was tough, but she never seemed to complain much. Like a trooper, Jana had a 6:00 A.M. workout, conditioning in the weight room at lunch, after-school practices three days a week, and then two-day tournaments every third weekend. On her days off, she would run three miles to stay in shape.

—from S. Kuchenbecker, case stories, Loyola Marymount University, 1998

Nine years into the gymnastic training program, Jana was so dominated by gymnastics that her thinking and feelings had been overlooked. If you asked Jana how she was feeling, she usually said, "Fine!" Did she feel hungry? "No!" Did she think she needed help? "No!" At eighty-five pounds and fourteen years old, Jana showed no signs of puberty; it was a sharp pediatrician who pulled her parents aside. Sadly enough, the whole family had been sucked into an imbalanced regimen that threatened Jana's health, but the problem went unrecognized until her physiological maturation halted.

TIP   **Keep your young athlete's performance in perspective; it is only one part of your child's life.**

Too Much Attention to Feelings

Unlike Jana's parents, some parents cater exclusively to their child's feelings. Loud and demanding, the child whose feelings run unchecked may coerce unwary parents into dancing to their emotional whims. "I'm hungry NOW!" "Where were you? You were supposed to pick me up right after school!" An emotionally intense child can quickly blossom into a fit-throwing young athlete whose complaints undermine his or her own success as well as the team's.

> "I don't *feel* like going to tennis practice today," whined Paula. "My wrist hurts and it's raining outside. Why do you want me to go anyway? The coach makes me feel bad. He corrects everything I do and last time I had to wait for the lesson before me and he ran over. I had nothing to do for a long time. It was boring. At the last match, I didn't get to play until the second round and then my stupid coach didn't even congratulate me after the game. He's terrible. I want a new coach."
> —from S. Kuchenbecker, case stories, Loyola Marymount University, 1998

Many young athletes whose parents see them as gifted soon learn that their talents earn instant attention from some coaches and possibly other players. For some parents, it's easy to fall into the trap of catering to the youngster's feelings, and in an increasing spiral, tremendous effort may be poured into helping the kid "feel" like he or she wants to play. Paula's suckered parents may buy a new racquet, a special wrap for the handle to reduce blisters, new socks of special material to increase foot comfort, or even a specialty electrolyte drink from the health food store—all coddling the supposed delicate feelings of the player. Frequently, the parents rationalize that the efforts are necessary in order to nourish their child's gifted talent, but in fact, the efforts only increase the young player's imbalance. Recent research supports the idea that the child praised for effort (versus natural talent) perseveres longer and thus succeeds more in the long run. In fact, parents' catering to "gifted abilities" may undermine the very effort their child needs to put forth to succeed.

TIP **Avoid creating prima donna athletes!**
Recognize effort! Don't credit natural gifts.

Too Little Attention to Feelings

When parents lose touch with their young child's feelings, they run the risk of pushing their child. In school, they push for more academic achievement. In athletics, they push for winning—at any cost. Much like a racehorse, the child is groomed and decorated, entered, and sent into one competitive event after another. Even painful injuries may be over-looked if they threaten to interfere with the child's competitive perfor-mance schedule.

> Rusty had been on the all-star soccer team since he was eight. A natural athlete, according to every coach, he often was responsible for bringing in the winning goal. In a shoot-out, his performance was usually crucial for success. After a particularly difficult shot on goal, which was blocked, he went down with excruciating pain in his foot. A yelp and he was taken out. His dad applied ice and was ready to double-tape it and send him back into the game, but a parent on the sidelines was a physician and in-sisted they take Rusty to the emergency room. Although he had often mentioned pains in his feet, a sore back, and sore legs, his parents largely wrote complaints off to growing pains. When the X rays came back, the doctor asked the family about the two other times Rusty had broken the bones in his left foot. The parents were at a loss. They never knew he had a broken foot. His parents proudly reported he had never missed a game in seven years. He never had a broken foot. He was fine.
> —from S. Kuchenbecker, case stories, Loyola Marymount University, 1997

The family paying too little attention to a child's feelings may ignore his or her injuries, illness, hurt feelings, and ongoing emotional needs. It is not uncommon for parents with emotional blinders to wait three or four weeks before having a child's painful injury examined—despite obvi-ous signs their child is suffering. Damaged, uncared-for tissues during childhood and young adulthood produce chronic trouble and pain at older ages as well as emotional damage from their being ignored. (Chap-ters 8 and 9 offer longer discussions on feelings and sports injuries.)

TIP   *Push* is a four-letter word.
Don't do it.

Too Little Attention to Thinking

Overestimating the value of athletic performance for some parents means underestimating the value of their child's cognitive development, which again spells imbalance for the young athlete. The child showing early athletic success may get pigeonholed by proud, button-popping parents and coaches as a "jock." Encouragement to practice an extra hour or two every day, often at the expense of schoolwork, means less time for the many other activities that bring balance to a child's life. By senior year of high school, a decade of substantial time on the basketball court, baseball or soccer field, and relatively little time studying leaves many young athletes with subpar grades and unimpressive SAT and ACT scores—and not a recruiter in sight who can consider recruiting him or her.

> Nick was a great baseball player. During the summers, he attended two sleep-away specialty camps. During the school year, his parents had him cut back his school schedule to the bare essentials for graduating so he could squeeze in extra time on the field to practice. During the school season, he usually stayed after practice and his dad helped him an hour more on some of the technical things he needed to improve. Eleven months of the year he played on a traveling club team. Three nights a week, his mom or dad drove him and stayed to supervise his individual lessons with a specialty coach from a neighboring high school. Nick and his parents knew there was little time for homework and school projects when he finally walked in the door at 10:00 P.M. They all agreed school was not so important . . . until the first recruiter asked him junior year how his PSAT scores had been. The look on the recruiter's face said it all. The combined score of 760 was simply too low to even consider. The recruiter mentioned the possible hope of an SAT prep class or special tutor before the SATs, but meanwhile, the recruiter moved on to other more promising candidates.
> —from S. Kuchenbecker, case stories, Loyola Marymount University, 1997

As parents will learn in chapter 14, college scholarships are awarded competitively, with academic success a crucial component. College recruiters know that education is an invaluable part of their package and that past educational success is the best predictor of future success. Game strategy and the ability to outsmart opponents depend on good critical thinking, and making it in school develops good habits for making it in life. Wise parents support their child's academic work, while shortsighted parents may overlook the value of an education, ultimately damaging their child's full personal potential.

Too Much Emphasis on Thinking

There is a split second in most sports when lightning-quick reactions make a crucial difference. While a pause to ponder the right move may be an asset in slower-paced chess games, that pause becomes a major handicap in games requiring physical speed. Regularly, overthinkers let the ball fly past them as they take an extra split second to review their next action and put the polishing touches on their cogitations. For overthinkers, the need for quick actions and feelings puts them at a disadvantage.

> Mara had everything going for her. She had the promise to be a superior player, if only she would "focus" (said the coach), "concentrate" (said her dad), "just play and have fun" (said her mom). Everyone had their ideas, but Mara was a student by nature and had gotten three books from the library on basketball technique. She studied the words of experts, memorized photographs of the perfect form for a free throw, and drew plays in the margins of her notebook. Each time she got onto the court, her head was full of planned actions and perfect maneuvers. Meanwhile, the ball whizzed past her in a direct pass while she was checking out the zone defense pattern of the opponents, and she double-dribbled regularly when looking around to find the best open player to make the three-point shot.
> —from S. Kuchenbecker, case stories, Loyola Marymount University, 1997

Nike would say that Mara should "just do it!" Not going overboard on thinking—too much or too little—but using just the right amount of knowledge and reflection permits quick, correct reactions and confident feelings during play. Too much cogitating while playing robs the player of her spontaneity and joy in the process, not to mention slowing down her reaction time.

TIP   **"Play and have fun"**
is good advice for kids who tend to overthink and lose joy in the process.

HOW TO HELP YOUR CHILD MAINTAIN BALANCE

How your child learns to balance thoughts, feelings, and actions becomes his or her way of coping in life. When lifespan researchers ask individuals who have coped successfully with aging what their secret is, many successful folks credit adaptability, positive attitude, and having multiple interests and resources. It's very easy for busy parents to overlook their youngster's need for balance, whether the child is very successful or struggling. Sometimes problems sneak up on families and kids. Sometimes peers throw in difficult complications. Occasionally, parents doing a great job run into stumbling blocks or breakdowns in communication they just can't get around. Sometimes, given the complicated situations of everyone's lives and the emotional intensity of some sports experiences, the need for professional help is simply inevitable.

It's time to consider professional help when troubling feelings, thoughts, or actions start interfering with normal daily living. If your child "forgets" to eat as Jana did or resists your encouragement to join healthy physical activities like Jeff, some professional assistance may be needed. If your young athlete seems stuck in self-absorption like Paula or is unable to break out of mind-lock because she's afraid she'll make mistakes, a professional's guiding hand may be helpful. It shouldn't take an emergency-room doctor to alert you to healed fractures that went unattended, like Rusty's, but that kind of wake-up call warrants prompt professional attention.

TIP **Seek professional help when troubled feelings, thoughts, or actions interfere with normal daily living.**

If you suspect a problem, let your child know you're concerned, then explore alternatives together. Letting your child know you're worried can be very healing, but there are times when Mom's or Dad's word won't suffice. Sometimes, someone else is needed, even if they say exactly the same things as Mom and Dad. Occasionally, a family member—an aunt, uncle, grandma, or sibling—or a minister, favorite teacher, or even family friend can help out. Gather information. If you talk with parents of kids of the same age and circumstances as your child, you may be relieved to find out that your child's responses are typical. Parent support groups can be helpful in establishing connections and letting parents feel comfortable about "normal" behaviors for the age. Seeking additional help, not too soon nor too late, can reduce the magnitude of the problem and its duration.

According to the American Psychological Association, a shopping list of common signs parents should watch for include

- feelings of hopelessness,
- deep and lasting depression,
- self-destructive behavior,
- substance abuse,
     alcohol, drug use,
     nicotine and cannabis use,
- disruptive fears,
- sudden mood shifts,
- thoughts, threats of suicide,
- compulsive rituals or obsessive thoughts,
- sexual or gender concerns.

I would add to this list any changes in school performance and study habits, shifts or conflicts with peer groups, unhealthy eating or sleeping patterns, and behavior that seems out of character. Any of these can be a signal or a call for help. We know that daily stressors as well as acutely stressful events can build up. Tense family life, difficult ethnic community relations, family financial worries, and living in poverty can all add to developmental challenges. Even your new work schedule can take a toll on your child's ability to function.

Ideally, you want to match the professional help you get to the nature and level of the problem. The alternatives range from psychiatrists (MDs with seven years of training) to community-based peer support programs:

Psychiatrist: These professionals are physicians who completed medical school (four years) and residency training (three years) in the specialty of psychological disorders. Treatment programs include psychotherapy, cognitive-behavioral treatment, and the option to prescribe medication for some problems.

Clinical Psychologist: Most psychologists have Ph.D. degrees (five to eight years) with expertise in research to gather and evaluate information, assessment tools, and therapy alternatives. Clinical Ph.D. psychologists offer therapeutic treatment for individuals or specialized groups. Some psychologists have Psy.D.

degrees with a clinical focus. About half of clinical psychologists work with agencies and half maintain private practices. Most specialize in a particular therapy mode and specific range of problems and may work in conjunction with physicians and social services to provide appropriate care for clients.

Clinical or Psychiatric Social Worker/MSW: Masters of social work programs (two years) prepare graduates to handle personal and family problems. Some work with agencies and about half are affiliated with the National Association of Social Workers as clinical social workers.

Counselors: Marriage and family counselors specialize in family relationship problems (MA-MFCC degrees; two to three years). Pastoral counselors, some of whom receive certification by the American Association of Pastoral Counselors, provide care to many. Specialized counselors are trained in specific areas including child abuse, drugs, anorexia, bulimia, overeating, alcohol, rape crisis counseling, youth crisis, AIDS, and dating violence.

School Counselors: Educational and personal counseling are provided within many school systems, and counselors usually have an M.A. (two years) or Ph.D. or Ed.D. (five to seven years). They provide support for school-related problems and can make referrals in your community for further treatment.

Peer Support Programs: Many communities and hospitals sponsor local peer support programs targeting specific needs within your area. Parenting and abuse programs are common, as well as local chapters of national groups such as Alcoholics Anonymous, Alateen, and Al-Anon. Additional programs may be available in your area. Please consult the national organization, your community hospital, or your nearby university for program referrals near you.

Parents looking for quality professional help might start with their family physician, pediatrician, adolescent medicine specialist, or school counselor. Be direct and keep the goal of finding the best help foremost.

During this process, you need to reassure your child that nothing is "wrong" with him or her. Let your child know you want to do a good parenting job and the process of seeking timely medical or psychological help avoids bigger problems down the road. While this may be hard for parents to hear, please realize that many problems children experience actually reflect learned familial or cultural coping mechanisms that are no longer working for the child. Let your child know that parents and kids often get help together so parents can learn how to better handle a problem successfully. If you have been one of those parents who liked the idea of maintaining a perfect image so your child will respect you, get over it. You and your child will both do better with a realistic perspective, for not only is it more accurate (you are not perfect), but it gets you the help you and your family need.

Finally, the fact of the matter is, not all professional help is created equal. Some professionals have the benefit of better training, better resources, or simply better empathy. Meta-analysis research indicates that no single therapy is ideal for all problems. It seems that the most important aspect of successful treatment is often the quality of the relationship between the therapist and the client. It comes down to caring and empathy. Thus, seek out help appropriate to your child's needs. Find someone who has successfully treated other individuals with the problem. Ask for a treatment plan and timeline, and understand what can be expected. Evaluate your child's progress and discuss realistic expectations. Be willing to find other help if the treatment plan isn't working.

IDEAS FOR BALANCE

Overall balance is the ideal goal. Many parents today find it is easy for one activity to take over, be it a sport, work, performance, or even leisure. Parents are wise to serve as balanced role models and remember to support their child's involvement in a range of activities: Theater, art, and music as well as other sports should all be sampled to help each child find avenues for their unique contributions.

Your child grows within your family and your family is a part of the community. You can help achieve balance through staying active in your community. One family I know requires their sons, outstanding basketball players, to visit a museum in every city in which they play basketball.

The guys have come to appreciate their travels a lot more. They say that the insides of a gymnasium looks pretty much the same everywhere, whether you are in New York or Guadalajara, but museums in different places tell a far richer story.

Another family spends every Thanksgiving serving dinners at the local Salvation Army. Their daily lives are so jam-packed with work, games, school projects, and practices that they don't have time to appreciate how lucky they are. Sharing their family time at Thanksgiving by helping others lets them give thanks together and grow in the process.

One coach I know commits his high-school players to helping out with a younger inner-city team every Saturday. The practices downtown are rarely missed by either teams' members, and both teams improve during the training sessions in more ways than just athletic development. This coach seems to know how much can be learned in the process of teaching . . . and the special relationships between the kids may make a lifetime of difference on both sides.

Some families make weekly time for community service through their church or philanthropic organizations. Many schools support community service projects, which your young athletes should be encouraged to join. Some families set aside the summertime for experiences to balance out the year's intense sports activities. It's up to you to have a commitment to balance and make it work for your family. You'll know you're on the right track when you watch the glowing face of your young athlete as she volunteers her time playing "duck, duck, goose" with *her* group of enraptured four-year-old Head Start "Sunbeams" during summer session. The balance gained from giving back to younger children keeps perspective and nourishes emotional growth.

4

All-Star Athlete Parents

Sunday morning, 7:15 A.M., Gahr High School, Cerritos, California, in the big gym, I zipped my checkered coat and shivered. The cold air soon filled with the *kathwump* sounds of volleyballs, and squealing athletic shoes heralded sharp turns as the players came out to warm up by the nets. A vibrating backboard echoed for a moment as the rim rejected a stray ball.

Parents exchanged their usual pleasantries over the paper cups of Starbucks, performing their own warming-up rituals. "Which one is your kid? How long has she played? How is your team doing?"

Signaling time to start, the ref blew the whistle and the server tossed the ball into the air. As the kids prepared to receive serve, I felt more than saw one of the dads come up beside me. Clapping for the successful dig by our team, I glanced out of the side of my eye to see a somewhat chagrined mustachioed dad looking at me apologetically. "My daughter says I have to come stand next to you." Huh? "She says I should take pointers from you during the game."

Was this the same yelling, screaming dad I had cringed from all season? I could still hear his voice carrying like a pained walrus when the ref made a call he didn't like: "Jeeez-zus!" His temper tantrums and constant berating of coach, players, and ref put me on edge just thinking about the next game day. Was this quiet, humble-pie guy the same person?

He wanted pointers . . . What on earth could I say? His daughter was a talented, brilliant, and sensitive player. On and off the court, her temperament seemed 180 degrees different from the dad I had witnessed. Where had the yelling guy and his tough attitude come from? Genes? Probably not—just bad habits learned decades ago in sports. And today was a new day.

During the course of the tournament competition, I learned he had been a baseball player through grade school, junior high, high school, and college, then went on into the minors while he attended law school at night. I discovered he had a sweet temperament matching his daughter's. I learned he yelled because he thought he was supposed to yell. He *really* cared about his daughter and he wanted to do a great job; apparently, his role models hadn't been so great. He didn't know any better. My heart went out to him and we both learned a lot that day.

What did I do that his daughter liked? What was I to teach this man with more years experience holding a baseball bat than his baby daughter? Where had I learned this thing I was supposed to teach? Only one thing was certain: I knew I had watched some all-star parents watch their kids.

FORMER STAR ATHLETES AS PARENTS

Have you ever watched a former star athlete—Olympic gold medalist, hall of fame member, top collegiate player, professional star-level athlete— watch his or her kid playing a sport? You may be surprised to learn that Kareem Abdul-Jabbar, Cathy Ferguson, Gerry Gregory, and Bob Klein all look very similar while watching their kids play. What do they do? How do *they* act?

Before I tell you, I'd like you to take a minute to remember your young athlete's last competition. What did you see? Do any of these sound familiar?

- A red-faced dad screaming, "You IDIOT! YOU I-D-I-O-T!" after a new player was subbed into the baseball game and struck out for the third time.
- A mom crying as she heard a dad scream, "You IDIOT!" thinking it was really directed at her son; it was really directed at the coach for telling the player to swing.

- An irate father jumping Rumplestiltskin-style on a raised wooden observation platform as his daughter was taken out of a game.

- A well-dressed father hissing between clenched teeth that the current lineup of players was a major rip-off! The family had paid their club money and all the players should be able to play. His son could miss a pass as well as the bozos on the field.

- A glaring mother and father stomping down the bleachers and out the gym door three-quarters of the way through the competition because their child had not yet been played.

- A row of three yellow-shirted mothers on the sidelines of a soccer game empathically kicking a phantom soccer ball as their seven-year-old players all clustered around the real ball, trying to get it away from one another and the goal.

- A grizzled father explaining to a twelve-year-old hockey player (not his son) that he had watched the videos of the previous games and he knew what was needed to fix the young man's skating problem. He proceeded to give a five-minute explanation of how to do it. (Please know, this dad had never played hockey, but had become a self-proclaimed expert in two years by videoing all his son's games, attending all his practices, and carefully listening at every coaching session his son attended.)

- An animated mother holding up three fingers on the sidelines to signal to her daughter that she would pay three dollars for every hit the twelve-year-old made that scored a point.

- A father shanghaiing a coach after a game and pinning him in the corner of the gym while he explained—index finger in the coach's chest punctuating every statement—what the coach should do if he ever wanted to make this team a winning team.

- An inflamed parent calling two levels of administrators at a school to complain that her daughter was an excellent athlete, but the coach had overlooked her and hadn't played her enough during the first seven games of the season. Lo and behold, in the next and last game of the year—the championship match—there was the daughter in the middle of the gym floor, cold off the bench and looking like a deer caught in headlights.

- A stuffy dad turning his back on the coach after the team lost a well-played game, because the coach had decided to play all the players, not just the top players.

- A mom complaining nonstop about a coach's decisions behind his back, then kissing up to his face.

Can you pick the all-star athlete dads and moms from this lineup?

If you selected any of them, you are wrong! All-star athletes as parents often share a very similar style watching their children play. They typically sit relaxed—sometimes leaning back, sometimes elbows resting on their knees, occasionally leaning slightly forward with hands folded together. Their eyes keenly follow the ball and the action. Once in a while, they may rest their chin on their hands. Each play receives careful study. They typically don't carry on extended conversations with people sitting near. The usual facial expression shows concentration. Smiling or frowning rarely, their raised eyebrows, widened eyes, or furrowed brows mark moments of heightened interest during important plays. When cheering, a single staccato clap recognizes excellence or a brief yell celebrates the team or a specific play. They *rarely,* if ever, cheer for their own young athlete. Whether their young athlete is playing or not, each part of the game, from start to finish, seems interesting to the all-star athlete parent. At the end of the game, their double handshakes, followed by bear hugs for their young athlete, have a genuine warmth in a shared moment that seems apart from the surrounding crowd. I've never heard all-star athlete parents criticize a coach in public nor make derogatory remarks about any aspect of the game including the coach's plays, substitutions, behavior, or performance of the young athletes. They are role models of sportsmanship.

In sum, the all-star athlete parents DO NOT

- scream at the kids;
- holler at the coach or referee;
- cry at mistakes their child makes;
- get upset at thoughtless remarks from the stands;
- shout instructions from the sidelines;
- march out of a game;
- throw a stomping fit over a substitution;
- rage about a game loss;
- criticize a coach in public;
- give advice to a coach unless asked;
- give advice to a player;
- use administrative pressure to change coaching decisions;
- undermine a coach's authority.

The all-star athlete parents DO

- respect the young athlete;
- respect the coach;
- watch every aspect of the game carefully;
- know the rules of the game;
- model maturity and sportsmanship;
- enjoy the process of watching the play.

YOU CAN BECOME LIKE AN ALL-STAR ATHLETE AS A PARENT

Five qualities serve many all-star athlete parents. They respect the young athlete, respect the coach, recognize that parents are not objective, learn about the game, and understand that development of an athlete takes time.

1. Respect the Young Athlete

All-star athlete parents understand what it's like to be a young athlete. As they listen and watch a practice or a game, their own experiences give rich insight into the internal emotional processes young athletes must go through. Their potential for compassion and empathy can center their respectful, appropriate encouragement of their own young athlete's development.

Caring about your young athlete requires more than understanding him or her. You can care about a trained Thoroughbred horse and watch a horse race without empathizing with the horse. Tragically, some parents treat their young athletes more like racehorses than developing children. I have seen horse trainers and owners have more compassion for their horse than some parents for their young athlete. Pushing a child comes easily to self-centered parents who feel only their own emotions and pursue their own needs (under the guise of doing what is "best for the child"), clueless as to how their young athlete feels. The nonempathic parent excels at bossing and bullying the young athlete: "Join this team." "Win that game." "Wear this pair of shoes." "Look good for this photo." "Run across this line for the video." "Do what I say." "Don't talk back."

Try on your child's emotional perspective. Walk in his or her emotional athletic shoes for a game or a practice. See what he sees. Feel what she feels. All-star athletes tell us the pressures on the young athlete can be overwhelming. By their model, they teach us to respect the process of emotional and physical growth in the developing athlete. Don't push. Don't prod. Don't rush. Give the time and space needed for improvement. Let your child grow in sports at his or her own pace.

2. Respect the Coach

All-star athlete parents respect the coach for several reasons. First, all coaches have different—and usually more—experience with the sport than the players they are coaching. It is that experience—however great or small—that is the first resource for their job as coach. Second, all coaches have been coached; they have gained experience on when, what, why, and how to teach from their own coaches. Like parents who parent as they were parented and teachers who teach as they were taught, coaches tend to coach as they were coached ... unless they have had some formal education, additional extension courses, training seminars, or other professional developmental programs to alter that style. Third, coaches are people with good days and bad. Everything from a broken duplicating machine before practice to the leaking water pipe at home can contribute to their behavior on a given day. Although professionally, coaches should separate personal problems from coaching, no coach is perfect every day, every game. It just doesn't happen. All-star athlete parents seem to understand the ebb and flow of coaching demands and are more patient.

Being a coach is a lot like being a teacher or a parent, but is made more difficult by the very public arena in which coaching occurs. Frankly, most parents have the luxury of making parenting mistakes privately in the confines of their own home, so they can go about fixing and undoing the problems before anyone really notices. Coaches are not so lucky. They have a public forum with a bevy of invested, emotionally intense parents watching their every move. Moreover, coaches have the confounding influence of crowd involvement with the intense feelings on all sides that competitive situations can magnify. Inappropriate coaching behavior and violation of players' civil rights are never acceptable (chapter 2; appendix A), but expecting coaches to always make the perfect coaching decision is unrealistic.

Learn from the all-star athletes as parents who

- respect the coach's knowledge;
- respect the coach's decisions;
- respect the coach's rules;
- support the coach's program verbally and nonverbally;
- show respect for their young athlete's learning process;
- enjoy the process of watching the athletic competition;
- show gratitude to the coach for contributing to their young athlete's development.

Probably not by accident, all-star athletes' children seem to wind up with some of the "best" coaches available. Many factors contribute. Athletic directors making assignments may conscientiously make more thoughtful matches for all-star athletes' children. Before team assignments are made, all-star athletes as parents may make more of an effort to search out the better coaches and arrange for a suitable placement. Having had many coaches themselves, they have watched their child and have an idea of their needs as well, they know whom to ask, what to watch for, and how to make assignments happen. But once the young athlete is on a team, most all-star athlete parents seem to step back most of the time. Each coach has some individual contribution that deserves respect. If you don't value what a coach has to offer, you won't be able to appropriately support your child's development. Follow the all-star athlete parent's guide. Do your legwork before the team assignments are made and do what you can to put your young athlete with a coach you do respect.

3. Know That Parents Are Not Objective

Many of the judgments made in athletics have subjective and objective components. All-star athlete parents know that objective evaluation of their young athlete is nearly impossible. Ironically, there are many parents who delude themselves into thinking they are objective, but the truly objective parent would exist only in the absence of empathy and emotional investment. Parents are intrinsically biased. The biases make some parents see no mistakes their young athlete makes and some parents see no successes. Most parents fall between the extremes.

Time spent second-guessing, judging, or criticizing a coach yields no profit and may serve only to deter your child from the really important learning process going on. All-star athletes as parents reserve their court-side judgments of their child's play and acknowledge their biases. In hindsight, a better alternative always seems obvious. "Well, if only (fill in the blank), then we wouldn't have lost the game." Playing armchair quarterback makes a lot of wannabe coaches think they're great.

4. Learn About the Game

All-star athlete parents make a point of learning the game. In addition to studying the game plays, they may also go to professional matches, watch televised games at all levels, get books and videos, and seek out camps and other growth opportunities to help their kids progress.

The all-star athlete parent frequently becomes the de facto expert to other parents on the sidelines, the one with the big picture while many parents are caught in the microcosm surrounding their own child. The earlier you learn to see the big picture, the sooner you'll be able to give your child sound support.

Coaches make decisions based on the big picture. Ideally, they use their knowledge of the game's fine points, rules, techniques, interactions of player positions, and strategy to make choices depending on the age and maturational skill level of the players. All-star athlete parents recognize from their own experience that many complicated factors weigh on coaching decisions. The more you learn about a game, the more comprehensible a coach's actions become. The more you appreciate the complexity of coaching decisions, the less likely you are to make unfounded critical judgments and the more respect you'll have for the decision-making process and the coach. Do your homework. Learn about the sport before you generate unfounded opinions.

5. Know That Athletic Development Takes Time

All-star athlete parents and coaches know that developing athletic potential takes time. Seeds of knowledge and technique planted in the spring need time to take root, grow, and mature. Don't try to harvest the crop early. Wait until the plantings have grown to their maturity and nearer their full potential.

If you show patience, your young athlete will, too. You do your child a great service by removing the pressure of time, which only increases the negative emotions likely in competitive sports.

TIP   All-star parents respect their child and the coach, and know athletic development takes time.

WHEN SHOULD YOU CALL THE COACH?

Each coach has practices, planning, scheduling, meetings, and games requiring more behind-the-scenes effort than most non–athletically trained parents know. Respect that time. Each call you make cuts into the coaching time, so screen your concerns and evaluate your calls very carefully.

When a problem arises, listen to your child before you pick up the phone. The more you've learned about a sport, the rules, regulations, techniques, and developmental levels, the better listener you'll be. Follow the guidelines in chapter 2 about types of problems young athletes face. Keep your eyes and ears open.

Of course, there are times when calling the coach is the best course of action. You should call the coach only after your child has exhausted his or her personal resources to solve a problem: Specifically, call if

- your child has an injury that prohibits or limits play in ways your child cannot explain to the coach;
- you need information that is otherwise unavailable through your child or other parents;
- your child is affected by specific coaching decisions that she or he cannot understand;
- you believe abuse or harassment may have occurred.

Many times, problems arise because of poor communication. Some coaches are gifted physically, but short on communication skills. Such coaches do better with a verbal assistant or parent who can share and disseminate information to the families. For ideas here, see chapter 6.

WHAT IF YOUR CHILD ISN'T GETTING ENOUGH PLAYING TIME?

According to coaches, the most frequent problem parents complain about is playing time. Why one young athlete plays and another (usually their child) doesn't rankles many parents into pre-game, post-game, and late-night calls to the coach. Calling coaches undermines the young athletes' individual responsibility and uses up the coaches' valuable time.

Given all the factors that go into playing-time decisions, the best approach is to view the issue as an opportunity for your child to grow. Encourage your child to approach the coach himself and ask, "Coach, what do I need to work on so that I can earn more playing time?" Two important communications occur:

1. You help your child take responsibility for the need to improve.
2. You help your child demonstrate a respect for a coach's knowledge to facilitate improvement.

This is a win-win situation. The young athlete and the coach now have the entrée to proceed with the development of valuable skills. This plan encourages self-efficacy, which parlays into athletic skill training, both foundations for winning games on the field and becoming a winner in life. If you take charge for your child and speak to the coach directly, your child gets the message she isn't capable of taking care of herself. You may negotiate this one situation for her, but what about next time?

HOW TO FOCUS YOUR ENERGY TO HELP YOUR YOUNG ATHLETE

If your son is new to T-ball and you know he knows nothing about the game—even whether he should run to a base, any base, after hitting the ball and you're not sure either, that's okay—you can grow together. After the game, he can explain what he's learned about his sport and you can dutifully take mental notes and learn as well. Not only is it teaching you something immensely affirming to your child, it taps into an aspect of parenting that makes the process wondrous for parents and kids alike—*reciprocal socialization*. You teach your child, and in the process, your child will bring you into new situations and have a lot to teach you as well.

The family behind me brought a complete set of pan lids and a long purple tube horn, which created a loud, memorable stadium moan. Difference was, this was an all-boys high school graduation ceremony. Never mind. Despite the principal's admonition "Hold your applause until all the graduates have received their degrees," the lady behind us and her large family celebrated various kids' names with toots, clangs, and bang, bang, bangs. She whispered over my shoulder she was holding back for her boy because she didn't want them to tell her to stop before they got to his "T" name. One handsome blue-gowned young man grinned winningly at her from the waiting line: "Would you cheer for me?" She laughed and nodded good-naturedly. A few minutes later when she tooted the purple horn, the grinning grad caught her attention. "I want *that* one, okay?" She nodded and he winked, giving a thumbs-up.

Joy pealed from this family when their young man received his diploma, clanging, tooting, and banging the good news to the crowd . . . and no, no one ever told her to stop. After the ceremony, the nineteen assembled family members clambered around the proud mortar-board-bedecked graduate. As various cousins, aunts, uncles, brothers, sisters, grandparents, even family friends grouped around to mug for the camera, all seem to share the same toothy grin . . . as if they each had contributed something to this young man's success. In a moment of light, I knew they had.

> —Shari Kuchenbecker, mother of three in her mom hat,
> Loyola High School graduation, 1999, Los Angeles,
> California

All-star athlete dads and moms who have been-there-done-that rarely reach the sublime ecstasy of first-time parents, but I'd wager their moms and dads did. Nor do all-star athletes manage to keep the deadpan face and loyal positive support profile all the time. They—like all of us—have celebratory moments and moments they would rather forget. They are ex-athletes, not saints, but their experience gives them perspectives that sometimes let the bitter pills seem less bitter. Like you and me, they are glad no microphone or camera is on their every move as they watch their kids play sports.

While the general rule of thumb says let kids grow and figure out a sport with their team and coach, no parent paddywagon will come whisk you away if your enthusiasm gets the better of you and you yell, "Run, Sam! Run! Run to first base! Yeaaaaaaaah!" The joy you share as a family on those weekend afternoons creates emotion-filled memories to last a fetime. Keep the lines of communication open, however, so you'll know when you have stepped over the edge. Your kid should be able tell you.

You can bang, clang, and toot, but use the wisdom when your real, personal disappointment starts to get the better of you. Stay positive. Failing that, use the all-star athlete parent as a role model to keep from acting out your negative feelings and damaging your kid's experience.

POSITIVE ROOTING

Two years after my positive rooting lesson at Gahr High School, I spotted my ex–apprentice rooter dad Sheldon at a high school game as his daughter, Ari, came bounding up to him, two steps at a time. Warmth was radiating between them. After a brief chat, she took off down the bleachers and I scrambled over to catch up. It was great to see him. He was sitting with his wife (she'd rarely attended the events in the old days) and he beamed. Everyone was doing well. His daughter had given up volleyball and was doing track. His face seemed softer now, less tense as he explained how much she loved sprint events and how well she was doing in school. He reassured me that he was cheering—positively—at every meet.

Find joy in the process of learning with your child in sports, but know the best cheering and greatest inspiration you can give your child happens long before he steps onto the T-ball field—by letting him know you believe in him or her. Be yourself, but remember the all-star athlete parents when your negative feelings get the better of you. You'll learn in the process and give your child a better chance of becoming successful both on and off the playing field.

5

"I Love to Play!":
Motivation and the Young Athlete

Why do I play? Because I love it! I love being outside . . . and I love the competition.
> —Kent Steffes, Olympic gold medalist,
> top money-earner for USA Beach Volleyball, 1997

I play and I coach because I love the game, but one thing was really important when I was a kid. If nobody was home, I used to turn on the national anthem music and pretend I was winning the gold medal. I'd step up on the platform and hear the crowd cheering. I used to practice again and again what it felt like to tip my head, feeling the ribbon go over and onto my shoulders. The weight of the gold on my chest was so real. In that moment, everything was just perfect! When I finally won the gold in the Colombia games, I had been there a thousand times in my dreams.
> —Chris McGee, 16s two-time Junior National gold
> medal volleyball coach, elementary school teacher

I don't play for the awards . . . I play because I love to do it. When I was born, God gave me a gift, and even though I was a pain in the butt half the time to my family, the gift was to be an athlete and specifically a soccer player. . . . We've heard a lot of superlatives thrown out, "greatest this, best that." Well,

I'm the result of the people I've surrounded myself with, the coaches
who are here today, my teammates, who, if I could handpick
nineteen people I'd want to hang out with, I'd pick them in a
heartbeat. I really am basically what they've given me. From that
team to my family. They crack me up every time I see them. I love
you guys so much. I'm just so happy you could be a part of this . . .
so thank you.

> —Mia Hamm, at the dedication of the Nike building in Beaverton,
> Oregon, quoted in the *Los Angeles Times,* sports section, 6/19/99.

Athletes play for many reasons—from loving the game to visions of gold medal ceremonies to promises of an ice cream cone. Ask a dozen young players, "Why do you play?" and you'll hear a dozen answers. Consider the following Saturday afternoon at Paul Revere Field, Pacific Palisades, California, girls AYSO soccer:

"We won, Dad!! Did ya see me?" yelled the grinning mud-covered sweeper as she sprinted toward the sidelines. Dad boomed back, running full stride, "I saw you! You were an animal." He lifted her up in a big bear hug as her coltish legs swung akimbo.

Next came the midfielder. She caught her brother's eye and slapped a high five. "You owe me, bro! Hot fudge *and* a banana! Pay up!" Bro gave a lopsided grin and began to negotiate whether she wanted payment now or would go for double or nothing after next week's game.

A red-cheeked goalie chortled enthusiastically, tugging the oversized glove off with her teeth. "Wasn't that the best save ever?" She finally pulled the other glove off as her mom wiped her wet bangs from her forehead. "I thought I wasn't going to be able to get it, but then I jumped and there it was! I've never jumped that high before!"

"New shoes! Right, Mom! Any ones I want. You promised!" The fullback and her mom exchanged knowing glances, smiled conspiratorially at Dad, who shrugged his shoulders, hands palms up, a big smile spreading across his face.

Meanwhile, the two forwards were sitting under the team umbrella figuring out their new ranking in the league. They decided next week's game was crucial. Beat the team next week and they had the gold medal nailed.

Off to the side, the coach was having a heart-to-heart with a player who had sat out the first and last quarters. The player had missed two practices. "First you come to practice, learn the plays, then you get three quarters of playing time. I can't put you on the field when you don't know your position."

Across the field, the voices weren't so vibrant and the faces not so animated. One girl was crying, her face buried in her dad's oversized shirt. The loss meant that they didn't go on to the play-offs. She loved to play. Her dad reminded her that the school season started right after Christmas and she would have plenty of playing opportunities in the future. He would make sure of it.

Another player was complaining to her dad that now she didn't have enough money to go to Disneyland with her friends. Her parents had been paying her ten dollars for each goal she scored, and she needed to score today and didn't.

MOTIVATION TO PLAY SPORTS

Watch any team. Watch any player. You'll see a number of motivations at work. Yet independent of the motives, each player shares the process of play and the final game outcome.

If you want to know who's going to stay in sports, watch the kids who come back week after week, year after year, win or lose. Who come early to practice and stay late. Who maneuver to the front of the line in every drill. Who want to win every drill, every race to the wall and back, every free-throw competition. Who want to try it "just one more time." Ask them why they play. They often answer, "I love to play!" "For fun!" "To get better!" "I like playing, that's why!" They let you know there is *nothing* they'd rather be doing. Across the board, the greatest, most enduring motivation for the young athlete is playing for the love of it.

ALL REWARDS ARE NOT EQUAL

As any coach or parent knows, what drives each kid is different. Motivation may be internal or external, differ from day to day and from year to year, and all rewards are not equal. Even kids who eventually become Olympic champions have had up seasons and down seasons, on and off times. You need to be aware and permit the normal ebbs and flows of what motivates your child over time. As most parents know, motivation doesn't function as a single, simple process, and when you deal with kids, their changing motivation must be interpreted through the perspective of individual development over time. After reviewing research and surveying coaches' and parents' experiences, I've summarized the kinds of rewards most commonly given. Note how the list moves from external rewards to intrinsic ones:

Hierarchy of Rewards

Level		Examples	Technical Term
1	Food	Candy, treats (granola bars, chips, crackers, cookies, raisins, soda pop, ice cream)	Primary reinforcement
2	Tokens/Money (redeemable for food)	McDonald's gift certificate, poker chips, scrip, or money	Secondary reinforcement
3	Toy	Soccer ball, plastic bug, ring, baseball bat, Star Wars Jawa, baseball	Concrete prize
4	Tokens/Money (redeemable— prize room)	Sport store gift certificate, scrip, or money	Prize room (choice of prize)
5	Trophy/Plaque/Pin	Trophy, participation team plaque, all-star pin, medal on ribbon	Symbolic reward
6	Praise	"Great job!" "You stuck to the drill and finished under time. Congratulations."	Praise
7	Grandma's Rule	"First you do what I want you to do, then you do what you want to do."	Premack Principle
8	Intrinsic Reward	The work itself provides intrinsic rewards (i.e., playing baseball is fun exercise and as a child plays, his or her skills improve, leading to mastery and self-efficacy)	Intrinsic reward
9	Self-Reinforcement	Telling yourself that you did the best you could do, even if it was average; you still learned a lot of good things even though the time didn't reflect how much you improved.	Self-reinforcement

Parents know a shiny gold trophy carries a lot of weight, especially if you get one with a marble base. The gold, silver, and bronze medals on brightly colored ribbons are valuable treasures hanging in most kids' rooms. Moving on up the hierarchy, coaches have long used behavioral contingency rewards like "first you come to practice, then you get to play." Psychologists call it the Premack Principle, but you might recognize it as Grandma's Rule. "First you do what *I* want you to do, then you get to do what *you* want to do."

Many aspects of athletics are intrinsically rewarding. Connecting with the ball after the pitch or timing a jump just right lets you know upon landing perfectly that you did everything well. Intrinsic rewards also come to the energetic kid who runs track and knows he feels better after he spins off some of his extra energy. Aerobic exercise not only gives a healthy workout and nice endorphin by-products, but reminds us that our muscles were designed to be used; it just plain feels good. At the final level of intrinsic reward, an athlete ostensibly experiences no benefit, gets no recognition, receives no trophy, no prize, no toy or goodie—but believes it was a good idea to do anyway. Self-reinforcement is the reward when athletes force themselves to do something, knowing that they need to try, but often end up with nothing to show for it other than the knowledge that they did it. Skills often build slowly, and some efforts seem to be false starts in the beginning.

In summary, kids' motivation to pursue sports often progresses from tastable, touchable, feelable, concrete things (candy, toys, trophies) to invisible, abstract rewards (joy of improving, knowing you tried). Rewards also go from external (outside the individual) to internal (feelings within the individual). Rewards usually start from an immediate, physical payoff and progress to a delayed, internal benefit. Thus, young athletes are more likely to be motivated by the chocolate strawberries for the team snack, while older players are more likely to be motivated by self-congratulations for trying.

The hierarchy of rewards helps explain why we see top athletes continue to be motivated to play despite team losses, injuries, coach and press criticism, and the natural ebbs and flows of their skills. Intrinsic rewards of playing for fun and improvement let the athlete ride more smoothly through the lean times of sparse victories and sagging coaches' encouragement.

WHAT IS THE *BEST* MOTIVATION?

What is the *best* motivation? Research by Leon Festinger, Ed Deci, and Bob Ryan of the University of Rochester as well as many others suggests that using too many rewards for young athletes may actually undermine their enjoyment of the sport and ultimately undermine their valuable intrinsic motivation to keep playing. It makes sense. The kids who keep playing long enough to become truly successful all-stars say they play *because* they love it. If we accept that intrinsic motivation—level 8, love of playing and joy of improving—is what keeps kids playing year after year, external rewards only serve to take kids *backwards* down the hierarchy to a lower motivation.

It works like this. If you give a kid ten dollars (level 2) to play a soccer game he already enjoys playing (level 8), then he thinks he's playing for the money. The money becomes the motivation. Take away the money and he thinks the reason to play is gone. The money gets in the way of *remembering* that he simply loves to play. My advice is to help your kids stay tuned into the intrinsic rewards for playing and keep your wallet in your pocket.

Young athletes should play sports for the right reasons. When parents swoop in with tantalizing rewards—a new pair of shoes, a trip to Disneyland, ten dollars for a goal—kids are vulnerable to *cognitive dissonance* and forget why they're playing. They thought they were playing for fun, but with the external payoffs some parents maneuver, it's really easy for kids to lose sight of the important natural internal rewards for playing.

Playing sports is fun. Pick any sport. Baseball, football, bowling, golf, tennis, archery—performing the skill is rewarding. It feels great when the player hits the baseball, catches a long pass, nails the landing, hits the green, returns a slam, steals a puck, makes a strike, or hits the bull's-eye. Improving a skill over time is great fun and adds meaningful challenges to life. Success is its own reward.

Long before Little Leagues had winners' trophies and participation medals, kids played sports. A back lot, quiet residential street, or neighbor's yard all served the purpose. A ball, a stick, and a few willing kids sufficed. Kids went sledding when a cardboard box was left in the snow. Barrel staves made fine skis. Home plate could be drawn in the dirt; no fancy bag was needed.

The commercial brouhaha over equipment clouds a lot of parents' and kids' vision. *Kids do not need* a seventy-five-dollar glove to catch a ball. One-hundred-dollar shoes *do not* make the run possible. Fifty-dollar shin guards may not be any better than the ten-dollar variety. And all those kids wearing fancy-label basketball shoes in the private gym will not get any better any faster than the kids on the blacktop in cheap variety-store shoes . . . unless they want to.

You can't buy success, and expensive equipment does not guarantee improvement. The young athlete's *desire to improve* and *time* are the tickets. (On the other hand, ill-fitting shoes, poor protective equipment, and avoidable injuries will cut into a player's fun, so when it comes to safety and fit, do your research and get the best value for the money.)

HOW THE REWARD HIERARCHY CAN WORK FOR PARENTS

Your job as parent is to support your child's interest, and the best way to support your child's development is usually to *sit back and let your child enjoy the process of learning the sport*. You really don't need to cheer (level 6)—though it's fun to—buy toys (level 3), or offer money (levels 2 and 4). That's bringing coals to Newcastle. Sports are intrinsically fun (level 8), and learning new skills intrinsically rewards the young athlete. Nature rigged it that way.

The way to make the reward hierarchy work for you is to understand the levels of reward and the goals for your young athlete.

> **TIP** **Encourage your child's intrinsic motivation.**
> (Play to have fun, to get better, to learn life's important lessons, and to enjoy healthy physical activities.)

Less Is More

In the world of rewards, less is more. The less often you give an external reward, the better. And when you give a reward, the less reward you give, the more internal rewards you let the players figure out for themselves. Intrinsic rewards shine through when not overwhelmed by external justifications.

The reward hierarchy comes in handy when intrinsic rewards aren't enough. The clues are often obvious—the child doesn't want to go to practice anymore; she's slow getting ready for the game on Saturday; or she starts complaining about minor aches and pains. Where is the negativity coming from? The first thing you need to do is really *listen*. Ask questions and accept what your child tells you. Hear his or her reality. You want to understand the problem.

Eliminate the Negative

You won't hear complaints about learning. Kids like to learn. That part is fun. Listen for complaints about things that get in the way of learning. By eliminating negatives that get in the way of learning, you let the intrinsic reward of learning shine through again. It makes sense. If your shoes hurt, it's hard to learn how to kick the soccer ball because every time you kick, you have to compensate for sore toes. If you're too hungry at the start of a game, you can't concentrate on doing what you need to do. If you're late for practice, you can't learn the plays you need to perform in the game. As discussed in chapter 2, there is a range of little things that come up which require your parental support.

TIP   Removing a negative can be a great positive!

Removing negatives motivates a player better than starting a reward program. The reason is simple. A reward is an add-on. The negative is still there and the value of the external reward must overcome the intrinsic negative dogging every practice or game. Watch carefully for those negatives that may be detracting from natural rewards. Some super-sleuthing parents have uncovered troublesome negatives like fuzzy vision (a child needs glasses or a stronger prescription), poor peripheral vision through glasses (the child needs contact lenses); sore arches (the child needs arch supports); even fear of wearing a skimpy racing swimsuit in public (time may help this problem as a shorter, less-developed child moves into puberty in the next few years).

Of course, playing sports has some natural negatives. Muscles do get sore, injuries do happen, and many long hours per week go into practices. That's just the way it is sometimes. Media and current culture seem to perpetuate an illusion there should be no effort, no pain, and no hard work without immediate payoff. These unrealistic illusions can be dangerous for kids. Many things of great value in life come through effort and hard work. Helping your child appreciate the work ethic has merit, whether it's through sports, academics, philanthropy, or household duties.

Positive listening helps with many problems. Help your child sort out problems and figure out solutions: "What could you say to let the coach know there's a problem?" "What are two things you could try that might make it turn out differently?" Put your child in charge of removing his or her own obstacles. Don't be surprised if the process of explaining the problem in and of itself leads to the resolution. Practicing clinicians, barbers, manicurists—everyone who listens—know that the process of telling a problem is helpful.

Caution: Don't Become a Crutch

Watch out for becoming too good a listener. One friend had her daughter on a very high-pressure club team, and each day after practice, the teen athlete would spend increasingly lengthy hours explaining what the coach said and did and how each of the girls responded. Cliques, innuendos, and favoritism all became major topics. Like the tines of a tuning fork, mother and daughter would resonate together over each seemingly growing problem.

Inadvertently, the well-meaning mom was rewarding her daughter for seeing problems. The more problems she could find, the more they resonated. While mutually rewarding in the beginning, the magnification of the many problems eventually overwhelmed the joy of playing. All the daughter could see were the problems instead of solutions, and it took the insightful mom some undoing to put the real problems in perspective again. Listen, but keep a mature perspective.

If the problem is inevitable and unchangeable, make an overall evaluation of the experience. Fully explore the problem. If the experiential value is high, but the motivation is in a slump, then the reward hierarchy can help you decide where and when to intervene.

For example, let's say your kid's soccer team is in a slump. Fewer kids are showing up at practice, they haven't won a game in weeks, and they're bored with the coach's drills. How can you help your child? Using the re-

ward hierarchy, remember that your first goal is to eliminate the negatives (in this case, boring practices and lackluster games) and then accen-
tuate the intrinsic positives (the joy of learning and improving—level 8).
If you are shy on skills and long on motivation, you're in an ideal position
to try one of several alternatives:

1. Offer to help the coach at practices. Offering to help the coach
in any way needed—shagging balls, making calls, running a drill in
one part of the gym, even holding the net—will free up important
coaching time. Being reliably available to the coach will let the coach
offer more individualized attention to improve kids' skills, which is intrinsically motivating.

*2. Set up a one-on-one session and let your child teach you what
he or she knows.* Fun for the young athlete, reverse-role teaching lets
kids teach you while simultaneously practicing the skills they have.
They'll be thinking about what they do, and in the process, naturally
building on their foundation skills. Playing the role of learner also
gives you good insight into the physical and emotional demands on
the young athlete. Playing and learning are both much harder than
they look.

*3. Arrange participation in an open gym, sport camp, or recre-
ation league to refresh your kid's enthusiasm.* As you develop your
watching skills, take a moment sometime to turn and watch the parents and coaches watching the kids play. Often, what you'll see is a
hothouse feverish scrutiny. For many young athletes, a chance to play
just for fun will be a great treat. Take your kid to play (really play) in an
open gym, a recreation league, or just let them hang out and play at
the local rec center or high school. Supplemental fun lessons or a
sport camp can also do the trick, but tend to be costly. Playing for fun
is a vital element to maintaining motivation, so keep your eyes open
for opportunities to bring fun back into your child's sport.

*4. Encourage your child to become an assistant to a team of
younger players or for the Special Olympics.* Helping others is a wonderful endeavor and reminds kids of the intrinsic reasons to play a
sport.

SETTING UP A REWARD PROGRAM

If you have exhausted all possibilities (removed the negatives, refocused on the intrinsics), the final backup plan is to set up an extrinsic reward program. Remember: Reward programs are to be used only as a last resort.

Situations possibly warranting a reward program would include:

- *Your child has committed to two sports, and midway through the season, he or she isn't enjoying one of them.* Partway into the season, feeling pressed for time, your kid wants to quit one of the teams. The social dynamics on one of the teams are really difficult. The coach can't sort out who gets along with whom and seems to make matters worse by running competitive drills pitting players against one another. Your young athlete is stuck playing a position he or she doesn't like and wants out.
- *The previous season was a tougher experience than you realized.* A minor injury, a coach who favored his own son on the team, and some petty between-player jealousy has your child doing a fast backpedal from starting another season. You know your child had some fun times before, but the bad taste from last season's negatives remains.
- *Your child has never played the sport before and fear keeps her from trying out.* Your child is twelve and has never played soccer. Other kids have been playing for six years. Your child likes to do well and hates the thought of being the worst on the team. She has friends on the school team and would love to play, but is afraid of making a fool of herself.

Each of these situations may warrant a reward program, but before you decide to begin one, sit down with your child and discuss the problem as you see it. Let him or her know the true value of trying or continuing. Explain the difference between intrinsic rewards and external rewards while making it clear that you believe there is value to the goal. Ask your kid what he or she thinks. You may be surprised to discover that even five-year-olds understand. Often just discussing the problem helps to remotivate a young athlete. If not, once you've established that your kid's motivation is sagging for a legitimate reason and there is nothing you as the parent can or should do to improve the situation, consider implementing a reward program. Ask your child for some suggestions about what might work as a little jump-start to get him or her going again. You want to shoot for the highest level of intrinsic reward, smallest amount of extrinsic reward, in a program lasting the shortest amount of time.

1. Use the Highest Level of Intrinsic Reward Possible

If the young athlete has been playing for the fun of it (intrinsic re-ward—level 8), explain the idea of perseverance. Many kids catch on to the phrase "When the going gets tough, the tough get going." Let them know that playing for fun when they're learning quickly is great, but they may have to hang in there even when they're not improving as fast as they want. Reassure kids that learning is fast sometimes and slower at others. Just knowing this can help them motivate themselves (level 9). Some-times a simple discussion will be enough to get your child back into the game again. If not, try praising your child for his or her efforts (level 6). You could also try Grandma's Rule (level 7): set up the schedule positively so that first your child goes to practice (what you want him to do), then he gets to do what he wants to do (go to the game on Saturday).

2. Use the Least Amount of Reward Possible

Remember: think small. The goal is to jump-start activity, not take it over; thus, offer the minimum reward. For example, to get your reluctant eight-year-old to try out for the soccer team, you don't need to promise a weekend at Disneyland. You can offer an hour of free play at the local park and often be just as successful.

The mom who gives five dollars to her four-year-old for cleaning up her room will be in real trouble by high school. It may take a wheelbarrow of money to get her to do her homework every night at those rates. For families who watch television, one hour of reward time instead of four hours follows the less-is-more-reasonable guideline.

3. Always Emphasize the Intrinsic Reward (Level 8)

Whichever level of reward you use, always include a word of reminder for your child about the intrinsic reasons for doing something. It should help your child stay in focus about the role of a reward program as a short-term aid.

> "You can be proud of yourself going to the soccer tryout. You've got a chance to learn where to connect your foot with the ball and your shots on goal got a lot more accurate."
>
> "You worked really hard practicing last week. Your free-throw percentage will be better in the next game, I'll bet."

4. Phase Out Extrinsic Rewards as the Intrinsic Rewards Take Over Again

Interestingly, phasing out a reward program often occurs naturally. As intrinsics take over, both the parent and the young athlete forget to follow through with payment of the earned extrinsic reward. As close as I can remember, I think I still owe our third child some prize or another for playing just one more soccer season, and that was three years ago. She is still happily playing, and neither of us remember why we decided to do a reward program or just what the reward was. Once she got into the second game that season, she liked playing so much we both forgot the deal until I started writing this chapter.

PARENT CHEERLEADERS

For several years, my daughter played on a team with one of the best cheering dads I've ever heard. George, a six-foot, eight-inch basketball-rangy dad, had a deep, rich bass voice that echoed off the gym timbers everywhere our girls played. George would boom, "Go, Harvard-Westlake!" and "Way to go, team!" When we eventually got onto opposing teams, I still wanted to cheer with George. When he boomed, "Come on, let's go!" everybody hunkered down a little tighter—including the parents in the stands. George was my role-model parent. He knew to

1. praise effort ("Great get! Nice try!"),
2. encourage teamwork ("Go team! Yeah! Go Tigers!"),
3. recognize excellence ("Great shot! Whatta block!"),
4. Cheer for sportsmanship (applaud the other team's successes, too).

Many parents find their excitement spills out in competition, particularly in close games. Most of us naturally get excited when the score on the board goes up, but young athletes need the most encouragement when the score looks the bleakest, not when it looks the best.

It is the process of playing well that earns the points. An old tennis coach used to tell the kids, "If the process is right, eventually the product will be, too!" Working on form laid the foundation for success later. "I don't care where the ball goes right now, just get the form right and eventually the ball will go where it is supposed to."

Cheer for effort, teamwork, excellence, and sportsmanship if you want to be a model cheering parent. Kids stay in sports when the process is right, and the process requires those four components I just listed.

Every criticism takes a lot of praise to undo. Marty Peterson at the University of Wisconsin at Oshkosh tells a wonderful story about praise and criticism. She had a team of excellent athletes and it seemed they should be winning more games than they were. A friend advised her to try the "acting as if" technique. By "acting as if" the team were winning and using more praise, Marty could help the team do better. For one week, Marty and her assistant coach ran all practices and drills with "Good job!" "Great effort!" "Way to be there" no matter the outcome, praising with no critiques. The team not only started smiling more, they won the next game and went on to win the state championship.

To be a successful cheerleader for your child, you don't need George's booming voice. Your quiet dialogues with your child before and after the game become the internal voices your child will hear during the game. The inner monologues your child carries into competition underscored by your encouragement may be more important than any sideline hollering you do. (If you want to hedge all bets and you have a weak voice, appendix D has instructions for how to whistle using four fingers when you really want to make a cheering statement!)

THE PERILS OF PLAYING TO WIN

If a kid (or parent) values winning above "playing to the best of your ability," losing a game becomes a significant negative experience. When playing to the best of your ability is more important than winning, losing is less relevant and the quality of the effort prevails. Nicely enough, individual players really can't control winning or losing, but they can be in charge of playing their best.

Encourage your child to value and cheer for the quality of play over winning a game. Individual effort is in the control of the individual player, but winning is influenced by a number of uncontrollable variables such as relative skill, past practice, coaching, team experience together, team mood, individual and team injuries, and referee calls.

Pity the young athlete who has one—or worse, a pair—of curmudgeons for parents. Folks who usually see the glass as half empty become grave burdens to the developing athlete. These parents seem to see only the mistakes their kid makes. The failures that they are quick to point out dwarf the few successes they seem to see. To these negative-thinking parents, the scores are never good enough, the wins are not by enough points, and there was always more that should have been done.

After many years of watching youth sports, I am sorry to report that the population explosion of curmudgeon parents was part of my initial motivation for writing this book. You can now hear them at most any competitive sports event. It's my experience that most of their children don't stay in sports long, but their time on the sidelines can significantly handicap their child as well as other team members. Regrettably, I have observed a growing cesspool of belligerent hollerers—anonymous folks from other teams—and the following are direct quotes from games I have attended in the last year:

Hollering for Curmudgeons (aka What *Not* to Say!)

"Kill 'em!"

"Go home, [team name]!"

"You Suck, Number 9!"

"Boooooooooooooooooooooooooooooo!"

"We are the goooooood team! That is the baaaaaad team!" (as led by the university cheerleaders)

"Sh——!"

"Use your heads!"

"You idiots. This is football, not pussyball!"

"Hey Batter, Batter, Batter! Hey Batter . . ."

"Hey Ref! You crazy? That kid can't play worth————!"

"Ref! Get some glasses!"

"Where did they get that big, ugly kid? The barrio?"

"Get your heads out of your butts and into the GAME!"

"We might as well go home if you're gonna play like that!"

"Coach, get that kid out of there. He can't hit the broad side of a barn!"

"You think that was a good win? You gotta be kidding yourself. They played like sh————."

Ironically, when you talk to some curmudgeon parents, they really believe they are "helping"! They seem proud of their self-appointed expertise and their ability to always know what's wrong with the team, a certain player, or the coaching. Stubbornly proud of their job as team critic, only a few hang around sports long enough to figure out how powerfully they contribute to a team's defeat. (Luckily, most coaches have it figured out, and curmudgeons' kids who reflect their parents' attitude get to warm the bench a lot. I am glad to say my kids have never been on such teams, but from folks I've interviewed, season end is a relief on teams with a cohort of curmudgeon parents and kids.)

If you're struggling with some curmudgeon feelings yourself (and most people do), put a copy of this positive script in your pocket as a reminder of what you need to do:

Holloring for Winners (aka What to Say)

"Go [team name]!"

"Good playing!"

"Yeah!"

"Bravo!"

"Great effort!"

"Way to hang in there!"

"Great job!"

"Nice teamwork!"

"Way to touch the ball!"

"Great defense!"
"Wow!"
"Whatta hit!"
"You're on top of it!"
"You're awesome!"
"Way to go, team!"
"Way to play like a team!"

Coaches Need Strokes, Too

It's no surprise that coaches potentially have a large impact on the development of the young athlete. Compare the amount of time you spend with your child to the amount of time he or she is with a coach.

In some studies, 35 percent of high school athletes place their coach's influence *ahead* of their parents'. Obviously, the choice of a coach is important. Coaches act as role models whose training potentially affects many aspects of the young athlete's future. A great experience can facilitate a lifetime of motivation, while a single bad experience can end a career in one season. Many college athletes credit one coach as being their inspiration, while those who leave the sport mention the last coach as the straw that broke the camel's back.

HOW TO PICK A COACH

What makes a successful coach? It depends on your child's development, the particular situation, and the team (ages and skills of players, friendships, and coach as a dynamic educator). You want the coach to be someone you respect, to whom you entrust an important part of your child's personal development. When selecting from several coaches, gather information about them from people similar to yourself who have children similar to your own. Make a point of going to watch a coach in action and form your own impressions. If you can, speak in person with the coach to find out his or her goals, style, and methods.

When kids say, "I can't miss practice. I love going to practice," they are telling you that what they are learning matches their needs. Their skills are improving, their understanding of the game is growing, and they feel good about practice. The quickest way to kill love of play is negative feelings. At practice and games, it's the coach who creates the emotional environment through praise (hopefully generous) and criticism. Building players' skills necessarily includes feedback and constructive direction, but how feedback is managed is what makes the environment a positive or negative learning experience. Keeping the emotional balance positive is an art and a science each coach must master.

The coach who praises growth, values effort, and regularly takes time to review each player's improvement encourages a superior positive learning environment. The coach who, win or lose, only rehashes players' errors makes a grave mistake. Negative focus quickly douses enthusiastic fire.

No coach should ever intentionally or unintentionally violate the psychological or physical rights of a player. All youth athletic organizations must abide by the federal guidelines regarding civil rights, and many have adopted harassment policies. A sample of a comprehensive youth athletic organization harassment policy statement is included in appendix A. Know that no coach, assistant coach, administrator, referee, or person affiliated with a youth sports organization may ever verbally, visually, physically, or sexually harass a player. Positive learning environments are free from discrimination due to an individual's sex, race, creed, color, national origin, ancestry, medical condition, sexual orientation, or physical disability. All communications (direct or by innuendo) must reflect respect for individual differences and support growth opportunities appropriate to age and developmental levels.

There is no place in athletics for inappropriate coaching behavior. Coaches who berate, degrade, or insult players not only undermine players' learning and self-esteem, they are violating the law. Harassing or inappropriate physical contact violates players' rights, and parents necessarily must monitor all adults with whom their child is entrusted. Your young athlete deserves fair and respectful treatment from all people.

I've heard parents say, "The coach is very tough. He yells and screams, but it's good for my kid." Wrong! Being yelled and screamed at is not good for anyone, and it is a violation of your child's civil rights.

TIP   **Screen coaches and staff.**
1. Watch the coach at practices
2. Watch the coach at games
3. Talk to parents of current or past players
4. Talk to players who have played for the coach
5. Talk to the coach in person
6. Check out the coach's training and certification

The Qualities of Truly Great Coaches

Look for these qualities when you're checking out coaches:

1. Teacher education training (bachelor's or master's program)
2. Special coaching certification classes
3. Good reputation
4. Goals congruent with your family goals
5. Successful win/loss record (more important for older and very talented players)
6. Extended coaching experience

Be open to accepting a coach who does not fit the exact profile, but who is an excellent match for your young athlete. The young, inexperienced, enthusiastic coach who loves the game may be the ideal match for the less confident first-time athlete. The older, hard-nosed coach may be too tough for the first-time athlete, but be an ideal match for the seasoned athlete getting a little cocky and lazy. Matching the young athlete's multiple psychological, social, and skill needs will require your mature, balanced perspective as parents.

Getting Assigned to a Team

In actuality, most of the time your young athlete simply will be assigned to a team and coach; you take what you get. Helping your young athlete learn to work with a wide range of coaches builds character and diversifies skills. While it's generally true that coaches with teacher education training, special coach certification classes, and much experience have superior techniques, this may not always be the case. There are a number of outstanding young coaches who shine in their very first coaching opportunity—probably a reflection of their own excellent coaches and parents.

Stepping Back Once a Team Assignment Is Made

Each coach has something valuable and unique to offer. Once your kid is on a team, step back and respect the coach's strengths. If there is a formative evaluation program in place, rest easier. If not, consider suggesting one to your youth sports organization. Your attitude toward the coach and your respect will provide a great role model and help your child listen and grow from the experience with the coach.

If you want to help nurture your child's relationship with the coach, you'll need to learn how to see the situation from the coach's perspective. When he or she makes decisions you don't understand, first try seeing the problem through the coach's eyes. Try to take into consideration the many variables he or she must juggle. Your child is but one part of the team. Other players, families, administrators, professional organizations, goals, budget, time, and so on each contribute to a coach's decision process.

If your youngster has a problem, have him or her take responsibility and ask questions. Few people, coaches included, respond well to strident confrontations. Take for example the young player on an ice hockey team who wants more playing time. She might say, "Coach, I know there are fifteen kids on the team and you have good reasons for putting people on the ice, so I was wondering what I might do to earn more playing time. What should I be working on?" Contrast that to the confrontational parent's approach who pokes his finger in the coach's face, saying, "Listen, my kid can miss the goal as good as any kid you have out there. We paid our dues and this is my daughter's third season. She deserves a chance or we're switching clubs now!" Walk a mile in the athletic shoes of your kid's coach before you become a coach critic.

TIP   Learn to see the coach's perspective.

COACHES COACH AS THEY WERE COACHED—
UNLESS THEY GET SOME TRAINING

Well-meaning but professionally untrained coaches will coach as they were coached. They'll pass on the strengths and the weaknesses of their own experiences unless the cycle is broken through education and effort. Most coaches never intentionally harm their players, but their coaching style may reflect antiquated theories. A coach subjected to verbal or physical abuse may pass the same along to his students, unaware that this could qualify as harassment or child maltreatment.

Usually, team assignments are made based on age, skill, gender, past training, and the fickle finger of fate. As I've said, do your homework before the team assignment is made, then step back. Helping your young athlete accept team assignments, learn from a range of coaching styles, and make the best of every learning opportunity are among the many valuable lessons sports have to teach. As a parent, you need to respect the coach's work. Your respect will provide an important role model and help your child listen and grow from the experience with each new coach.

Coach Training and Certification Programs

More than 3 million people coach in the United States. According to some statistics, five out of six—2.5 million coaches—have no training to do the important job of educating young athletes.

Before parents get too worried about coach training, the 17 percent of coaches with some training surpasses the near 0 percent of parents with parent training. Educating coaches about appropriate methods, techniques, and skills-building is in its infancy. Many youth athletic organizations have budding programs, but most coaches thrust into the job of coaching still have limited resources to form their athletic and educational curriculum.

With the increasing popularity of youth sports, a concurrent parallel movement to professionalize coaching should give parents some peace of mind. Many youth sports organizations including Pop Warner Football, American Youth Soccer Organization (AYSO), and United States Youth Volleyball League (USYVL) have active coach-training programs, harassment policies, coach-screening procedures, and may be considering in-service formative evaluation programs. Check with your youth athletic organizations to find out about special training programs for coaches and ask about parent workshops as well.

Appendix C lists some current organizations offering coach-training programs or coach in-service workshops. If you know of additional programs, please share them with other readers at doctorshari@raisingwinners.com. New resources and programs will be updated regularly and made available to interested parents and coaches.

Screening Coaches

Wise parents will also check out the youth sports organization policy for screening coaches. Fingerprinting and government record checks are slow and require as much as six to eight weeks to process each file. Instead of searching nationwide databases, many states use only local manually assessed information. Individual evaluations are often limited to the state in which the search was initiated. You've got to be watchful when entrusting your child to others. Support organizational policies that encourage and monitor appropriate behaviors among coaches and staff to benefit participating youth and help put parents' minds at rest.

Formative Evaluation

Formative evaluation is a new tool being used by some organizations to help encourage positive coaching techniques consistent with program goals and decrease harmful treatment of players. I've devised the Sports Proactive Information Formative Feedback Inventory (SPIFFI), a simple tool available for the professionalization of coaching (appendix B). Using the SPIFFI, coaches and parents are advised of the organizational goals early in the season to help everyone promote quality experiences for the kids. Specifically, many youth sports' goals include promoting sportsmanship, valuable practices, positive coaching, fair playtime, and positive development overall. Inquire about your youth organization's positive coaching procedures. The Positive Coaching Alliance, a nonprofit organization, believes in "transforming youth sports so sports can transform youth." Check with your child's potential coaches and see if they're following positive SPIFFI guidelines.

POLICY: TWO ADULTS AT ALL TIMES

The Boys Scouts of America has a firm policy of having two adults present at all times. Other youth organizations have similar policies. Parents might consider encouraging implementing the two-adult policy in their local sports organizations as a safety net for their children. Professionals note a growing trend for parents to use a drop-and-run policy at children's games and practices as their own overextended schedules cut the time they can be with their children. Regrettably, a drop-and-run policy increases the exposure and risk to children, especially where professional screening may be marginal or inadequate.

As with all situations in sports, keep your parental common sense about you and monitor your child's experiences. Whether an organization has an adequate coach screening, training, and monitoring program or not, it's up to you to keep your child safe.

WATCHING OUT FOR YOUR YOUNG ATHLETE

With the range of coaches on display in professional and college sports, it's no surprise that parents have a confused picture of what constitutes quality coaching. Many parents just keep their mouths shut. Some parents say very little. A few don't know when to shut up. Well-informed parents have an obligation to know what to expect, when to speak up, and when to be quiet.

Is Your Kid's Coach Abusive?

Why do some parents demand references on a baby sitter, ask direct questions about a teen's friends, even harangue their bank about a four-dollar charge, but never think to question a coach's behavior?

I have witnessed parents standing passively by as a coach verbally hollered top volume at their grade-school child. I have seen a tantrumming coach throw a metal folding ball cart against a sports arena wall as passive spectators looked on. Slamming a clipboard on the ground has become a permissible national symbol of a coach's frustration. I've seen rag-

ing, red-cheeked, pug-bodied men standing eight inches from a teenage
player backed against a railing and yelling nonstop in her terrified face. I
have heard stories of worse.

It's alarming that parents can stand by during such inappropriate incidents. Psychological, verbal, and physical maltreatment are simply unacceptable.

A coach's job is to develop the young person's athletic skills and, in the
process, build an individual in personal as well as physical ways. There is
no room in this process for tearing down years of personal growth and
self-efficacy. Coaches who use demeaning methods while offering ratio-
nalizations for their abusive behavior need professional help. If a coach
makes any of the following statements, you might offer that coach a copy
of *Raising Winners* or talk to your sponsoring organization about signing
the coach up for some positive coach-training workshops.

"But that's the way I was taught! Look at me. I'm fine!"

"No pain, no gain. You have to work till it hurts."

"There is only good pain."

"Sports make men out of boys."

"If it doesn't hurt, it isn't doing any good."

"A good coach is a tough coach!"

"You have to yell at a kid to get him to do anything."

The old school, traditional coaching style was based on old ideas about
athletic development. The boot camp athletic training mentality included
a lot of yelling, mandatory silent obedience, walking off injuries, playing
on sprains, and the notion that fun was out of place in the learning
process. Research has shown that boot camp ideas are simply wrong! Psychologists and sports medicine specialists recognize that abuse isn't developmental. It is simply abuse.

In the old school, coaches worked to weed out the wimps. Only the
"tough" survived the rigors of an old school training program. The boot
camp mentality left a core of young athletes whose parents supported the
rigors and believed in the gains. We now know they were misguided. The
core of young athletes surviving were indeed survivors, survivors of abusive treatment.

As we move from a culture that largely supported the old school
methods to a new culture with research-based methods to educate
and train the young athlete positively, it is no surprise that we witness a tremendous range of coaching behaviors. As things change and

the range of experiences increases, parents are more important than ever in helping to assure that their young athlete receives quality experiences.

Even good parents can easily get sucked into a boot camp mentality and forget the overall perspective. Yesterday, I heard of an ice hockey parent prowling emergency rooms looking for someone to remove the cast from his son's broken wrist (broken in the semifinals the night before) just two hours before the 7:00 P.M. championship game. The dad reassured the ER staff with a straight face that it was very important; the team couldn't win without his son on the ice.

When a key lacrosse player went down in a recent high school game, everyone wanted to keep the kid on the field—including the kid. The trainer assured the coach and parents that taping the turned ankle firmly would keep the swelling down, but the risk of increased injury was real. The parents didn't bat an eye as they ordered the tape job and patted the kid on the shoulder as he limped back into play.

Parents need to be aware that coaches, families, trainers, and teammates may push players. A wise parent knows that pain is a healthy signal telling a body to stop. Determining the severity of an injury may be a tough call for trained medical staff with specialized equipment, much less a young, inexperienced athlete. Don't shirk your responsibility to listen to your child's needs here.

In the old boot camp mentality, it was common pre-game practice for college team physicians to shoot Novocain and steroids into sore ankle joints, knees, and shoulders to get the kid onto the court. It still happens, but taping has become the more frequent remedy. Kneecaps inflamed with tendinitis are prewrapped and taped tight. Bruised ribs are lubricated with ointment, prewrapped, and bound. Swollen aching ankles are massaged with compound, sprayed, prewrapped, stirruped, and strategically bound in adhesive. Training rooms get tape by the case. Each injury takes a toll, and the severity increases with frequent damage. Calcium deposits build up in injured joints. If you want to get a convincing argument, visit a thirty-year reunion from a top football or basketball team trained in the old school plan. Limps and canes are common.

Take a word from these older and wiser folks: err on the side of caution and make decisions to preserve your child's lifelong health.

Too Much Parental Intrusion

One bonus of the old school of coaching included the unquestioned respect for the coach's decisions. Parents and players accepted that playing time was earned through the quality of past performance. Game strategies were the expertise of the coach and no one questioned the decisions necessary to carry out the program. Fairness was defined by the coach's judgment.

In the current climate that encourages parent involvement, finding a balance between too much and too little involvement challenges many parents. Many teams now seem to have one or more self-appointed parent experts. Heaven help the coach who has more than three. Occasionally, parents will speak to the coach regarding decisions benefiting the whole team, but most of the time, the advice usually primarily benefits their child. Offering suggestions, jawboning about game strategy, and suggesting increased playing time for your child are all too much. Remember the value of self-efficacy training for your child and that all-star athletes as parents (chapter 4) respect the coach and stay out of the coaching process.

When the coach makes a call you don't understand, check in with your child. Quality coaching includes establishing and explaining rules and consequences. When a child doesn't start a game as usual, many a chagrined parent has been embarrassed to learn from the coach that the kid was late to practice and it is a team rule that the starting lineup is earned by being on time to practices.

To support communication, encourage the coach to have a regular team meeting with all parents and players to update everyone on policies. Some coaches even create a brief newsletter. Planned meetings and notes are particularly important when there are one or two parents who appoint themselves as the team spokespersons. Parents who unilaterally dominate the ear of the coach can set the tone and pace for a team, but regrettably, all self-appointed parents do not have unselfish nor necessarily positive perspectives.

What Can You Do About a Terrible Coach?

In the first place, how do you know the coach is terrible?
Coaches come in many different psychological sizes and shapes.

Among professionals, acceptable practices include a range of techniques and methods. If the coach engages in sexual, psychological, or physical harassment, it's an easy call: dump the coach and take action to protect others from harm. But what if you think the coach simply isn't measuring up to coaching standards?

Parents should know there are no perfect coaches for all players of all ages. Within broad guidelines, picking a coach is a matching process. Before you criticize a coach or make any big decisions to leave a team based on few facts, see what you can do to help your young athlete learn from the coach. I find that almost every coach has something valuable to share. Few parents objectively evaluate their child's abilities, and even fewer can claim a balanced view of overall team needs versus a single player's needs. If there is a problem with a coach, encourage your child to handle it by himself or herself before you ride to the rescue. I've found that most cases of "terrible coach" turn out to be misunderstandings of the coach's goals or the child's desires and needs. Often, breakdowns in communication are an important element contributing to poor coach evaluations.

TIP   **Support your coach's participation in professional development workshops and programs.**

COACHES HAVE A TOUGH JOB

Most coaches are probably doing the best they can with what they have. Money, time, and resources are all limited. Stress increases with each of the limitations. Remember this.

Limited Money

Most organizations have limited budgets for staff, equipment, and assistant staff salaries. Pay is often modest even in the best of situations. School coaches frequently have an academic teaching load as well as their coaching duties, and by the time they juggle game schedules, orders, grades, and rosters, the pay per hour is surprisingly low. In some organizations like AYSO, the coaches are all volunteers with no payment at all for coaching.

Limited Time

A coach may spend from one hour to as many as sixty hours or more per week on coaching and duties associated with the coaching job. Time with your young athlete can be extensive, but additional administrative paperwork, scheduling, regulations, organizational compliance, and other demands each take huge chunks of time, too.

Limited Resources

Equipment and facilities both need tending. Maintenance of property takes time. You can get an idea of the pressure by watching many coaches scramble after the equipment kids leave out. Coaches are responsible for managing limited equipment budgets, and each lost ball becomes another expense some administrator somewhere may question.

SUPPORTING THE COACH

Finding ways to support the coach so his or her time with the team is high-quality time has advantages for everyone. The coach benefits because he or she can focus on the job of coaching. Young athletes win because they have better-quality experiences. Parents win because they are able to support quality experiences.

A word of caution. Supporting a coach does not mean kissing up to a coach. Most kiss-ups would be amazed if they knew how obvious they are. At the 1997 Junior National Championship volleyball pre-game warm-up, I was taking some photographs near the net. A parent from the opposing team sidled up to their coach, who was standing within earshot. First the coach's hair, then the last game, finally their shoes received unctuous compliments from the obsequious parent. The unfazed coach, eyes still on the warm-up drills, nodded her head each time and kept watching the kids. By the fourth round of compliments, the coach turned and faced the parent and laughingly said, "Would you like a straw so you can really suck up?" The nearby ref and I both burst out laughing, tipping our eavesdropping hats (or ears, as the case may be).

TIP   Support the coach's work, volunteer help, but don't be a suck-up.

NINE PRACTICAL IDEAS TO HELP MOST COACHES

1. Say Thanks

Coaches often receive little recognition for the tough work they do. In our heavy-duty win-oriented culture, many coaches *only* receive recognition when they produce winning scores. The day-to-day scheduling, the drills that led up to the game, the drudgery of paper shuffling get nothing for the coach. Most kids rarely realize how fortunate they are to have an adult, much less a skilled coach, helping them learn. Parents often get so wrapped up in who is playing and their own child's progress that they forget the fundamental importance of recognizing all the work that has gone into their child's learning. Parents need to remember to say thanks and remind their kids to show their appreciation too. (P.S.: Don't forget the assistant coach.)

2. Pass Along Genuine Compliments

If a coach has a team of parents who say nothing until they have a complaint, the coach has a constant diet of complaints. Even the well-trained coach attempting to use praise and encouragement with the young athletes will be hard-pressed to be a wellspring of positive feedback if all she herself hears are criticism and complaints.

3. Remove the Negatives

In the typical athletic program with minimal support services, anyway you can act to remove negatives from a coach's job will be welcome. Be willing to do those tedious tasks (big negatives that get in the way of quality coaching time). If you look at a top collegiate program or the Olympic Training Center, you will see an important support staff helping the coach out. An assistant coach (or two), administrative staff, student academic coordinator, weight trainer, strength coach, nutrition consultant, psychological consultant, and media-relations people all let the coach get down to the business of working with the young athletes.

For those of you consciously deciding to suck up to the coach in nonobvious ways with the goal of getting better treatment for your child, forget it. Coaches usually see through self-serving efforts. You should help a coach because the quality of the experience for all the players, including your own kid, will be improved.

4. Make Up a Team Roster

Make up a team roster for each team family with addresses and phone numbers so team members, parents, and administrators can quickly reach one another. As a bonus, tell the coach you will be responsible for making team calls. For big teams, recruit another parent to share calling duties or set up a phone tree.

5. Field Cheering Rosters

Make multiple copies on three-by-five-inch note cards listing each team member's name, jersey number, and parents' names. Bring brightly colored copies to the first several games to encourage parents' positive involvement. It will help parents communicate once they know one anothers' names; as an extra bonus, include reminders to parents of positive cheers on the back.

6. Game and Practice Snack Schedule

Make up a calendar of dates, places, and times of practices and games. Check with families, then assign a team snack date to each family. Tell the coach you will be responsible for calling and reminding the parents of their snack date.

7. Car Pool and Practice/Game Schedule

A car pool and practice/game schedule is easy to do if you have the team roster. Note where the players live and make a few calls to help get parents organized into sharing driving for practices and games. It's a lot easier for all the families when everyone shares the driving. Since young players are dependent on adults for rides, helping to form car pools will keep attendance up.

8. Be a Team Manager

Offer to help the coach as the team manager in whatever ways are needed. This usually includes organizing phone trees, doing a few mailings, making some phone calls, arranging for trophies, and being a resource to other parents. You might get a list of important phone numbers from the coach (e.g., uniforms, insurance, national organization) and give out your phone number to team families. You serve as the clearinghouse for the coach to disseminate information as well as help refer problems to the appropriate party. This leaves the coach more time to coach, with less hassle.

9. Chaperone

For teams that travel, offer to chaperone. Become the designated responsible parent who truly takes the worries off the coach so he or she can coach. This is a lot of work when done well. It means setting down the ground rules with players and families, having emergency numbers, accounting for each player at all times, arranging meals, drinks, water, and snacks, as well as supporting the players psychologically.

FOR COACHES WHO GO ABOVE AND BEYOND THE CALL OF DUTY

On occasion, you will get a coach who gives far more than expected. For those special coaches, consider organizing a little extra something.

1. Coach's Award

Arrange to make up a certificate of appreciation for the coach with all of the players' signatures. If you don't have a calligraphist or a computer-savvy parent on your team, local copy stores and national chains often have folks available who can create a certificate for around seven dollars. Combine the certificate with a nice speech of thanks at the last game. Alert each player beforehand to have prepared a brief word of thanks for one special thing the coach did for them and you have a great closure to a season.

2. Season Party

Arrange a potluck supper at the gym, field, local recreation center, or at a team member's home. The friendships that come from team sports are some of the most valuable benefits, and getting together reinforces them.

3. Team Photo

Offer to take team photos. Select a time before a big game and get out your camera. Nothing fancy is required. A point-and-flash disposable camera works well for the equipment-challenged. Pick a shady area (so the kids aren't squinting), line them up with feet together, hair tidied, and shoot using the flash for a sharp, shiny front-flash fill photo. A five-by-seven-inch picture can be a valuable memento of a team's season. Total cost for film, developing, and a copy for each player on a team of fourteen plus the coach is between twenty and thirty dollars and is a great way to save valuable memories of friendships formed. (The kids may want to have two photos taken, one serious and one crazy. You probably know which one is usually the favorite.)

4. Chip In for a Coach's Gift

Remembering volunteer coaches and the very slim salary most paid coaches receive, organizing a team gift can be a wonderful gesture. The effort need not be expensive. Parents can organize personalized letters from each player and put them in a notebook at the season's end. Homemade cards with notes from each player make a treasured memento for most coaches. Gift certificates with contributions from families have the one-size-fits-all advantage, but don't be shy about gathering ideas from the families for a more personalized present.

Being a coach can be tremendously enjoyable, but it can also be very tough. Your offer to help in little ways or crucial ways will be valuable assets to the team in general. Remember to teach your child to recognize and appreciate what people do for them. Remind him or her to say thanks for the coach's time and energy. Your support and commitment to development will increase the coach's likelihood of doing quality work. Coaches take some cues from parents. Parents take some cues from one another, and kids follow. When parents encourage positive learning by helping the coach out whenever possible, everyone benefits.

7

Eating and Sleeping Right to Play Well

Sitting on the pavement, I could see eighteen pairs of shaven legs progressing quickly across the courtyard toward the picnic spread. The Nikes and Reeboks and Asics jockeyed for positions near the display of snack goodies. A big wooden bowl of bananas, grapes, and orange slices sat on the checkered blanket next to a platter of sliced chicken, turkey, and bagels, two bowls of cream cheese, peanut butter, and jelly along with an assortment of plastic spoons and forks. Orange juice, Cranapple juice, bottled water, and a rainbow of Gatorades quickly found pourers and cups.

More like a bunch of puppies than teenage girls, they stretched and rested, leaning on one another's backs, legs, and stomachs. The team mom moved silently among the clusters of girls refilling cups and offering more turkey. Refueling, the young women ate and drank—some more, some less—just what they needed. Each made good choices, and the alternatives available were all healthy. Three cheers to the team mom—and to home lives that had helped these girls develop.

—Shari Kuchenbecker, volleyball mom hat, 1998

These young athletes' powerful calf and thigh muscles are refreshing in a culture skewed by media images of waif-thin, stick-legged models. Their defined biceps and triceps showing as they grabbed for another slice of chicken made a great statement. Commonsense rearing had nurtured these young women to develop healthy eating, drinking, and sleeping habits.

HEALTHY HOMEOSTASIS FEEDBACK MECHANISMS

We all come equipped with a number of beautiful feedback mechanisms assuring overall *homeostasis,* or balance. Critical centers for physiological survival nestle deep within the brain stem, telling us when we need to breathe, drink, eat, sleep, increase or decrease our body temperature, and more. Our bodies let us all know—unequivocally—what we need and when.

"Body wisdom," say researchers Thomas Scott of the University of Delaware and Bart Hoebel of Princeton University, comes from brain mechanisms reinforcing behavior that will help us achieve homeostasis. With eating, our brains foster behavior that will lead to good nutrition via taste. Have you ever found yourself craving a specific food? Has your child ever been wild about the flavor of a certain food? Body wisdom may well be at work.

When my then six-year-old tasted Grandma's rhubarb pie at a restaurant, her eyes lit up. Smacking, smiling, she polished off half of Grandma's dessert, nabbed a piece of her own, and talked us into buying a whole pie to take home. For a few days, her hankering for rhubarb seemed insatiable. What did she want for breakfast? Rhubarb pie. Lunch? Rhubarb pie. She even volunteered to come to the grocery store to check out fresh rhubarb. I called the pediatrician. Was this okay? Dr. Eileen Yager, then at the UCLA School of Medicine, was delighted with the story. Did I know that rhubarb was very high in calcium? No. My six-year-old had a milk intolerance and in recent weeks had probably been running low on calcium—thus her craving for the rhubarb pie. Dr. Yager explained that when the need was satisfied, the craving would pass. True to her predictions, with a healthy array of foods available, a reminder to listen to her body, and an extra platter of meats, my daughter's craving for rhubarb eventually faded. Fifteen years later, it's occasionally the dessert of choice, but for that brief time, it was instrumental to naturally rebalancing her own nutritional needs. By listening to her taste, she wanted the very thing she needed—calcium—and played out a valuable lesson in body wisdom.

> **TIP** "Body wisdom" may be at work when a kid craves a single food.

Nutritionists and pediatricians recommend teaching children good habits and trusting that children know what they need. Think of nutrition over a twenty-four-hour day (and sometimes over many days), each meal and snack just a part of the whole picture. Experts tell us we'll help meet our kids' balanced nutritional needs if we provide a healthy array of alternatives and respect a child's ability to make good choices.

Of course, you wouldn't drop your ten-year-old off at the candy store to get some lunch. Similarly, you'll need to look at where you and your family are in the process of building good habits. I have known some moms and dads begin healthy habits right from their child's first year and other parents who only came to understand the importance of healthy eating after a painful clinical problem brought them to the doctor's office or mental health clinic.

FOOD GUIDE PYRAMID

The Food Guide Pyramid looks a lot different from the nutritional recommendations when most parents were in school.

The broad nutritional foundation includes bread, cereal, rice, and pasta (six servings daily); vegetables (three servings); fruits (two servings); low-fat milk, yogurt, and cheese (three to four servings); and meat, poultry, fish, beans, eggs, and nuts (two to three servings). Fats, oils, and sweets sparingly grace the top. Serving sizes vary by age, size, and activity of the individual, with adults' servings about one to two cups; preschoolers, one-half cup; and toddlers at one-quarter cup.

Ask your kids what they know about the Food Guide Pyramid. Many schools offer information they'll be happy to share with you. Learning the

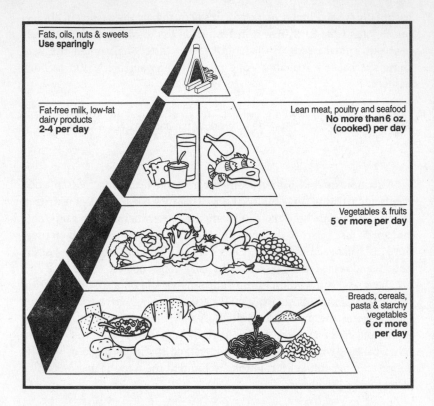

Fats, oils, nuts & sweets
Use sparingly

Fat-free milk, low-fat
dairy products
2-4 per day

Lean meat, poultry and seafood
**No more than 6 oz.
(cooked) per day**

Vegetables & fruits
5 or more per day

Breads, cereals,
pasta & starchy
vegetables
**6 or more
per day**

newest findings about nutrition should be a priority. *The Yale Guide to Children's Nutrition* by William Tamborlane, M.D., includes information on kids' eating habits and needs at different ages, nutrition for athletes, how to read food labels, the truth about organic foods, vitamins, and specialty problems such as diabetes, phenylketoneuria, attention-deficit/ hyperactivity disorder, and more. If it's been a while since you brushed up on the latest in healthy eating, visit your library, bookstore, or browse the Internet. Be a critical reader and evaluate the sources. Nutrition experts at quality institutions deserve priority.

Once you have solid knowledge based on the latest research, you should feel more confident and involve your kids in decisions about meal planning. Many families enjoy learning about nutrition and grocery shopping together. Not only do you have an opportunity to learn your children's individual food tastes, but you create a forum to discuss healthy eating habits. While shopping, you might be surprised how good the fresh fruits look to kids, a great substitute for cake, cookies, or brownies.

RESPECT

An infant's parents seldom question whether their child knows when he or she is hungry or has to pee or poop. He or she just does it. No questions asked. At the age of two, however, when kids normally gain weight more slowly and seem to be eating less, many parents start to worry. Sometimes conscientious but uninformed parents may go to extremes, including formalized home policies and strict rules about home and away-from-home eating.

> **TIP** **Avoid rigid rules controlling your kids' food choices (they undermine staying in touch with their own needs).**
> Rules Not to Live By:
> Clean your plate. • No candy. • Eat the veggies before the pasta. • Don't drink sodas. • Don't drink water when you eat; it expands your stomach. • Wait for dinner. • Never snack. • Don't eat past 6:00 P.M. • Bread is bad for you. • No dessert until you finish your meal.

WORRIED ABOUT YOUR KIDS' NUTRITION?

If you're worried about your kids' nutrition, welcome to one of the biggest parent clubs I know. We're all trying to raise our kids in a complicated culture where researchers find that, at present, about 45 percent of women and 32 percent of men are on diets and Americans spend more than $30 billion a year on weight-loss products, $8 billion on exercise clubs and spas, $10 billion on diet sodas, and billions more on artificial sweeteners and low-calorie foods. Susan Nolen-Hoeksema at the University of Michigan reminds us that this should be compared to the $30 billion per year spent by our federal government on *all* education, social services, training, and employment programs. Dollar for dollar, what statement are we as a nation making?

MAKE HEALTHY CHOICES EASY

Fast food is so convenient. Most families know how hard juggling every-one's schedules for meals can be, and this is especially true for kids in ath-letics. Practice lets out at 5:30 P.M. Dad and Mom coordinate pickup of one or more kids. Game days sometimes run until 7:00 or 8:00 P.M. Someone often gets hung up at work or the traffic is bad. What about dinner? Fast foods are not only expensive, they are often poorly balanced and high in fat. What can a family do?

Knowledge and planning seem to be most busy families' secret to suc-cess. By organizing the day ahead of time, many households make creative arrangements that are both convenient and healthy. Lean roasts with potatoes and carrots wrapped in tinfoil and baked at a low temperature greet your family with delicious smells the minute you open the front door in the evening. Simmering Crock-Pots of vegetables and chicken can be started in early morning, as can lean briskets covered in onions and au jus mix. If you have the makings for a fresh salad, a loaf of bread, and some fruit for dessert, you have honored the Food Pyramid teachings.

Home Snacks

Regrettably, convenience food makers make unhealthy eating easy. The wrapper on the candy bar barely slows the muncher down; bags of chips burst open with a modest tweak; and a finger's pull removes the flip top from the soda can. Problem is, all of these quick choices can develop into bad habits. The good news is that parents can rig their family's health for success by keeping a low shelf in the refrigerator filled with healthy al-ternatives from the time kids are little. Many families wash the vegetables and cut them into bite-size pieces when they first come home from the market. That way, a plastic bowl with peeled baby carrots, celery slices, cut-up broccoli and cauliflower, and some slivers of peppers stand ready for hungry kids. You can cut up fruits like apples and pears and store them in a sealed container as well (put a few drops of lemon juice in the water when you rinse them; they won't brown as quickly). If you have two or three of the small sport-top water bottles, refill them with low-fat milk and you have a drink as handy as a can of soda and much more nutritious. In the kitchen, set aside a low shelf for crackers, raisins, dried fruit, granola bars, and cereal for snacks and be sure to include special treats everyone likes. Lunchtime sharing taught my kids about Craisins (dried cranberries), bagel chips, and a host of treats far superior to potato chips and soda. I was always eager for their healthy suggestions, for not only did it get them thinking about choices and involve them in the process of selecting foods, the novelty was fun for all of us.

How to Be a Pro-Level Team Snack Parent

For those new to athletics, you'll recognize the entry-level team snack parents by the two brown grocery bags they hover near during the game. Fancy snack parents have a cooler, and the pro-level snack parents have a deluxe-cooler-on-wheels that rolls across the gym at a speed putting Indy drivers to shame. How you move from entry-level snack parent to pro level is all training done via word of mouth. The differences are subtle, but for those of you wanting to look pro level early on, here are a few handy pointers:

Healthy Is In

Use the Food Pyramid to create a healthy team snack. For short games, go with fruits and vegetables. For longer games, add alternatives from the bread, grain, and pasta group. And for day-long tournaments, add from the protein, dairy, and fats groups:

1. Seasonal Fruits Cut into Bite-Size Pieces Are Always Hits!

   Apples, bananas, watermelon, strawberries, and grapes are excellent standards, but don't be hesitant to try novel choices like pineapple, kiwi, and papaya. Pair a new fruit choice with the all-time favorite orange for the best shot at success. Use the gifted method (see box) for cutting the other fruits, including pineapple, kiwi, and papaya. Platters with plastic wrap or sealable plastic bowls or boxes keep fruits fresher.

2. Vegetables Cut into Bite-Size Pieces

   Celery, carrots, broccoli, and cauliflower are the staples, but creative parents have successfully tried jícama, cucumbers, soybeans, fresh green beans, peas in their pods, zucchini, and even vegetable juices like V-8. Again, platters and sealable bowls are a good way to keep things fresh.

TIP   **Gifted Method for Cutting Oranges—and Most Fruits (Thanks, Mrs. Mirman)**

Place the orange on a cutting board with the belly buttons pointing side to side.

Slice off each belly button end about one half to three quarters of an inch in.

Stand the orange on one of the two sliced ends. Slice it down the middle.

Place the two halves end to end on the cutting board.

Slice each half into three or four three-quarter-inch slices (you'll be cutting across the center cord).

Now, hold up a slice and uncurl the rind. You'll see the little triangles of pulp stand up ready to be eaten cleanly from the rind, which can then be thrown away.

3. Breads and Cereals

For long games, pick whole grains low in fat and high in fiber, which means skip the granola with coconut oil and high-fat muffins and go instead with rice cakes, pretzels, bagels, saltines, graham and animal crackers.

4. Milk, Yogurt, and Cheese

For tournament days or events lasting more than one game, the nutrition and fat in this category gives kids extra staying power. Small cubes of assorted cheese or cream cheese and bagels add a nice complement of calories and nutrition. Yogurt, low in fat compared to ice cream, is a first-rate treat, and frozen yogurt bars on a hot day will make the snack parent an all-team favorite.

5. Meat, Poultry, Fish, Beans, Eggs, and Nuts

Turkey and chicken are many athletes' first choice because of the low fat content. When a snack parent has tournament-day duties, full-meal refueling can include creative touches like hummus spread (garbanzo bean paste) for pita bread and peanut butter for crackers, but don't count on too many of today's kids wanting deviled eggs.

Set Up an Attractive Snack Spread to Suit a Wide Range of Needs

A cast-aside bedspread from the linen closet or thrift store can be a wonderful home base for a team. If you find something in the team color, all the better! Family style or buffet style works best when you have a range of needs to meet. From the littlest kids to the biggest adults, each should be able to have as much as they need of what they need.

Recycling Is In, Waste Is Out

Remember to bring a sack for trash and try to minimize trash waste when possible. Year after year, all-star soccer team mom Debbie Held (also Region 69 commissioner) watched as too many paper plates got tossed. She invested in inexpensive bright yellow durable plastic plates and cups to be used every game. The initial cost was very close to the cost for the tossable plastic. Heavy sport water bottles were purchased and marked with each girl's name and brought by the family with snack duty to the game each week. Coordinating plates and water bottles was all family teamwork.

Coolers and Coolers on Wheels

Very fancy, bulky, and pricey. You can do a lot with bags of ice and well-packed grocery store plastic and paper bags. If you as a family can use the cooler for trips to the mountains, beach, river, or Grandma's, then go for it, but otherwise, wing it until you know it's worth the money.

Snack Pros Know to Check with the Coach, Child, and Other Families

It's great fun to bring your own skills and talents to team snack duties, but when in doubt, double-check with the coach, your kid, and other families. Wondering if home-baked cookies for Halloween will be okay as a treat? Ask. Before you make ants-on-a-log (celery stuffed with peanut butter and a row of raisins on top), ask your child. No kid wants to have the dorkiest snack parent. There is a certain family pride here if you can manage to coordinate a healthy, fun, and tasty snack when it's your turn.

GROWING IS KIDS' BUSINESS

Healthy infants double their birthweight by four or five months of age and triple it by twelve months. As girls approach eighteen months and boys twenty-four months, physicians use a rule of thumb guestimating them to be near half of their adult height. The rate of growth slows around the second birthday, but still advances about seven pounds and two and a half inches per year until puberty (ages ten to fifteen for girls and thirteen to seventeen for boys), at which time there is a tremendous growth spurt, after which bone epiphyses close and growing ceases. Of course, these are overgeneralizations from which many normal kids vary, with some starting puberty at eight and others growing on into the late teens and early twenties. The important point for parents to remember is the reassuring wide range of normal.

During all ages and stages, your child's personal homeostatic balance is continually being readjusted. Especially during growth spurts, there are so many variables—the amount of energy expended, the size of the child's last meal, its calorie content, even cultural differences—that it can be tough for your child to know what to eat, especially when he or she has no control over breaks and mealtimes.

Youngsters in athletics need to be especially careful to replace the extra energy they expend. Nutrition experts recommend adhering to the basic Food Pyramid, with carbohydrates supplying 50–55 percent of the total calories. The reason is simple. Carbohydrates are used to replenish muscles during exercise. Protein can serve as a building block during growth, but excess protein will not be helpful.

You probably don't need to worry about your child's overall vitamin and mineral requirements if you're providing him or her a balanced diet; in this case, professionals reassure us that supplements of any form are usually not necessary. Check with your pediatrician if you're concerned.

FLUIDS AND ELECTROLYTES

Our bodies are 60 percent water, and water is crucial for temperature regulation and a host of metabolic functions, including digestion and blood pressure regulation. Staying hydrated during physical activity boosts performance, and performance stalls can often be traced to water deficiency. According to Los Angeles researcher and soft-tissue specialist Joseph Horrigan, D.C., and others, elite ice hockey athletes on an adequate hydration program outperform those with poor hydration. Wise parents and coaches encourage athletes to drink water. Nicely enough, excess fluids are simply excreted as urine, and water intoxication is an extremely rare problem.

TIP   **Water is crucial to your child's health and performance.**
Kids need to drink water before they get too thirsty.

Electrolytes, particularly sodium and potassium, are sweated out during physical exertion and can be replaced by adequate nutrition or supplemented by any of a number of sport drinks. Gatorade, 10K, and others all want to take the lion's share of the athletic market, but the fact of the matter is, each has a slightly different profile of flavor, calories, carbohydrates, and nutritional value. Find the one your child likes, and balance intake by encouraging him or her to drink equal volumes of water and electrolyte drink. Teach your child not to wait until he or she is thirsty at the end of the workout, but to sip fluids during breaks in the practice or game.

PERFORMANCE SUPPLEMENTS

When it comes to supplemental products aimed at enhancing young athletes' performance edge, most add-on products bring a share of risk, and to date, most have not been proven to aid performance. Nothing supplemental your child eats, drinks, injects, or absorbs can take the place of hard work and training. Moreover, parents are wise to take a cautious approach and reassure their kids that how they are naturally is ideal. Extra protein, extra creatine, and even extra vitamins can actually hamper overall performance and harm health. Take a conservative line. Let your kids know they are just right the way they are; tell them that each artificial enhancement seems to produce a loss somewhere down the road. Even creatine, a natural substance in the body, in excess can increase dehydration and muscle cramping and has been associated with kidney and liver damage.

IN THE PURSUIT OF THIN,
SOME SEEM TO BE GETTING PLUMPER . . .

Despite concerted efforts and large financial expenditures, adult obesity—being at least 20 percent heavier than your medically recommended weight—increased more than 50 percent between 1960 and 1980, and the number of obese teens doubled from one in eight to one in four between

1980 and 1997. Soberingly, more than 70 percent of girls say they have dieted by the age of ten. And how successful are the diets? Across studies, from magazine polls to well-controlled medical experiments, a majority of dieters seem to gain the weight back two years down the road. Often, folks gain more weight than they lose, only to start another diet and move into a cycle of yo-yo dieting.

. . . AND A FEW AREN'T

Based on statistics, girls and women report more dissatisfaction with their bodies and have a greater likelihood of developing clinical eating disorders: Anorexia nervosa (1 percent incidence; 90 percent female), bulimia nervosa (0.5 percent incidence; 80 percent female), and binge eating disorder (2 percent incidence in the general population and as much as 30 percent of the dieting population; 32 percent of college women and 29 percent of college men). The high incidence of eating disorders among females worries most parents of girls, but the numbers of young men in the last decade also falling victim should be of growing concern.

Anorexia Nervosa

Anorexia nervosa is a persistent lack of appetite that endangers the individual's health, with the lack of appetite arising from emotional or psychological factors rather than organic disease. The typical individual suffering with anorexia is an upper-middle-class adolescent female who was normal or somewhat above normal weight for height, yet who dieted until significantly underweight (15 percent or more below normal weight). Victims often have a distorted body image and frequently claim to be "fat" despite obvious evidence to the contrary and reassurances from others that they are not.

Far from a benign psychological problem, common medical complications of anorexia make the disease fatal in 15 percent of cases.

Complications of Anorexia Nervosa

Slow heart rate	Susceptibility to bleeding
Irregular heartbeat	Decalcification
Fluid in pericardium	Tooth decay

Heart failure	Amenorrhea
Yellowing of skin	Lack of sexual interest
Impaired taste	Impotence
Hypoglycemia	Salivary gland swelling
Dehydration	Acute expansion of the stomach
Weakness	Constipation
Tetany	Hypothermia
Anemia	

K. D. Brownell and J. P. Foreyt, eds., *Handbook of Eating Disorders* (New York: Basic Books, 1986).

News stories like Barbara Huebner's in *The Boston Globe* received headline attention across the nation in 1999 in "Eating Disorders: The Most Lethal Psychiatric Disorder of Them All." She reports Boston ballet dancer Heidi Guenther was twenty-two when she died, apparently one of many young dancers in 1997 dieting to be thin. The ninety pounds for her height seemed low-normal, but for Heidi, it was lethally light. Christy Henrich, U.S. gymnastic Olympic hopeful, missed the U.S. team by 0.118 of a point in 1988 and reportedly spiraled into anorexia and bulimia following an offhand comment by a judge about her weight. She weighed forty-seven pounds a few days before her twenty-second birthday, when she died. Singer Karen Carpenter was eighty-five pounds when she died of cardiac arrest after struggling with anorexia for seven years.

Bulimia Nervosa

Individuals suffering with bulimia nervosa engage in binge eating followed by purging to get rid of the excessive food. A "binge" occurs in a discrete period of time and includes eating large amounts of food, significantly greater quantities than most people would consume in a similar time and situation; anywhere from six hundred to twenty thousand calories can be consumed. While bingeing, the person feels out of control and compelled to eat even when he or she isn't hungry. Afterward, the person might engage in self-induced vomiting, fast, exercise excessively, or use laxatives, diuretics, or purge medicines. This pattern also has significant health risks.

Complications of Bulimia Nervosa

Dehydration	Tetany
Kidney disease	Softening of bones
Gastric dilation	Skin pigmentation changes
Inflammation of the salivary gland	Reduction in blood magnesium levels
Elevation of the enzyme amylase	Fluid retention
Pancreatic disease	Malabsorption syndromes
Excess uric acid in the blood	Colon abnormalities
Lowered blood potassium levels	Susceptibility to bleeding
Alkalosis	Electroencephalogram abnormalities
Acidosis	
Tooth enamel erosion	Abnormal thyroid hormone and growth hormone response
Tooth decay	
Reduction of blood calcium	

K. D. Brownell and J. P. Foreyt, eds., *Handbook of Eating Disorders* (New York: Basic Books, 1986).

Binge Eating Disorder

Struggles to control appetite are common among teens and young adults. Most can remember a time they wished they had been able to resist a special food or extra helping, but some become plagued by feelings that their eating is out of control. Defined as compulsively overeating, either continuously throughout a day or in discrete binges, binge eating disorder seems to be growing in our diet-conscious culture. Kids who binge eat are often plunged into the cycle of greater diet control efforts.

YOUNG ATHLETES AND DISORDERED EATING

As parents intuitively know, kids who do more need to eat more. Growing bodies need refueling with the right balance of nutrition at the right time. Perhaps because of the higher volumes of food required or the more delicate balancing and rebalancing needed in kids with heavy exercise programs, studies show that as many as 15 to 62 percent of female athletes and a growing number of male athletes have pathologic weight control problem behaviors. Athletes in certain sports seem more vulnerable. Researcher J. Sundgot-Borgen found that 29–35 percent of participants in aesthetic or weight-dependent sports—including diving, figure skating, gymnastics, dance, judo, karate, and wrestling—have eating disorders. Eating disorders nab 20 percent of participants in endurance sports, including cycling, running, and swimming. As many as 14 percent of golf and high jump participants (in the so-called technical sports) and 12 percent of volleyball and soccer participants (in the ball game sports) also fall victim.

One investigation of bodybuilding found that 46 percent of men binge after competitions and 85 percent gain significant weight in the off season. Among female bodybuilders, 67 percent are "terrified of being fat" and 58 percent admit food obsessions. When K. Brownell and Judith Rodin of the University of Pennsylvania asked *Runner's World* readers about their body weight and dieting concerns, 4,551 responded. Of those, 64 percent of women and 45 percent of men described binge eating, and nearly one half of the women and one quarter of the men confessed to being preoccupied with the desire to be thinner.

Here's where you can be an especially valuable resource for your child. When J. Sundgot-Borgen interviewed athletes, ten significant factors emerged as triggers for eating disorders. Here are the signs to watch for, and the percentage of athletes with disordered eating who report each trigger event:

Prolonged periods of dieting/weight fluctuations	37%
New coach	30%
Injury/illness	23%
Casual comments by others about weight	19%
Leaving home/failure at school or work	10%
Problem in relationship	10%
Family problems	7%
Illness/injury to family members	7%
Death of significant other	4%
Sexual abuse	4%

Female Athlete Triad

In the last decade, three interrelated problems have been identified as a clinical syndrome, often appearing together among active young women athletes: disordered eating, amenorrhea, and osteoporosis. Termed the *female athlete triad,* this syndrome typically affects an adolescent or young woman with perfectionist tendencies, driven to excel and believing that a low weight will help her do better. She develops an eating disorder. Her menstruation ceases (amenorrhea) as body fat and estrogen levels drop. Premature osteoporosis (thinning and weakening of bones) may leave the young twenty-year-old with the bone density of a woman in her fifties, a possibly irreversible health loss.

Prevention and early identification of these problems are essential. The American College of Sports Medicine's women's task force has devised a slide series and script for primary care physicians and other health care professionals (317-637-9200), and the NCAA has a video on eating disorders and athletes (800-526-4773). Cathy Rigby and other athletes, ex-athletes, and celebrities have come forward with their own personal stories to help bring the problem to the public's attention. Awareness is the first step toward a solution. Timely support and professional referrals (chapter 3) when appropriate can avoid bigger problems down the road.

HOW TO HELP YOUR KID DEVELOP HEALTHY EATING HABITS

Many experts conclude that the harder we as a culture pursue the external value of thinness, the further away we shove our children and ourselves from internal cues. Research supports a body's wisdom and the ability to develop healthy eating habits, but your support as parents will be crucial.

> **TIP**   Help your children learn to respect, treasure, and maintain their own health.

On a personal level, you should:

1. evaluate your own beliefs and attitudes about weight (your own, your spouse's, parents, siblings, family of origin);
2. become a good role model of healthy eating and fun exercise for lifelong health;
3. take your children seriously for what they say, feel, and do, not for their physical beauty or physique;

4. discuss the attractiveness messages in the media aimed at women and men;

5. support activities building physical self-efficacy;

6. empower your young athletes with knowledge and respect for healthy habits.

SLEEP: AN ESSENTIAL PART OF BALANCE

Experts tell us sleep *is* important. To begin, people spend one-third of their lives asleep, but the total amount of sleep needed decreases with age. Newborns log in seventeen hours per day, with sleeping gradually diminishing over the lifespan to roughly six hours in old age. Far from a quiescent, comatose condition, sleep is known to be a very complex process with important balancing functions.

Have you ever watched a baby's eyes as he or she becomes drowsy? Eye movements slow, then become a fixed stare, then eyelids flutter, droop, and close. Similarly, the brain waves as seen on an EEG go from an active, awake gyration into slower patterns as the child drops into stage one sleep. Within a short time, stage two sleep appears, with even slower waves and a few brief bursts of activity called sleep spindles. Stages three and four follow with increasingly slower, wider brain waves. About ninety minutes into the night, at the depth of stage four sleep, there is a rapid shift in brain pattern back up through increasingly faster waves into the onset of rapid eye movement (REM) sleep. At this point, the brain activity on an EEG looks the most awake, but in fact, the sleeper is the hardest to awaken. Also paradoxically, while the brain looks the most similar to an alert brain, the person's voluntary muscles are the most relaxed. Most individuals awakened during these periods of REM will report dreaming.

Dreams last a few minutes early in the night but become longer and closer together as morning approaches, ultimately occupying about 20–25 percent of the adult's night. Newborns dream for more than half of the night. Sleep researchers tell us that dreaming is a crucial function of sleep; via body wisdom, the individual's brain is jockeying to get the business of sleep completed before having to rise and begin a new day. Supporting this idea is research showing that individuals become irritable, have slight tremors, reduced comprehension, impaired judgment, and lessened creativity when deprived of dream sleep. It seems that dreaming may be a counterpoint function to learning and memory, sorting and hard-wiring the material to be kept while discarding the unneeded. Increases in physical activities, such as sports events or marathons, cause complementary sleep increases in stage four sleep.

During a normal twenty-four-hour period, your child's body has a full cycle, a *circadian rhythm,* of body functions, including arousal levels, metabolism, heart rate, body temperature, even hormonal activity. The body reaches its coldest in the wee hours of the morning. As dawn approaches, temperature slowly rises, as do heart rate and arousal levels. Growth hormone is secreted during sleep. While research continues to unfold regarding the many functions of sleep, most coaches and parents have a lot of commonsense experience demonstrating the simple fact that sleepy kids don't do as well as well-rested kids.

William Dement, celebrated sleep researcher at Stanford University, has documented a major tendency of college-age students to be sleep-deprived. Most folks ages eighteen to twenty-two need about nine hours of sleep a night, but get only five, six, or seven. If you or your child falls asleep within five minutes of hitting the pillow, or can't remember walking to bed, you probably suffer from sleep deprivation. If your child falls asleep in class, on short car rides, or while watching TV, he or she probably is not getting enough sleep.

"The national sleep debt is larger and more important than the national debt," laments William Dement. The Exxon *Valdez* oil spill, Union Carbide's Bhopal, India, disaster, the Three Mile Island and Chernobyl nuclear accidents all occurred after midnight, when decisions were being made by folks at their sleepiest. Furthermore, sleep deprivation magnifies the effects of drugs and alcohol. One beer is a more powerful soporific to a sleep-deprived person than someone well rested.

While a slumber party the night before a ten-year-old's soccer game seems harmless, the loss of sleep and the impaired functioning can be disappointing. Body wisdom teaches kids important lessons. Many kids a few years into sports are quick to protect their sleep, having learned for themselves that their peak functioning can only be achieved when they are well rested.

TIP   **Getting enough sleep is crucial for physical and mental health:**
Encourage kids to care for their sleep needs.

When I talk to parents about kids' balancing mechanisms on breathing, temperature, even pain, most nod in agreement. When it comes to eating and sleeping, the reactions are mixed. Some parents eagerly affirm their children's wonderful ability to balance and maintain healthy habits for themselves, and other parents become very concerned. Some want to exert parental rights and control their children's choices, but this desire may well undermine their child's own learning.

Kids who play sports for very long, given a chance to learn, will develop a pretty good program for themselves. Nature rigs natural reinforcements this way. If kids eat too much sugar a couple of times, they really don't feel good. They don't do it again. If kids go without sleeping, they feel bad. They learn from their own natural response. Having chaperoned many teams and been team parent at away tournaments from Dallas, Texas, to New Orleans, Louisiana, I can tell you that the kids who start young and learn at young ages to listen to their body's natural feedback on food, sleep, breathing, water, and so on can and do make good choices. The kids who go hog wild and sneak to spend all their free money on candy are often the ones whose parents have laid down the firmest rules about sweets, but the kids didn't really understand why. The kids who run wild in the hotel corridor at 3:00 A.M. or stay up all night their first week in the freshman dorm are often the kids coming from the homes with little understanding and the strictest bedtime rules. Had the kids had some chance to learn for themselves *why* the rules were important or experience the consequences, they simply wouldn't have the same rebound reactions when restrictions were removed. Parents who try the strict-rule approach without explaining the reasoning or validating kids' natural learning and body wisdom run a risk of undermining their child's body wisdom and personal self-efficacy.

Ironically, the healthiest message for a young athlete to learn is to trust his or her body and its powerful homeostatic mechanisms. When it comes to all choices, knowledge is power, experience is a great teacher, and kids will make better choices when parents support the understanding and thinking behind healthy behavior.

8

Feelings: Competition Brews a Thick Hormone Soup

The night game's stadium lights cast sharp shadows across the field as frozen faces stared in disbelief at the football sailing cleanly through the goalposts. Across the way, cheers erupted, bells clanged, and the sound of the crowd surging onto the field was matched by an equally intense, dark silence where we were standing. No one moved. Wasn't this game OUR game? We were winning just one minute ago. We had the ball and then . . . a fumble. Of course his fingers were cold. We'd get the ball back. But the other team made an impressive march down the field, right up to the end zone, and kicked the winning field goal just as the horn blared, ending the game. Tears brimming in a girl's eyes spilled over the edge and down her cheeks as she clutched her arms around herself. I heard someone else catch his breath, then moan. We stood a long time in the cold watching our players gather up their gear as if in slow motion. Heads hanging, eyes downcast, we started to move automatically down the wooden bleachers. Shuffling across the frosty grass, one fan said it all: "Bummer!"

We felt the electricity as a celebrating throng merged into our shrouded retreat. Celebratory voices ringing high and clear recounted the last minute's march over our team with morbid clarity. Faces wearing exaggerated grins yelled and whooped, ignorant of our presence. Backslapping and spontaneous bear hugs blocked the flow of our crowd through the tunnel passageway. We pulled back from their ebullience. We wanted to be alone in our misery.

—Undergraduate football fan after a Notre Dame–USC game

SPORTS ARE ALL ABOUT EMOTIONS

The best of times. The worst of times. From the crowd to the athletes, we are sucked into the galvanizing emotional contagion weaving through sports participation. The athletes feel their pounding hearts, flushed faces and hands (physiological arousal) as their team jogs into the gym wearing school warm-ups; a slight tremulous worry before taking the first shot (usually not visible, but a feeling some athletes call "pre-game jitters"); and the spontaneous, elated jump into the air when the first shot swooshes into the home basket (behavior). As a parent, you also experience your own pounding heart, flushed face and hands as you climb the bleacher seats (physiological arousal); your fluttery stomach when your kid enters the gym (a feeling no one can see, but you call "nerves"); as well as pumping your fist exalting "Yes!" when the first basket is good (behavior). In actuality, it's hard to separate the intuitive experiences of physiological arousal, feeling, and behavior. All add together to create the magic electricity of playing and watching sports.

Not all the emotions are positive. With the adrenaline pumping, parents and athletes alike work themselves into fever pitches. Currently, there are two to three assaults on umpires per week, according to the National Association of Sports Officials. NASO president Barry Mano acknowledges that "assaults are much more common at the Little League levels" than elsewhere. Verbal abuse, shoving, spitting, stabbings, and shootings have become so prevalent that NASO now offers its nineteen thousand members assault insurance. Officials are not the only targets of aroused wrath. Spouses, other parents, coaches, kids, even the ice cream truck man have been brought into the fray.

In the beginning, when our kids were tots, sports were cute. Everyone agreed. Snack was the most important part of the experience. Parents cheering alternated between giggles and exalted yells when some kid actually made deliberate contact with the soccer ball. Clusters of knee-high kids moved in Brownian motion back and forth between goals (who knew whose was whose). Most parents laughed and made self-effacing gestures as their kids tripped over dandelions or got distracted by a fluttering rise of white butterflies, wandering off the field the one time a ball dribbled into their zone.

With time, the Saturday mornings added up. Practices got a little more serious and technical. "Positions" and "strategies" were some kids' first three-syllable words. Parents' faces started to change, too. The yelling lost its humor. Some parents started announcing to the team (louder than the coach) what should be done. One Saturday morning AYSO game, it dawned on me that the eight-year-olds would *really* benefit from little microphones in their ears telling them exactly what needed to be done next (especially if they were still chasing butterflies). I liked the idea for a good three minutes before I knew I had fallen over the edge. Eight-year-olds *should* chase butterflies.

Sobered, I listened to parents around me. "Play like an animal, Caitlin." Everyone laughed. Good. But not for long. As time, age, and experience increased, the pressure mounted. Words like *battle* and *defense, kill,* and *no mercy* cropped up. Was this a miniature war? Was this a battle of some symbolic significance to be won? Some parents seemed to think so.

INSTINCTS AND SPORTS

Some sociobiologists argue that the drive to beat others, to win, can be traced to a single force: survival of the fittest. Competition is the name of the game and always has been. As parents, we not only want our children to survive, we want them to thrive. That's normal. Is this why we want them to be acclaimed "winners"? The rich mix of parents' and kids' drives makes sports a very thick situation. Take a few pinches of testosterone, add three squirts of adrenaline and thyroid-stimulating hormone, stir in a measure of growth hormone, and add a whiff of old gym T-shirts. What do you have? A powerful soup of hormones and instincts yielding emotions that make athletic events potent potions for some awesome (or horrendous) social behavior. Athletes, parents, fans, coaches, referees—everyone involved is potentially vulnerable to the hormonal jangles and emotional contagion.

Three decades ago, researchers wondered if kids could "let out their aggression" by hitting a Bobo doll. Albert Bandura, Dorothea Ross, and Sheila Ross discovered that the more a kid watches hitting, the more hitting she and especially he are likely to do. Not only does the kid become a more practiced hitter (not calmer, less aggressive), but watching other hitters teaches him or her new, unique hitting techniques as well as the emotional style of the hitter. While the catharsis "let-it-out" hypothesis had some intuitive appeal, it was a blind alley. Take a kid to shoot paintballs and the kid becomes a better shot with a gun. Take a kid out to tackle the dickens out of his teammates and the better tackler he gets to be. We do what we see. The more we do it, the better we know it and the emotional learning is probably as powerful as the physical.

On the positive side, the very physical kid with aggressive tendencies who plays sports gets a chance to exercise (that does reduce aggression); to work with a team (team membership can teach cooperation); and to learn some good game rules about how to play and use his or her body in a sports setting.

Experience and Feelings

The experiences we provide (or passively permit) for our kids become the curriculum that shapes and hones their emotional workings. Enrolling a child in after-school gym class, fencing, or soccer inevitably provides rich emotional learning opportunities. The more you know about feelings, the better you will be able to balance the experiences for your child's overall well-being. While the following isn't meant to be a comprehensive guide to your child's emotional highway, it is meant to give you a solid foundation for making informed decisions.

Your Child's Temperament

Researchers currently believe that each child comes with genetic wiring and formative prenatal environmental experiences that determine early arousability. Called *temperament,* included here would be the child's physiological startle response to noises and regularity of habits. Some infants are more placid and sleep more. You know this already. One kid wakes up from a nap, feet already churning to hit the playground. Another child doesn't nap at all, while another moves at half speed until recess.

Harvard psychiatrist Jerome Kagan and others show how effectively parents can encourage learning experiences to balance their children's early natural temperamental tendencies. Sports is one of the choices parents intuitively make to round out their child's development.

HYPERAROUSABLE TEMPERAMENT

Jeffrey needed sports. Recess was his favorite part of school, and without Little League, he would have driven me nuts. He was so volatile. Some kids sit and watch TV. Not him. He NEVER sat still for longer than three minutes. It used to make his teachers crazy, but we all learned when he came in from recess or practice, he was okay for a while. That's when I got him on to his homework and his teachers were clued in to use his post-exercise down time, too.

Later, Jeffrey took charge and set his own schedule. He just needed to spin off some of his extra "Jeffreyness" before he could sit still and do written work. On through high school, he made up his own work-out program. He would lift weights every afternoon from four to five-thirty, then come in, sit and do his math—algebra, geometry, calculus—for as long as needed before dinner. After dinner, he would sometimes run or do crunches before he could sit down again to do his reading. It was not uncommon to see him pedaling the stationary bike while reading a chapter for history.

—Mother of high school and college track and field athlete

QUIET SUSIE

I watched as the dad walked into the gym with his daughter a half step behind. Awed, she looked up at the ceiling and visibly drew back as the crowd suddenly yelled and cheered for the entering team. She was probably ten or eleven years old. The seams of her dress were stretched to their limit with the waist scrunched high above two little inner tubes of chubby. A cardigan sweater pulled tightly across her shoulders and she tugged at the front self-consciously. Her feet took a wider stance to keep her balance and her extra weight made walking awkward.

Her dad didn't seem to notice. He proudly led her up the bleachers. As she sat down gratefully, he motioned to the sideline where the women's team was warming up. She glanced over to see one of the team members catch her eye. "She sees you," said Dad. The college volleyball player grinned and waved a big wave. Suddenly, the self-consciousness disappeared as she waved and grinned eagerly back. They knew each other. Throughout the game, the young girl watched the college girl's every move, entranced. After the game, the college player came up and hugged her. "You'll be at practice on Saturday? Great. We'll have fun with our team. You'll see." Can a child grow emotionally in one evening? I watched a more confident, hopeful girl walk out of the gym than walked in.

—Shari Kuchenbecker, UCLA volleyball spectator hat, 1995

Playing Emotions Like a Well-Tuned Instrument

Learning about feelings is another valuable lesson from athletics, not only the absolute presence of specific feelings, but how feelings rise and fall as well. Too little arousal, and performance is muted. Too much arousal, and performance falls apart.

Some coaches seem to work at maintaining the balanced mid-levels of arousal. For example, Coach John Wooden didn't like to see his athletes get too worked up or too relaxed. Steady was his ticket. He seemed to agree with the researchers on emotions who document that what goes up must come down. What goes up fast often comes down quickly. Research on the hormones cortisol and adrenaline tells us that big expenditures early are likely to leave players depleted later.

Sports researchers have shown that there are actually at least two different arousal curves: one curve for easy tasks that have been well learned and a different curve for more difficult tasks. Easy tasks benefit from just an extra zap of stimulation. With a cute girl watching, the young male basketball player making a lay-up enjoys a higher jump and a cleaner swoop into the basket. Thanks, adrenaline. Difficult tasks often get their best show when the pressure is off. It's easier to do amazing three-point shots when the guard from the other team isn't breathing down your back and slapping at your sides.

Playing to the Opposition

The two curves help explain the phenomenon of "playing to the opposition." When the opponent is seen as easy, highly skilled players may let down (low arousal) and stop pushing to perform well-known skills, missing a lay-up in basketball or mis-hitting easy balls. When the opponent is seen as tough, kids have more trouble executing newer, more complicated skills, and the three-point shot caroms off the hoop.

Thank goodness coaching decisions and timely substitutions often intuitively take the ebb and flow of emotions into consideration to put the best team possible out to play. The young, eager freshman may get some playing time against the easier opponent when the senior lets up. The same eager freshman, under the pressure of a big game, may witness her newer skills fall apart and get pulled back to the bench, permitting the more seasoned, older player to execute well-practiced drills less affected by the immediate pressure. Bravo, coach! No kid feels very good knowing he or she isn't performing well, and the truly talented coach takes the time to explain emotions, play, substitutions, and coaching choices.

Emotional Self-Efficacy

As a parent, you need to remind yourself that your child's greatest opportunities in sports are to learn about himself and learn how to work with others. No matter how clearly you tell your sixteen-year-old basketball player about easy and difficult skills, low and high arousal, he or she may not get it or even be interested. Even with curious kids, some learning only happens when they experience it vividly. Talk all you want—many young athletes need to feel and learn for themselves. After the process, you *may* be able to explain what you understand, but maybe not.

TIP Kids can build emotional resilience through sports. (Both positive and negative experiences teach emotional lessons.)

Positive Affect

Kids learn best when:

1. their learning is rewarded (intrinsically or extrinsically),
2. they and their teachers maintain a positive learning environment.

Bottom line, a kid in a positive frame of mind learns most things quicker and better. Even modest shades of negative, such as expecting or fearing failure, cause significant impairment. If you create clearly defined behavioral goals in small, doable steps, it makes it more likely that your child will attain those goals, but positive affect is often crucial.

It makes sense. When a kid is afraid of failing, he or she thinks about failing and "what will happen if . . ." There is that much less time to think about the problem at hand, whether it is a math test, a penalty kick, or shooting a free throw.

Losing begets losing. Winning begets winning. The team that hasn't lost a game only knows how to win. Last year's championship team carries that winning memory into every new competition. How powerful is the winning memory in generating another win? Positive emotions provide much better foundation than suiting up in a defeatist attitude.

Coaches in our research cited 81.5 percent of damage to a young athlete's potential comes through negative emotional processes: undue criticism, constant negative feedback, emotional pressure and pushing, bad attitude, hostility, negativity and self-doubt, cockiness, lack of positive guidance, lack of love, winning overemphasized, anger, blaming others, irresponsibility, and poor sportsmanship. Coaches say "parents," one word with no elaboration, constitute 8.5 percent of the problem, "poor coaching" 6.1 percent of the problem, and "drugs" 3.9 percent. Of course, when parents respond, more point fingers at the coaches, but all agree about the damaging effects of negative emotional processes.

The message is clear, we need to nurture more positive emotional processes in sports. But how do we do it?

TIP Coaches say kids who love to play and have positive attitudes are the real winners and pressure and undue criticism damage a young athlete most.

Coaches know that kids who take losing too hard or who are sore losers become their own worst enemies.

EMOTIONAL CONDITIONING

Nature rigs us with some superior self-protective mechanisms, and our survival instincts help us avoid painful things like flames, stings, and blows. We don't need to learn to avoid these *unconditioned stimuli*. Under all conditions, unconditionally, when exposed, we do what we need to do to withdraw from or minimize further harm.

Nature also rigs us with a personal radar, an emotional alarm system. The sight of the hot flame makes us pull back. The sound of the bee makes us wary. In academic terms, a signal that directly precedes or leads to the unconditioned stimulus takes on the unconditional stimulus's emotional feelings. At the sight of the bee, we withdraw. Upon seeing someone who has hit us, we pull back. This is called *classical conditioning*.

Sights, sounds, and smells are all potentially very powerful signals of what is to come, things we have learned at a gut physiological level to expect. You may have had it happen to you. If you are a former basketball player, try walking into your old high school gym. Brace yourself for a flood of feelings and memories. Triggered memories can come anytime, anyplace. This simple signal system can explain some otherwise inexplicable emotional responses. The kid who gets a stomach virus (unconditioned stimulus) after the team party of sausage pizza (conditioned stimulus) may suddenly feel nauseated the next time the team orders pizza (conditioned response). The growing kid may start disliking after-school soccer practice (conditioned stimulus) because she goes from noon to 5:00 PM with no food (unconditioned stimulus) and feels faint and weak (unconditioned response). Kids quickly learn to avoid physiologically aversive events. Being hungry is aversive. It just so happens that soccer practice happens at the same time, so soccer practice gets nixed as well.

Parents can be on the lookout for anything causing physical pain. Classical conditioning can happen with football cleats that are too tight, uncomfortable jockstraps, football pads that rub skin raw, scratchy sports bras, neoprene shin guards on allergic skin, even the new fabric softener that makes the warm-up T-shirt itch. Kids dealing with these irritants find themselves disliking the sports that generated them.

PUNISHMENT AND EMOTIONAL CONDITIONING

A slap, a hit, a spanking all fill the bill as physical unconditioned stimuli. Kids don't need to learn that slaps, hits, and spankings hurt. Physical punishment covers a range of actions from the obvious spanking to the less obvious indirect infliction of pain. *Direct punishment* includes any painfully intended physical contact between individuals (e.g., hitting someone else's face with the hand). *Implement punishment* is any physical contact using an implement intended to cause pain (e.g., using a fly-swatter to hit a child's buttocks). *Indirect punishment* means mandating behavior that causes an individual to get hurt (e.g., ordering a kid to dive onto the floor after a missed hit; cinching a seat belt too tight; ordering a kid to run excessive laps after missing a free throw). *Verbal punishment* includes loud yelling or screaming or foul language. *Physical restraint* means holding or binding an individual, which can potentially cause injury. A *withholding punishment* occurs when an individual withholds appropriate clothing, heat, light, or food (e.g., sending a child to sit on the snow-covered field for missing a practice; making a child go without dinner).

In each case above, the inflicted physical pain and natural response to the pain form an unconditioned stimulus–unconditional response pair. Parents should know that *anything* that precedes the pair can become a signal or conditioned stimulus. Imagine a coach who forces a player to do fifty crunches every time he or she misses a free throw. The sight of the basket, the sound of the coach's voice, the color of the coach's jacket, even the smell of the gym and the sound of the ball bouncing off the rim can become a signal of the pain to come, and the kid's love of the sport dies a little more with each blow.

On the superficial level, many coaches will tell you that they make the kids do the crunches to "teach them a lesson not to miss baskets." In actuality, what many kids learn at a deeper level is to avoid the situation leading to the painful crunches, and that means they quit going to games and practices. Whenever a coach or a parent resorts to physical punishments (direct or indirect) to teach kids a lesson, they are heading into risky territory.

Reasons Not to Use Physical Punishments

There are five fundamental reasons not to use physical punishment:

1. *Physical punishment only suppresses a behavior, it does not eliminate the behavior.* Many physically punishing coaches seem surprised when they leave and the assistant coach takes over; unless the

assistant coach wields the same big stick and threats of punishment, "all hell breaks loose." The kids unleash with wild abandon all the things the coach has been so diligently punishing. Why? Simple. When the coach goes, so goes the punishment, and from learning research we know that the removal of a punishment acts like a reward. The kids are thrilled to do all the stuff they have been suppressed from doing.

2. *Physical punishment does not teach kids what they should do.* Many coaches fall into the habit of punishing the bad behavior every time it crops up, but give little time to teaching positive behavior. Teaching time can rapidly spiral into a whirlwind of don'ts and punishments with little positive forward momentum.

3. *Physical punishment associates the punisher with pain and negative affect.* The coach can become a conditioned stimulus. Many punitive coaches find their relationships with players quite wary for the obvious reason: Kids don't trust them. It's fairly stupid to entrust your feelings to someone who squashes you with punishment. The best thing to do around people who hurt you is to go on emotional alert. Importantly, emotional alert (provided by cortisol and other stress hormones) does not necessarily lead to improved playing—indeed, it often causes poorer playing—and the punishing coach loses his or her status as a valuable positive emotional resource.

4. *Punishment teaches kids to be punishers.* In research on the effects of punishment, kids trained with punishment often turn around and become punishing teachers. Interestingly, the more a kid was spanked, yelled at, or punished in a two-week period, the greater was his or her incidence of punishable behavior the following week. Punishment seems to beget punishable offenses and kids who like to punish others. Negativity breeds negativity.

5. *Punishment misses the fundamental, logical reasons to do or not do most things.* Almost everything we want a child to do or not do has logical, valuable reasoning behind it. Even two-year-olds can get it, but teaching them takes time and energy. For a child starting to run across the street, a quick whack will set the kid to crying. We have a short-term success, but a long-term failure. Teaching the child why the street isn't safe goes a lot further than the physical spanking. Moreover, when you aren't there, the child will know how to stay safe (self-efficacy).

Injury and Pain

Research on pain intensity tells us that the more pain you know, the more you know how to endure. Kids who have been spanked regularly have "higher pain tolerances." Called the *contrast effect,* kids learn how to deal with pain by experiencing it. A slight slap to a child who has never been hit is a powerful event. The same slap to a child spanked regularly is nothing. We know that hit kids learn to adjust to the pain and often "need" increasingly larger amounts of pain to effectively suppress their behavior. Spanking parents will often glibly relate how they have had to hit harder and harder "just to get their point across."

Let me be clear: Physical punishment is primitive and abusive. Physical punishment for undesirable behavior won't foster quality learning and begins a cycle of learning how to tolerate increasing pain. Please remember that your children need to learn to trust their bodies and recognize pain as the healthy sign it is. If an ankle hurts when moved, it should not be moved. If a finger hurts to bend, don't bend it. If kids behave badly, model what they need to do better, don't hurt them.

Struggling with frustrations yourself or a history of physical abuse? Many parents who make a choice to hit their children quickly defend the practice as a parental obligation and right. In fact, it's a ritual often learned during childhood, a ritual that must be stopped. The Child Help USA hotline (800-422-4453) offers supportive counseling twenty-four hours a day if you or someone you know needs help. If you are worried about the coach's or assistant coach's behavior, check out chapter 2's guidelines on how to handle the situation.

Yelling at Kids

Have you ever seen a baby when a door slams? BANG! The infant's arms and legs fling open, then pull in, the body curling into a ball. His or her face screws up and the baby starts crying—*loud.* This response is a natural startle reaction, critical for survival. It says, "Come pick me up. I need help. Something loud and dangerous is near." Peeking inside at the hormones, you would see a responsive adrenaline burst.

As kids get older, they learn from experiences. Kids in loud, banging households become less and less startled by loud noises. Kids in houses with yelling adults become less and less alarmed by yelling. Kids from quiet, soft-spoken homes startle much more than kids from loud homes. They simply are not accustomed to the noise. Stand two kids on a baseball diamond, yell at both, and the kid from the quiet home will usually burst into tears first.

Some coaches talk about making kids "emotionally tough." I have heard super-nice parents say, "Oh, it's good for her. She needs to be yelled at." Parents should know that there is a hair's breadth difference between *emotionally tough* and someone so emotionally toughened as to reach *true jerk* status. The balance between endurance in the face of emotional stress and learning to ignore other people's words and feelings is a judgment call. How much is too much? How little is too little? Insensitivity to others' feelings may sometimes be an adaptive coping mechanism in the face of past abuse.

Of course, it's immeasurably valuable to be able to stand, arms at your side, legs in the parade rest pose, and take a dressing down by a superior. One up-and-coming woman ref in the NFL says:

> I've learned in acting classes how to relax in front of an audience and how to do your best and stay focused. Let me tell you, that comes in handy when coaches are screaming at you and you've got to determine whether there is a clipping penalty.
> —Chrystal Nichols, quoted in the *Los Angeles Times,* 11/15/98, p. D1

"Sticks and stones may break my bones, but words can never hurt me." Chanting across playgrounds, grade-schoolers often wish words had no effect. In fact, others' words can be powerful, and kids do need to learn how to handle verbal taunts appropriately. One of the worst insults a child can sling is "crybaby." *No* kid wants to be a crybaby.

> During her senior year of high school, my middle daughter didn't go for a ball sailing within a few feet of first base. As she was the softball team captain, the coach thought it was a huge mistake. He flew into an emotional tirade, took her out of the game at the next inning, and yelled at top volume for five minutes in her face while she stood, blank expression, and stared through him.
> I wasn't at the game, but my wife was and parents who saw it said

they have never seen such composure and dignity under fire. When the coach was finished, he sent her back in the game and she returned to playing as if nothing had happened. Parents on the sidelines were both astonished at the severity of the reprimand and at my daughter's composed demeanor.

Of course, the coach was sorry later. He apologized to her and gave her a miniature doll, a Velcro tear-apart referee, in front of the team the next day. My daughter understood. She had played for him for a number of years, knew him well, and had the big picture. What no one really understood, however, were the numbers of hours that had preceded that five minutes of public behavior. My daughter, wife, and I had had countless discussions, long before that fieldside moment, hours of listening, supporting, and debriefing. She had not always felt so invulnerable under attack. When she was younger, her tears had welled up more times than I could remember over peoples' thoughtless remarks, cruel jokes, or just mean digs . . . but she had grown through it all.

It was not the road I would have chosen for her, but the emotional toughness she learned across sports experiences gave her a foundation richer than the coddling I would have preferred. When parents asked me what I had done, I could only credit her on choosing a very challenging path with much to learn along the way. I only tried to help her see other people's point of view while protecting hers. (And as an aside, none of the parents watching the dressing down knew how my wife and she had cried that night. Through laughter and tears, I had promised my daughter if it ever happened again, I would have the coach's proverbial balls on a platter ready to turn into chicken feed.)

—Father of five, high school and college softball player

Not Making the Cut

Some parents freak out when their kid gets cut from a team. They want to fix it. A few phone calls, some begging, some pleading, even some emotional bribery, and some parents get the kid reinstated. I think this is a mistake. There is a valuable lesson to be learned, but the "helpful" parents just short-changed their kid. The fact is, no matter how great your kid is, there is another kid, sometimes just around the block, who's better. No kid is fabulous at everything all the time. Kids need to learn from the hard lesson of disappointment.

TIP Parents of very skilled young athletes frequently ask whether they should "play up," which usually means joining a team of older players. Many times, a skilled youth may earn a spot among older players with comparable abilities, but his or her emotional and social maturity will not match the older players'. I would caution you strongly not to overlook your child's emotional development. Research indicates that it is usually best to put your kids with peers of the same age and similar skills rather than push them up the ladder. If you have to choose between matching age or skill level, age matches usually work out best in the long run. Ask the coach for his or her advice and insight here.

Stress = Wrong Kid, Wrong Time, Wrong Place

When our son was fifteen, he got onto a team that was a lot more physical than the teams he had played on before. Everything was a lot more intense, from the minute he got to practice to the minute he got in the car to come home. They were all over each other all the time, and the coach really encouraged it. He had them run at each other full speed to just smack chests and bounce off. He even told the kids to remember "no pain, no gain." He told them they should hurt.

We just weren't sure what to do. Our son wanted to be one of the guys. He is not a quitter. In the beginning, he seemed to steel himself for practices and games. We could watch him sitting in the backseat slamming his fist into his leg again and again saying to himself "See, it doesn't hurt. I'm tough." During the first month, he jumped out of the car and grabbed his gear, pads, helmet, bag and trotted toward the field. By the second month, he had slowed down. He quit hitting himself and instead seemed to always have his fists clenched. "Wound up tight" is the way Beth's mother described him. Too tight. He was grouchy with everyone—me, his little sister, even his friends. By the third month of the six-month season, he was really different. He got real quiet and would just sit in the backseat, mouth in a firm line, jaw jutting out and looking into space. He hardly talked at all. Coach never played him in games, so he said it didn't matter. He just went through the motions. When his schoolwork went down, we knew it was time to get him off that team. We should have done it two months before, but we just didn't know how bad it was going to get.

—Father and mother of high school football player

Stress is a slippery concept these days. Tossed around casually, it's sometimes used to describe threats or challenges and other times to explain our responses.

What if we could get rid of all your child's stress? Don't be so quick to cheer. A stress-free life would offer no puzzles to solve, no challenges to overcome, no difficulties to surmount. In short, take away the challenges and you take away some of the richest moments of life. Strip away stress, and you would have a life without texture and with little growth.

Stress per se is not the problem, but *how much* stress your child experiences. This is where the art of parenting truly shines. Reading your child's experiences lets you understand and support his or her growth, temper overly stressful situations, and facilitate your child's maturation process. It makes sense. What is one child's "fun of a lifetime" puts another child over the edge.

Researchers T. Holmes and R. Rahe propose a list of stressors among college age kids, including death of a close family member, death of close friend, divorce of parents, jail term, major personal injury, marriage, being fired, down to trouble with parents, change in living conditions, lower grade than expected, and even minor traffic violation (*Journal of Psychosomatic Research*, v. 11, No. 2. pp. 213–218). Their Social Readjustment Rating Scale (1967) scores events with standard points from most to least distressing, but parents know all kids are not alike and all events are not similarly stressful. Wise parents watch and listen with their hearts.

"Stress is not disturbing if people believe they have the means to relieve it. It is not the occurrence of perturbing thoughts that is anxiety-arousing, but the perceived helplessness to turn them off," explains Albert Bandura, the David Starr Jordan Professor of Psychology at Stanford University.

Understanding both your child's stress and your perceived stress as a parent is an important step. It will help you more effectively provide balance and be on the alert for your child's experiences of extreme stress. Burnout, covered in chapter 12, is a "syndrome of emotional exhaustion, depersonalization, and reduced personal accomplishment." According to leading researcher Christina Maslach at the University of California at Berkeley, even modest amounts of unmanageable stress, before reaching burnout, can be detrimental.

> **TIP** **Be alert for signs of extreme stress.**
> Support your child's ability to manage feelings and maintain balance.

THE POWER OF OPTIMISM

According to Martin Seligman at the University of Pennsylvania, thinking style plays an important role in emotional health and happiness. Optimism has three general characteristics:

1. Attributing illness or problems to specific causes (not general tendencies)
   "I feel fine except for a little pain in my ankle."
2. Blaming the problem on controllable external conditions
   "I twisted it the time I came to practice without my ankle braces."
3. Assuming the pain or problem is temporary
   "It won't last long. Once I get warmed up, it won't bother me. I just need to stretch it out."

The pessimistic thinker, in contrast to the optimistic thinker, tends to see the problem as global, internal, and long-lasting. "This pain is awful. It's going to ruin my whole season. I'm so prone to injuries. It's depressing to know I have such rotten luck."

Research tells us that there's a real bonus for those who are optimistic, even if the optimism *slightly* distorts reality. Perhaps this should be called rosy glow optimism. This is not the crazy-over-the-edge-ga-ga-optimism: "My god, you are going to be an Olympian by the time you're eighteen. I'm your dad, just ask me." It's the commonsense, realistic, this-is-just-a-temporary-setback attitude that says things will look better in the morning and you'll be fine in the long run. Cultivating optimism in your kid will give him or her one of the strongest assets on the sports field and in life. Dr. Martin Seligman's book, *The Optimistic Child,* offers valuable suggestions to help you support optimism.

> **TIP** **Parents should encourage a child's positive, optimistic attitude and minimize negativity.**

Mary's Wager

Positive attitude and hope are precious commodities that coaches and parents can dispense. If a coach pumps a team up and tells the players they can win (generating a lot of positive feelings), the players access good emotions and good playing memories. When the players go through the game emotionally pumped, they play better. If, at the end, they still lose the game, at least they played their best. Moreover, what did they really lose? If they played as well as they could, they should count the game as a personal win. If they play down on themselves and perform poorly, they not only lose the game, they lose a personal competition. Most of all, a positive attitude gives the players more fun in the process. Don't forget, 32.7 percent of coaches identify positive attitude as a key quality of a winner and 43 percent celebrate young athletes who love to play.

The research busting-at-the-seams to be done in sports focuses on the power of the positive attitude to *create* winning. As I see it, it is a win-win research opportunity I'll call Mary's Wager. Based on Pascal's Wager, Mary's Wager is simple. Do whatever you do with a good attitude. Hope for the best. If positive attitude supports success, great. If positive attitude is irrelevant, you've lost nothing and had more fun anyway. Named after my grandmother, Mary Piety Slaughter Stevenson, Mary's Wager says be positive (merry=Mary) and you'll find joy along the way, and I bet win more games in the process. Notably 45.7 percent of our collegiate coaches identify "loves to play" and 37 percent cite positive attitude as characteristics of a young athlete who's a real winner . . . and a fair proportion of the sample came from Stanford University, who just won the Sears Cup for the fifth year in a row. The characteristics these coaches presented are literally of the top collegiate winners in all senses of the word *winner.*

In the absolute sense, optimism is both a thinking strategy and an affective outcome. Applied to athletics, it means that you're in charge of providing your child with information. In other words, you can train your child for optimism or pessimism. Mary's Wager makes sense; research gives the thumbs-up to optimism training. Probably the best path is one supported with balanced optimism. Not too much, not too little. If you get a child's expectations way beyond his or her immediate successes, the frustration will be too great. Watch. Listen. Balance.

Fundamental Attribution Errors

People commonly believe their successes are due to their abilities and their failures are due to the situation. This is called the *fundamental attribution error.* There ought to be a name for the similar parental phenomenon as well:

> "My child's successes are due to his or her superior ability (and my great genes).
> Your child's successes are due to coach favoritism and luck."

> The flip side of this:
> "The coach favors my child because he or she really is superior."

Let's call it the *fundamental parental attribution error (FPAE).* It can work for and against your child. When your child needs a boost, your rosy support helps. When your child gets too cocky, your FPAE may keep him or her from learning an essential truth about life: Sometimes people are responsible for wonderful success and sometimes they are lucky—in the right place at the right time—and come up smelling like roses. Truth is, both are accurate.

TEACH YOUR KIDS TO COPE WITH STRESS

Even if you've bathed your children in optimistic attitudes, there will be times when the stress of their sport gets to them. There are five major resources you can explore to help them cope: aerobic exercise; social support; self-relaxation techniques; biofeedback; and cognitive-behavioral appraisal.

1. Aerobic Exercise

Sports can provide powerfully good feelings. It's exhilarating to exercise. Breathing deeply, blood pulsing, heart pumping, a body comes alive. "I am hooked on my endorphin high," confess many lifelong athletes. Some researchers say aerobic exercise may be nature's best antidepressant and anti-stress remedy. Encouraging your kids to exercise also has a major bonus: emotional self-efficacy. When kids and adults stay active, they simply cope better. Getting kids into athletics helps give them a great handle on stress management. (Of course, you'll still need to watch out for those sports situations that undo the good stuff aerobic exercise fosters.)

2. Social Support

Let your child know you support him or her. Believing in your kid (no matter what) can reduce your child's perceived stress in everything from a missed ball to a poor mark in school. A number of large studies confirm that social support and multiple social ties help people weather the stressors, even adding years to life.

Peer support can also be important, but my inclination is that you should be your kid's first line of support, not the chorus. Peers have a complicated role in kids' lives. Other kids are the other pickles in the pickle jar; they often lack the maturity to handle tough situations for themselves, much less others.

3. Self-Relaxation Techniques

Not surprisingly, sports participation provides the potential pressure of competition. Few kids ever make it through their sports careers without succumbing to the potentially overwhelming pressure of wanting to win.

VARSITY PRESSURE

My middle child truly enjoyed a charmed career in sports from the ages of five to fourteen. He played every sport with ease, handling wins and losses with equanimity and never seeming to have a nervous moment . . . until he made the varsity football team as a freshman. When the quarterback got injured in the first game of the season, the coach made the quick decision to bring him in off the bench. I guess my son had done everything well in practice. He said everything was going well and his passing was better than ever, but I could tell right away that day something was wrong. The coach signaled to my son as they carried the first-string quarterback off the field. He looked nervously off to the right then the left as the coach signaled to him. He couldn't believe it was him. Reluctantly, he stood up and walked at half his normal pace. I have never seen him scared on a football field before. Disoriented, he jogged

awkwardly to the middle of the field. When everyone went into down position, he stood up a good three seconds longer than everyone else until
the ref started to blow the whistle and then he scrambled. He butterfin-
gered the ball and it slipped right out of his fingers. Luckily, one of the
other players just landed on it. It only took a few more plays until the
halftime, thank god, and the coach put in the junior. After that day, my
son worked on a deep-breathing technique the coach recommended for
a month before he even got back into a game again. It was a good two
months before he finally got it together to play decently again.

> —Mother of three when her middle son was a quarterback
> on varsity football, Los Angeles, California

Many athletes discover self-relaxation techniques for themselves.
They may hear about them from one another or the coach, but anyone
who stays in sports long enough learns self-calming devices to help with
big-pressure situations. Some use progressive muscle tightening and relaxation, others find breathing helpful, and many have a warm-up ritual.

EASING INTO THE GAME

I always feel jittery at the start of a game. It usually starts out that I just
don't feel like eating for a couple of hours before the game, so I always
get a big breakfast on game days. Next, when I come into the gym, I always make sure that I go for a few easy shots to warm up. I would never
try a three-pointer first. That would blow my whole game if I missed it,
so I start easy. I do one lay-up, then a few more, depending. Next, I try a
couple of shots from the free-throw line. Finally, I will go for the three-
pointer. Same thing once the game starts. First the easy, then the
tougher shots.

> —College basketball player, junior year

Self-Relaxation Exercises

Add these to your bag of tricks if you or your child needs help in this
area:

SIX-SECOND QUIETING RESPONSE

1. Draw in a long, deep breath through your nose.
2. Hold it for three seconds.
3. Exhale slowly through your lips for a count of three.
4. As you breathe out, let your face, jaw, shoulders drop. Feel relaxation flow into your arms and hands.

QUICKIE HEAD, NECK, AND SHOULDER RELAXATION

The muscles that most often tense up under anxiety, anger, or emotional strain are in the neck and shoulders.

1. Contrast tense-relax exercise: Consciously tighten up neck and shoulder muscles. Hold it for five to ten seconds, then completely release the muscles. Repeat this process while focusing on the contrast between tension and relaxation.

2. S-W-E-N head: Slowly tilt your head forward until your chin touches your chest (S); move to the left (W); to the right (E); and to the back (N). Repeat.

PROGRESSIVE RELAXATION

Start with the tips of your toes and move up. Spend ten seconds tightening each muscle group and then ten seconds relaxing.

During tightening, tense completely. During relaxing, focus on positive release. Begin with the toes, then move to calves and feet, stomach, thighs, butt, midsection, back, neck, shoulders, biceps and triceps, hands, mouth and tongue, and forehead and eyes. Finish with breathing.

4. Biofeedback

When kids learn self-calming gimmicks for themselves, they've shown they've learned how to listen to their bodies. For advanced levels of athletic training, biofeedback provides a more formal method of tuning into a body's responses using specialized equipment to monitor such physiological functions as blood flow, electrical skin conductance, and brain alpha waves. For kids with major attacks of nerves, parents can consider exploring biofeedback. Working systematically with licensed professionals, a child can learn techniques to relax under increasingly anxiety-provoking stimuli. By the end, their emotions have been tamed and they've mastered their feelings.

5. Cognitive-Behavioral Appraisal

As I explain further in chapter 10, it's not an event per se, but a child's appraisal of the event that makes it stressful. For the young quarterback in the earlier story, his appraisal of playing varsity and the pressure resting on his shoulders was immensely stressful. He knew how much the position meant to him and how much winning meant to the school. All told, his assessment was on target, but ruminating on the importance of the game interfered with his ability to think about playing. In addition to the breathing exercises he began practicing, he also started a visual focusing strategy. Paying close attention to the ball and to the position of his other teammates let him get out of his self-absorption and over his case of nerves.

TIP   Behavioral tricks to cope with emotional stress include aerobic exercise, social support, self-relaxation, biofeedback, and cognitive-behavioral reappraisal.

TAKING PRIDE, FINDING HAPPINESS

Your child may be as happy now as he or she will ever be. The pro athletes, making thousands or millions of dollars per season, are not necessarily any happier now than they were when they were playing Little League in the park. Help your child enjoy the moment now and savor the many positive feelings coming through sports. Treasure each and every opportunity. Ken Anderson, a trophy company owner from North Hollywood, summed it up well:

WHAT IS A TROPHY?

Is it just a piece of marble, a wooden column and a baseball figure? No, it is much more. A trophy is a symbol of your success.

Your participation trophy is your personal symbol of having completed a successful season. This success is not measured by your win/loss record, but by your memories. It is measured by your satisfaction that you always did your best for your team and always worked to further your organization's goal of good sportsmanship. In future years, this trophy will remind you of your friends, your coaches, your moments of glory, and, believe it or not, your moments of failure. Be proud of these memories.

A first-place trophy recognizes success as a member of a team. Through group effort, your team was able to show that it was the best. This trophy should always remind you that many important goals can only be accomplished by cooperation with others.

The all-star trophy recognizes individual success as a result of many hours of hard work and practice.

We love the recognition that awards symbolize. They serve to remind us of life's best moments. As you go through life, don't concentrate on the trophies. Do your best, practice hard, and cooperate with your fellow man. The trophies and the success will follow.

—Ken Anderson, Anderson Trophy Company,
North Hollywood, California, 1999

Don't be surprised when trophies, ribbons, pictures, and paraphernalia enjoy front and center stage in your kid's room. Good memories and positive feelings shine in reflected lights falling on these earned medals and commendation plaques. More are woven into the fabric of the old jersey now pinned carefully to the drape—proof positive that sports can help bring emotional fulfillment and balance to your child's life.

9

The Growing Athlete:
Injuries, Prevention, and Time

I hear his feet shuffling across the tightly woven rug. Slowly, deliberately, painfully: slide-step, slide-step. Perhaps it isn't the noise that tells me how much he hurts, but the set of his mouth, the downward gaze, and the ever so slightly furrowed brow deepening with each forward movement. So it is every morning when the alarm goes off at 6:10 A.M., the slow shuffle to the bathroom starts off another day on his sixty-year-old body. Bones, joints, and muscles that once played in peak physical condition now hobble with time and old injuries. Champion! Star! Winner! Phenomenon! Top school tackler, a record made and held for thirty years, celebrated on a dusty plaque in the dark athletic department hallway.

Was it worth it? How many team victories for the pains? How many championships earned on yet another swollen sprained ankle? When does the past justify the present? "Get out there and play, boy. We'll ice it up after the game. You'll be fine!" A slap on the butt and in he went again. How many moments of glory does it take to counterbalance the slow shuffle step he now makes every morning? Oh, in twenty minutes or so, after a hot shower, the calcium chips in both his ankles loosen and find a more comfortable hiding place for the day. He can walk at almost a normal pace for a while, but by late afternoon the damaged knee cartilage, even after one operation, still grinds, and he favors it as evening comes on. The fact of the matter is, most people have no idea. He never complains. He just gets really quiet and a bit more sensitive about little stuff. But I know. Sometimes I bring him tea or serve him dinner in his favorite chair, but time and rest in equal measure help the most.

> —Wife of ex–high school, college, and
> eight-year pro football player

Would this aging athlete—or thousands of other athletes like him from the past—have played if he had realized the fate ahead? How could he know? His coach said he would be fine—some ice, a couple of aspirin, and a tight tape job and he was back running with the team. The crowd called his name. The team needed him.

If it's any solace, this old warrior's not alone. Drop by any college or pro football team reunion. The field heroes of the 1950s, 1960s, and 1970s wear their injuries like badges of courage. Shoulders, knees, hands, ankles are all hot topics. Some have canes. Some have walkers. Most speak knowledgeably about torn ACLs, PCLs, ligament damage, rehab options, advances in cartilage regeneration research, and the latest in orthopedic surgery.

LESSONS LEARNED

The good news comes in the lessons we have learned at the expense of these athletic warriors of yesteryear. The young athletes today potentially have wiser counsel, better care, fewer injuries, and fewer long-term problems.

The obvious fact stands out clearly. It's up to parents to learn about and negotiate healthy outcomes for their children in athletics. Your kid only gets one body. Somewhere between *wussy, hypochondriac,* and *tough-balls jock of yesteryear* resides a broad spectrum of potential physical activities that are healthy and developmentally appropriate. Knowing what is safe and preventing, spotting, then appropriately caring for injuries means paying close attention to your child and his or her athletic training program.

TIP   **Your child only gets one body.**
Help him or her make choices supporting lifelong health.

RECOGNIZING AND TREATING COMMON INJURIES

Stress Fractures

I love cross-country. I still run every day. My daughter Kim is a great soccer player, a first-class swimmer, but I must admit, I was especially happy when she decided to go out for track. She was only a ninth grader and they had her working out with the varsity straightaway. I was mighty proud. Two weeks into the training on a pretty rigorous schedule, Kim started complaining about a sore leg. I didn't pay much attention. We all get aches and pains. I figured she was fine. She sort of quieted down about it, but the next week after practice she was pretty adamant that she hurt. I asked her where and she pointed right to her hip. I told her she didn't know anything about pain—wait till she was forty-eight! By the following week, she mentioned she sat out two practices and I asked her why. Kim was near tears as she explained that her leg hurt all the time, even walking from the car to the house.

I finally made an appointment with an orthopedist. He said he couldn't find much but would take an X ray of her hip just as a safety measure. In hindsight, she was pretty stoic. When the films came back, it was really obvious. She had a stress fracture of her right hip.

—Cary Spalding, Dad of three, accountant, Santa Monica, California

Stress fractures, an apparent epidemic among young athletes in the 1990s, occur as a simple function of muscle load on bones. Visible on X ray, they show up as a detectable break in the fundamental bone matrix with accompanying pain and malaise. Most sufferers have no single traumatic event they can recall that would have caused the injury.

Stress fractures actually develop slowly over the course of time and physical exertion. The specific pain in the area overloaded with muscle stress typically progresses through three stages:

Stage 1: Pain only during the specific drill or activity that overloads the site.

Stage 2: Pain with activity that lingers for increasing time after the activity ends.

Stage 3: Chronic pain extending throughout the day and into the night, possibly disrupting sleep.

According to authorities, stress fractures are largely self-limiting. With time and rest, pain abates and normal activities can be resumed. In the last three weeks, I have heard of stress fractures in kids as young as thirteen—hip, foot, ankle, back, and wrist. What worries me is that I didn't find these stress fractures written up in a literature review at the medical library or on the Internet. I heard about them in casual holiday conversations with other parents.

None of these kids has bad parents. All of them are just like you and me. Our kids are in sports and we support what they're doing. We listen and we give the advice we think is right. We try to do our best, but something is amiss. How can so many kids be getting stress fractures? Three years ago, stress fracture was an orthopedic sleeper that emerged in an athletic triad associated with eating disorders. Now it seems to be cropping up all over.

Over-Training

According to Dr. Bert Mandelbaum, member of the Association of Professional Team Physicians, medical director for the Women's Professional Volleyball Association, national team physician for U.S. Soccer, and recent USA World Cup team physician for France '98 and for the Women's World Cup '99, current research suggests that the increased incidence of stress fractures, youth injuries, and pain is a function of the increased total hours of practice—more hours in the gym, more hours on the field. It is a "dose-related" phenomenon. Apparently, many of our kids are getting bigger "doses" of sports participation than their young bones and muscles can handle. The results are stress fractures, injuries, and bony nodules. A number of studies by sports medicine specialists point to over-training as the culprit.

Unlike adult sports medicine, youth sports medicine deals with kids whose bodies are changing rapidly. From research across ages and sports, we know that low-intensity exercise builds bone density and increases muscle endurance and strength, but apparently too much exercise can overstress and disturb dynamic bone growth. Kids' bone growth plates are open, their organs are enlarging, and gender-specific reproductive changes are in action. The mix is unpredictable and highly individual.

At this point, I would love to give you a chart to put on your refrigerator detailing in black and white the *right* number of hours of practice in each sport at each age. Absolute rules that take no thinking to implement always make our job as parents so much easier. The problem is, such a chart would necessarily be wrong most of the time. Two hours a day of baseball pitching practice for one eleven-year-old boy might be fine but too much for another kid exactly the same age whose growth plates are more open and thus more vulnerable to "Little League shoulder" overuse syndrome. Once-a-week weight training might be ideal for one fourteen-year-old but overwhelming to another in the midst of puberty's develop-mental changes.

Interestingly, coaches, parents, and even physicians often have proved to be poor judges of physical maturation. The obviously tall, clearly physi-cally shapely thirteen-year-old girl with good coordination may be judged ready to compete with the sixteen-year-olds. Upon commencing the longer, more rigorous workout schedules, the youngster complains of aching joints. One MRI later, wide-open growth plate epiphyses, swollen in self-protection to shield the vulnerable growing edges of her bones, are the cause of the pain. Just looking at her, no one knew. Without the MRI, the only real clue was her own report of pain.

Common sense and sports medicine specialists tell us that young ath-letes need adults' guidance and knowledgeable support to help them judge their own ability to participate. This is a huge responsibility and not one to be left unattended. Your child needs your help to make good judg-ments.

Begin by teaching your child the fundamental premise of respect for his or her individuality. "It is your body. You only get one body." If you as a parent honestly and consistently have taught your child to attend to and care for himself or herself, listening to your child's personal feedback sig-nals of over- and underuse will be discernibly easier. On the other hand, if you are like most of us and flounder in your own mixed messages from childhood ("Stop if you hurt, honey, but no one likes a quitter"), you will have to monitor yourself.

CLAY FEET

I flounder. I don't mean to. It always surprises me how badly I can blow it. For weeks, it seems, I say the right things. "Listen to your body." "You know when it hurts." "Make the choice that is best for your health in the long run." "Take care of yourself."

Then, right out of the clear blue sky, my fourteen-year-old will catch me off guard, and old, old memories wash away good sense. She tells me after the soccer game that the reason she didn't play was because she told the coach before the game that she couldn't play the field. Her ankle worried her. She hadn't had any trouble for two years, but last practice it twisted a little. "What do you think, Mom?"

Out of my mouth, before common sense takes charge, my fifty years of experiences (good and bad) let out, "I think you sound like a WUSS."

"Mom!" she howls. Oh god. I'm such an idiot. I'm being two-faced, speaking good, healthy parent jargon for months and in a weak, unguarded moment, my own ugly rearing escapes and says something awful, so I apologize. I say she is right. She must protect her ankle. I know her confidence was undermined when she twisted it again. Of course she shouldn't run on the uneven field if she is worried about the lateral stability of her ankle.

I explain I am hamstrung by a medieval past. *She must take care of herself.* "Please forgive my flip, thoughtless answer," I beg.

I do fifty mental lashes, one for each of my damaged years, with a wet tennis-shoe lace. I am sorry, Karalyn.

—Shari Kuchenbecker, soccer mom hat, 1999

If you suspect you're child is suffering from a problem brought on by over-training, consultation with a physician is *essential* for complete evaluation and medical treatment. You will find it interesting to note that the treatment in each case is often similar and has an easy-to-remember mnemonic—RICE:

Rest: Stop the particular activity or activities that cause pain.

Ice: Make an ice pack using double plastic bags filled with about three cups of crushed ice. Commercial ice bags are okay. Apply ice packs to the area for periods of no longer than twenty minutes apiece. You can hold the ice pack in place with a three-foot stretch of kitchen plastic wrap.

Compression: Use a compression bandage (not too loose, not too tight) to support the injured area after you're done icing.

Elevation: Elevate the extremity above the heart to reduce swelling by increasing the venous blood flow return.

Dr. Kevin Ehrhart, father of three, volunteer team physician for Loyola High School, and Santa Monica orthopedist, notices that it's easy for parents to get kids to slow down or stop an activity when they have a very painful injury. As the pain fades and energy returns, kids want to know "When can I play again?" The longer the rest, explains Dr. Ehrhart, the more time the body has to recover and reknit injured tissues, so it is up to parents to convince their children to stay off an injury as long as possible. Sometimes physical therapy is valuable. Gather information about the injury and help your child understand the importance of following doctor's orders. Many physicians have free colorful pamphlets fully explaining different problems. When there are options, get your child's input and discuss pros and cons of treatment. Be consistent in your focus to protect your child's long-term health.

Problems Peculiar to Young Athletes

Little League Shoulder

Little League shoulder is "pain felt during the end of a hard throw" related to use, widened epiphyses, and demineralization of bone. According to pediatric textbooks, with rest and ice it should resolve in about six weeks.

Little League Elbow

Kids, often pitchers and catchers, who do a lot of throwing may start to complain of pain during practice. As the season wears on, the pain may extend throughout the day. Little League elbow includes changes detectable on X ray in the radial and humeral bones of the lower arm. More common than you might think, one study of young pitchers found that 23 percent had bone damage visible on X ray, even among some kids not complaining of pain. Rest lets the healing process begin.

Gymnast's Wrist

Young gymnasts often complain of wrist pain, an increasingly common malady correlated with the introduction of the Urtchenko vault. One study of college athletes found that 75 percent of men and 33 percent of women acknowledged the presence of weight-bearing pain. Among young gymnasts with a mean age of 11.7, Dr. Bert Mandelbaum found 72 percent reporting pain lasting longer than four months. Rest and time off from training are required to begin recovery.

Osgood-Schlatter Disease

Among young athletes between the ages of nine and fifteen, pain associated with running, jumping, or kneeling localized below the knee may be a traction-induced inflammation or small stress fracture of the tibial growth plate. Tenderness, swelling, and pain may occur during a rapid growth spurt; it should be evaluated and treated with reduced activity, possible immobilization of the joint, anti-inflammatory medication, and ice. Osgood-Schlatter disease or pitcher's knee may result in a bony bump or "tibial tubercle," which may be cosmetically unattractive, but is otherwise unremarkable.

Jumper's Knee

Pain below the knee is common among basketball players and athletes in other sports with frequent high-impact jumping, and is known as *patellar tendinitis*. Treatment includes reduced activity and ice to minimize swelling.

Shin Splints

When a youngster complains of an achy lower leg pain that gets worse as the workout continues, shin splint syndrome may be the culprit. Sometimes the young athlete will complain of tenderness up and down the inner lower leg or specific spots of particular pain. A physician will need to rule out stress fracture, but shin splints are treated with rest, ice, and anti-inflammatory medication. As the pain abates, activities can be resumed.

Achilles Tendinitis

Pain over the Achilles tendon appears most commonly among young runners. The inflammation and injury may represent little tears in the tendon, which need time to heal. A minimum of two weeks' resting from running or exacerbating activity is recommended.

Consult with Your Doctor

As with all injuries, a physician's evaluation of these syndromes is essential. Getting a second physician's opinion also makes good sense for more serious injuries. With orthopedic injuries, a specialist in sports medicine is very handy, and I have found that a consultation with a foot specialist (podiatrist) can be very helpful if there is any indication that foot, ankle, and knee alignment are adversely affected by foot problems, such as arches that are too low or too high. On occasion, a consultation and shoe insoles or inexpensive arch supports can avoid painful and costly injuries down the road.

Concussions

"Coaches and players need to understand there is no such thing as a minor concussion. While you can put ice on an injured knee or pulled muscle, you can't 'ice' the brain," states Jay Rosenberg, neurologist with Kaiser Permanente's San Diego medical center and co-author of a recent report in the *American Academy of Neurology,* in a *Los Angeles Times* article, March 13, 1997. A current pediatric textbook states "concussions occur frequently in contact sports, and determining an athlete's ability to return to play afterward can be difficult."

There are three levels of concussion. A grade 1 concussion occurs when a person with head trauma does not lose consciousness, but may lose balance, "see stars," suffer a transient disorientation or disturbed concentration or a second of confusion, with all symptoms resolving in less than fifteen minutes. A grade 2 concussion is diagnostically similar, but the above symptoms linger more than fifteen minutes. A grade 3 concussion is diagnosed whenever there is any loss of consciousness, either brief (seconds) or prolonged (minutes). The symptoms at the time of injury may indicate the extent of brain trauma, but careful monitoring for twenty-four hours is always important. Parents should know that the greatest threat is accumulation of blood or fluid within the skull, creating intracranial pressure on the brain, which can kill brain cells and destroy function.

Based on the increasing number of injuries in youth sports, Rosenberg and other head-injury specialists mounted a campaign to adopt uniform guidelines for assessing and treating concussion injuries. According to the 1997 *Los Angeles Times* articles, Brett Lindros, former pro-hockey player, and Harry Carson, pro-football linebacker, both bear the lifelong burden of cumulative head injuries that now limit their functional abilities. Lindros and Carson support the American Academy of Neurology's new guidelines, which are also endorsed by the American Orthopaedic Association, Brain Injury Association, National Athletic Trainers' Association, Pop Warner Football, USA Hockey, and other groups. The proposed guidelines should help coaches, trainers, and parents make more accu-

Recommendations to Youth Sports Coaches for Evaluating Concussion

GRADE 1 CONCUSSION

SYMPTOMS

- Transient confusion (inattention, inability to maintain a coherent stream of thought and carry out goal-directed movements).
- No loss of consciousness.
- Concussion symptoms of mental status abnormalities on examination resolve in less than fifteen minutes

RECOMMENDED RESPONSE

- Remove from contest or playing field.
- Examine immediately and at five-minute intervals for the development of mental status abnormalities or post-concussive symptoms at rest and with exertion.
- May return to contest if mental status abnormalities on examination resolve in less than fifteen minutes.

GRADE 2 CONCUSSION

SYMPTOMS

- Transient confusion (inattention, inability to maintain a coherent stream of thought and carry out goal-directed movements).
- No loss of consciousness.
- Concussion symptoms or mental status abnormalities (including amnesia) on examination lasting more than fifteen minutes.

RECOMMENDED RESPONSE

- Remove from contest and disallow a return that day.
- Examine on site frequently for signs of evolving intracranial pathology.
- A trained person should reexamine the athlete the next day.
- Neurologic examination by a physician to clear the athlete for return to play after a full week with player asymptomatic at rest and with exertion.

GRADE 3 CONCUSSION

SYMPTOMS

- Any loss of consciousness, either brief (lasting seconds) or prolonged (lasting minutes).

RECOMMENDED RESPONSE

- Transport the athlete from the field to the nearest emergency department by ambulance if still unconscious or if worrisome signs are detected (with cervical spine immobilization, if indicated).
- A thorough neurologic evaluation should be performed, including appropriate neuroimaging procedures.
- Hospital admission is indicated if any signs of pathology are detected or if the mental status of the athlete remains abnormal.

Source: American Academy of Neurology; Kaiser Permanente.

rate decisions about the nature of the head injury, reentering play, and appropriate referrals for hospitalization.

"Losing Consciousness"

Physicians often have great difficulty in determining whether someone has in fact "lost consciousness." To help decide, three types of amnesia (memory loss) associated with loss of consciousness provide clues to aid in diagnosis:

1. *Retrograde amnesia:* forgetting extends to events predating the head injury by some years (usually temporary)

2. *Permanent retrograde amnesia:* missing memories encompass the few seconds or minutes that immediately preceded the injury

3. *Post-traumatic amnesia (anterograde):* missing memories after the injury reflect impaired ability to form new memories usually lasting for some hours

Coaches on the scene should ask a child suspected of having a head injury his or her name, day of the week, and more specific information, such as "Do you remember getting hit?" "What happened?" "What was the play just before you got injured?" Often, duration and type of memory loss can be a useful guide to diagnosing head injury severity. If the answers or symptoms are indicative of head trauma, immediately go to the emergency room. Keep notes so you can share the information with the treating physician.

Occasionally, hours or even days later, postconcussional syndrome will develop. This is characterized by headache, dizziness, visual disturbances, irritability, nervousness, trouble concentrating, and other emotional, cognitive, or behavioral problems and should be brought to the attention of your doctor. Nausea, unequal pupils, or difficulty rousing from sleep are more worrisome and warrant a phone call to your physician and possibly a visit to the nearest emergency room.

Most Kids Worry About Getting Back into the Game

It's good news for parents that the most important thing on most kids' minds is when they can get back into the game. As you will note from the guidelines for a grade 1 injury, the athlete should be removed from the game and examined at five-minute intervals for any abnormalities including changes in sensation, differential pupil size, nausea, and headache. Return to competition is okay if symptoms resolve in fifteen minutes or less. For grade 2 injuries, the athlete should be kept under supervision on site for any emerging intracranial problems. Kids should never be sent off to the showers or back to the locker room alone if there is a chance of head injury. They need a neurological examination and clearance as well as one week without symptoms before they can return to competition. Watch out for the seriously injured athlete who, not thinking clearly, demands to get back on the field. Some coaches simply withhold necessary equipment (racquets, helmets, jerseys) to ensure the athlete remains quiet while a thorough evaluation can be completed. Grade 3 injury merits transportation to the nearest hospital, a thorough neurological exam, hospitalization, and monitoring for any changes suggesting rising intracranial pressure.

Luckily, the human body is very resilient, and most kids recover from a concussion uneventfully, but it is still important to watch them for the first twenty-four hours. Follow your doctor's specific advice, which may include the suggestion to wake your child every few hours during the night and make him or her respond to a few questions. A few kids may have lingering problems, but monitoring and early treatment reduce the chances of unfortunate outcomes.

Tragic Outcomes

According to a *Los Angeles Times* report (3/17/1997), dizziness and tingling were Eric Hoggats' only complaints after a normal high school football game. He was found dead the next morning. Adrien Taufaasau, seventeen, never regained consciousness after a Newport Harbor High School game. Neither death seems to have been the result of a single blow; rather, they were the cumulative result of several insults.

Notably, some physicians feel that three concussions in a sport and the youth should quit. Does that mean that another sport with concussion potential is out, too? Do you get three ice hockey concussions, three football concussions, and three skateboarding concussions? Is that the same as nine ice hockey concussions, a clear no-no? Who decides if something truly qualifies as a concussion?

I am a parent. To me, it's simple. One concussion is one concussion too many. Two concussions? Give me a break. The risk is too great and the payoff too small. *No* concussions should be the goal. If your child has a head injury and you have any doubts, take him or her immediately to an emergency room or private physician for professional evaluation. If the risk of further injury is present, carefully evaluate the situation. Watch your child for ongoing signs of postconcussional syndrome and stay in close contact with your child's physician. Be open to having a neurologist or pediatric neurology specialist examine your child if there is a doubt about resuming play or even continuing in a sport.

Neck Injuries

Neck injuries and the risk of lifelong paralysis due to spinal cord trauma are high on my parent alert list. Whenever there is a loss of consciousness, there is the risk of vertebral column and spinal cord damage. Up to 10 percent of such injuries incur tragic compression during the initial emergency care, thus exacerbating the original injury. The importance of proper care in transporting and moving accident victims cannot be stated too strongly. When in doubt, *do not move the victim*. Wait for a professional. Prognosis improves with reduced compression, prompt treatment, and anti-inflammatory measures.

How Serious Is the Injury?

The Glasgow Coma Scale is a three-to-fifteen-point index assessing visual, motor, and verbal abilities. The higher the score the better. Ideally, the child spontaneously opens his or her eyes (4), obeys motor commands to move fingers and toes (6), and converses normally (5).

Glasgow Coma Scale

Eyes opening	4	Spontaneously
	3	To verbal commands
	2	To pain
	1	No response
Best motor response	6	Obeys command to move fingers and toes
	5	Can indicate where it hurts
	4	Flexion withdrawal from pin prick
	3	Flexion abnormal (decorticate activity)
	2	Decerebrate extension
	1	No response
Best verbal response	5	Oriented and converses
	4	Disoriented and converses
	3	Inappropriate words
	2	Incomprehensible sounds
	1	No response
	3–15	Total

Having immediate professional medical help available on all youth athletic fields is unrealistic, but well-informed coaches and parents can support appropriate care until emergency professional care arrives. Sadly enough, the intuitive choice for many uninformed people at the scene of an accident is counter to good care. Many well-meaning helpers finding an unresponsive victim immediately want to move or shake them. The best choice is to *assess the victim first* using the Glasgow Scale. Ask "How are you?" "Where do you hurt?" "Can you move?" Establishing whether a victim can be moved is the professionals' first job. Well-informed folks need to protect victims and adhere to proper procedures. *Stop less informed people from making a mistake that may increase damage.*

Breaks, Sprains, and Strains

Further down on my parent worry list are breaks, sprains, and strains. Traumatic at the time, with rest, ice, treatment, and tender loving care, most can return to "as good as new."

There was a cluster of kids in front of the goal, and the coach bolted toward one child lying motionless in the grass. They were waving for me to come onto the field. My seventeen-year-old was down.

The whole process on the field only took ten minutes. Thank god one of the dads was a doctor! After certifying he was safe to move, they carried him off the field. I got our van and drove to the corner of the field for a trip to the emergency room. As they lifted him in through the back sliding door, they kept the ice bags in place along with his ankle tape and shoe. They said compression reduced swelling. He didn't talk much as we drove.

Check-in at the ER was quick. Copy my card. Fill out some papers. Get into the treatment room. I got the first look at his ankle when they eased off his shoe and cut the tape. Rapidly swelling to the size of a base-ball, one side seemed to have no bones. His foot turned at an odd angle. The next two hours were long. The final X ray and MRI said things like, "There is evidence of what is believed to represent an ostrigonum poste-riorly." "Extensive soft tissue swelling overlying the anterior talofibular ligament . . . local hematoma . . . soft tissue edema . . . a complete tear of the anterior talofibular component to the lateral collateral ligament complex . . . with the calcaneofibular component of the ACL appearing thickened."

The worst part was the look on my son's face. He tried to be stoic, but he looked so utterly dejected as he told me that this meant he could not compete this summer. College recruiting was out. All these years and it was over in a single play. Luckily, the ER gave us written instructions, because I don't think either of us heard what the doctors were saying. We read at home about the avulsion fracture and the very severe sprain (tearing of joint-supporting ligaments). Casting was to be later when the swelling went down. Ice often. Stay off it. Elevate. Use crutches.

How could I put a crutch on his broken heart?

—Mother of high school varsity soccer player, injured junior year

Broken Bones

Some breaks are evident early. When your child's arm or leg bends at a new angle or turns on a new fulcrum, an X ray confirms the obvious.

Some breaks, however, are marked only by shortening or lengthening of the limb, swelling, bruising, or mottled skin discoloration. Hair-line fractures may show up only on X ray.

Short of X-ray vision, it is often hard to know the severity of an injury, and many times medical evaluation will be required. Discomfort and pain are subjective. Knowing your child helps. Some kids are consistently stoics. Some kids have low pain tolerance. Some kids cry wolf often. Some never say peep. Use information about pain tolerance and emotional style as well as common sense to seek a medical examination when indicated.

Sprains

A sprain is an injury to a ligament or joint capsule. When your doctor says your child has a sprained ankle, that means that the bones and muscles are largely okay, but the ligament that attaches the muscle to the bone has been stretched or torn.

Grade 1 sprains occur when only a few of the fibers are torn in a ligament, with little pain and swelling and a full range of motion. A grade 2 sprain has many torn fibers, laxity, with moderate swelling and pain. Grade 3 means marked laxity and significant swelling and pain.

Strains

A strain is technically an injury to the muscle. Like sprains, they are also graded 1, 2, and 3, from a few fiber tears to a complete muscle rupture. Treated with RICE and TLC, time will heal the damaged muscles.

Jammed Fingers

Pain on movement is nature's signal to stop moving. Swelling is nature's cast. When a finger gets jammed, fluid often accumulates around the injury site, and care should be taken to reduce the risk of further injury. One quick trainer trick is to gently tape the jammed finger to its neighbor before seeing the doctor. This gives it some support and effectively reduces movement and further injury.

Iatrogenic Problems

Iatrogenic problems occur when the treatment itself causes damage. The splint that immobilizes a sprained elbow reduces the pain, but left too long lets the muscle atrophy and the ligaments heal shortened, losing mobility. The medicine that reduces pain in the swollen joints in excess may destroy the stomach lining and cause bleeding ulcers. In treating any problems, the physician, parent, trainer, or coach should remember the Hippocratic Oath: First, do no harm.

Other Common Problems and Home Remedies

Bumps, Lumps, and Bruises (Unbroken Skin)

Ice has wonderful properties. First, ice slows the bleeding and thus the size of the hematoma (blood blob) under the skin. Second, ice reduces the sensation of pain by sending cold messages along to the brain. Finally, it reduces the inflammation that causes pain sensations. Mostly it is one of those great mom-grandmom home remedies that really work and cause no harm if done correctly.

Rules for Icing

- The best ice packs are made of one-inch or smaller chips in a very flexible container.
- Never apply ice directly to the injured area; it's too chilly and might stick and damage tissue. (Commercial ice bags with nice cloth covers are easy to use and durable, but you can create the same effect out of heavy-duty plastic bags wrapped in an old T-shirt. A one-pound bag of frozen peas, corn, or mixed vegetables is actually quite effective if you're in a rush.)
- Ice for twenty minutes maximum at a time (too long and you'll deep-freeze and damage tissues).
- Repeat as often as desired at twenty-minute intervals.

While your kids may be reluctant to try icing, its effectiveness for pain relief usually convinces even the most skeptical. Tell them to check out most college teams after a game and you will see a majority of the athletes sporting ice-filled plastic bags wrapped to various appendages with clear plastic wrap just like you buy at a grocery store.

Abrasions and Infected Wounds (Broken Skin)

Whenever skin is broken, the body's shield to harmful bacteria has been broken as well. The blood and moist tissues exposed are very vulnerable to infection. The first task is to clean the wound. Rinse the area well using a stream of water, clean, sterile gauze pad, or small sterile brush. Remove all debris, dirt, hair, etc. Add an antibacterial agent such as Betadine or antibacterial dishwashing liquid to a large bowl of warm water. Soak the affected area. Be sure to keep the area immersed for twenty minutes and you can repeat the procedure up to five times a day until swelling, tenderness, and redness disappear. When obvious signs of infection are gone, you can cut out soaks and use the antibacterial ointment alone.

After soaking and cleaning the wound, cover the area with a sterile dressing. Add a small amount of antibacterial medication such as polysporin ointment or Betadine ointment. Secure the dressing, but leave room for air to circulate. If you seal it off, the sweat and moisture collecting under the closed dressing will help the bacteria grow, and moisture may irritate the site further. If you note pink or red streaks spreading from the wound, call your doctor; this could be the sign of a serious infection.

Scaling or Itching Skin

For garden-variety dry itchy skin or hives, use a lukewarm bath with a half cup of cornstarch or oatmeal added. For specific irritants, treat with appropriate medication:

Athletes' foot: Clean the area well, then apply antifungal medication. Be sure to add treatment to athletic shoes and street shoes as well. Remind your child to wear flip-flops in the showers and gym area, not only to avoid spreading the problem, but to diminish exposure to other germs that may make their way in through the cracked skin.

Impetigo: Spread by fomites, *Staphylococcus aureus* or *Streptococcus pyogenes* can get under the skin and cause distinctive crusts. Wrestling and gymnastic mats can be washed to reduce the spread of this irritating skin disorder. Infected participants should not compete until wounds are dry and noncontagious. Systemic medication can be used.

Herpes gladiatorum: Named after high-contact sports like wrestling, this disorder is caused by the *Herpes simplex* virus, with infections lasting five to seven days. Oral acyclovir has been used by some for speedy recovery. Until all fluid-filled blisters are crusted over, participants should be disqualified.

Cramps, Aches, and Pains

There is nothing like a hot bath to reduce overall aches in tired muscles. For spot relief, a hot water bottle or heating pad can be applied to cramp sites, effectively permitting the muscle toxins to disperse. Add a towel or T-shirt around the hot water bottle or pad to avoid burns, and be sure to monitor the heat.

Sore bottoms (hemorrhoids, fissures, and the like) also respond well to hot soaks. The moist heat increases the circulation in the area and lets nature clear up the problem. Ask your physician to recommend changes in diet (high-fiber, more fluids, etc.) to eliminate the problem in the long run.

PREVENTING INJURIES

Stretching

Fitness and exercise programs recommend a three-prong total body wellness approach. The cardiovascular portion of a wellness program can be completed in thirty minutes of total activity that causes sustained raised heart rate (briskly walking, running, jogging, or biking) three times a week. The strength component specifically targets certain muscle groups for development, building strong arms, legs, shoulders, etc.

The stretching component is, however, a crucial foundation of a wellness program across ages. Not only does stretching keep a body working well, but the process has unexpected benefits like stress reduction, body toning, and maintaining range of motion necessary for diverse activities. It can also help prevent injury.

America's leading fitness expert and mother of two Kathy Smith offers four fundamental tips on stretching to help performance and prevent injury.

1. Warm up muscles five to ten minutes before stretching. Muscles are somewhat like taffy. When they are cold, the fibers are more brittle and can tear more easily; when warm, the more pliable fibers stretch and elongate more easily.

2. Stretch each part gently. Don't bounce or jar.

3. Hold a stretch for fifteen to thirty seconds to get the full result.

4. Spread out stretching across the day, take several quick stretch breaks (take stress and muscle relaxation vacations when tension starts to build). Kathy's book, *Getting Better Every Day* (Warner Books), has valuable tips for fitness applicable across the life span for both you and your child.

Always Wear a Helmet

My oldest daughter Jane has always been fearless and usually the first to try new things. Believe me, it took a lot of talking to convince her she HAD to wear a helmet when she rode her bike. We live in a small city and she didn't think there was any chance she would get in an accident. She tried to convince me of her superior bike-riding abilities. She had never fallen off. She never lost her balance. She had perfect vision. She always followed all the rules. She watched out for drivers who didn't.

In the end, I prevailed. I told her it wasn't her abilities I didn't trust. It was the other drivers. The people in cars on the road around her were unpredictable and very dangerous. They had a ton of metal surrounding them to keep them safe. She had nothing.

As I tell the story now, it still is hard. She was an avid bike rider. All through grade school, high school, and even when she went off to college, she always lugged her helmet with her. As she grew or the old one got particularly beaten up, I would take her down to replace it with a new improved model. When she joined the bike club at her college, they all got matching helmets. She called just before the end of fall semester to tell me about a bike trip in Europe that several kids were going to do that summer. In the end, we were all excited for her to go.

The flurry of activity to get her bike checked out and get the bedding, knapsack, and other equipment ready was exciting. I waved good-bye standing beside my wife and two other daughters.

When the phone rang at 3:00 A.M., my heart started pounding. I knew something was wrong. The voice on the phone explained that Jane was in the intensive care unit in a German hospital. She was in a coma. She had been in a collision with an auto, thrown twenty feet through the air with a massive head injury.

My wife and I were on the plane by noon that day. We walked into the ICU at 8:00 A.M., about forty-eight hours after the accident. A nurse was checking a chart. Jane looked so small. There were plastic tubes from her arm and her head was half shaved. My heart leaped as she opened her eyes and gave a cock-eyed smile. "Oh dawd, I'm sowrry." The nurse explained that she had awakened last night and her speech was just returning. There was some paralysis on one side, but we would have to wait and see.

The story came out later that they had just gotten off the train and unloaded their bikes. She always wears her helmet, but this time as she struggled with the big backpack and bedroll, she just hung her helmet on the handlebars. It was only two blocks to the youth hostel, and this car came out of nowhere.

It has been two years now and she still goes to speech and physical therapy. The doctor says she may be able to go back to school next year, but she still has a little trouble concentrating. Meanwhile, we take each day one day at a time.

> —Father of college-age cyclist accident victim,
> now twenty-seven years old

"Every day in the U.S., one child dies and fifty suffer permanent brain injuries from bicycle accidents," says Dr. Abe Bergman, professor and physician at the University of Washington Medical School. One study in the *Journal of the American Medical Association* (Rivara, Thompson, and Thompson) documents that helmets can reduce the incidence of head injuries by 85 percent.

Brand or price of the helmet are irrelevant as long as the helmet is approved by ANSI (American National Standards Institute) or Snell Foundation. Proper placement of the helmet is atop the head, not canted forward or tilted back. Snug straps properly fitted keep the helmet secure in the event of an accident. The most important part of the helmet is remembering to put it on . . . every time.

Dr. Bergman tells of one particularly outstanding retailer who placed a tag on every bicycle saying "This bicycle is missing a part." The tag was redeemable for a reduced price on a helmet. Further talks with one of the nation's largest toy-store chains brought low-cost (less than twenty-five dollars) helmets to parents.

Now you can get a helmet for only ten dollars. Prudential Healthcare and Troxel, a leading manufacturer of helmets, have a special program to make protective helmets available to adults and children. Call 800-694-3258.

Regrettably, many kids believe that only "geeks" or "nerds" wear helmets. You'll see only a few helmeted kids on many college campuses today. How can smart kids make unsafe choices? Simple. It's not cool to wear a helmet in some communities. As social psychologists explain, being cool and being a part of the peer group is an immensely important force. The solution becomes to make wearing a helmet cool. Dr. Bergman and Dr. Rivara propose a community-based head injury prevention program, which you should consider for your neighborhood. College kids should consider bringing the information to their educational community as a healthy role model to the nearby high schools, junior highs, and elementary schools.

Dr. Bergman and Dr. Rivara's
Head Injury Prevention Community Action Program Plan

1. Form a coalition of interest groups with enthusiastic representatives from each (PTA, health-care providers, hospitals, insurance companies, bicycle clubs, retail shops).

2. Find an underwriter to offset costs of helmets (i.e., bicycle shops, manufacturers of bikes or helmets, health-care organizations, HMOs).

3. Develop written handouts specific to your community, briefly telling about the benefits of helmets (gather samples from other communities and adapt them to your needs).

4. Use local radio, newspapers, TV stations, and public meetings to share information.

Helmets in Athletic Activities (In-Line Skating, Roller-Skating, Skateboarding, Street Hockey)

Regrettably, some of the most passionate and articulate spokespersons on behalf of helmets are parents of children who have either sustained preventable head injuries or died because they weren't wearing a helmet. Hindsight is always clear, and the logic is obvious. If your child plays any sport where high speed and hard surfaces potentially interact, make wearing a helmet mandatory. Whether it's biking, in-line skating, roller-skating, skateboarding, wrestling, boxing, snowmobiling, football, or street hockey, don't play the odds with your kids' lives or well-being. Give them the information. Help them understand the importance. Get other parents to cooperate. Raise your community's consciousness *before* your child is the one injured.

Knee Pads, Wrist Guards, Elbow Guards, Mouth Guards, and Other Safety Equipment

Most kids think they're invincible. Most parents know they're not. Knee pads, wrist guards, elbow pads, mouth guards, and other pieces of safety equipment have been developed *because* someone has gotten injured. The equipment functions to reduce injury and keep the wearer safe from harm.

Each sport has a shared base of safety equipment. Be sure you learn about and obtain the properly fitted safety devices when your child plays any sport.

Water and Fluids

As simple as it is, drinking enough water before, during, and after games and practices provides a crucial mechanism for preventing injuries. Research shows that adequate hydration prevents muscle cramps during games, reduces muscle soreness after games, improves play, and even positively affects the number of points scored. A water-deprived athlete is more likely to make poor decisions, make errors, and be more vulnerable to injuries. The better-hydrated athlete does better, feels better, and suffers fewer problems.

Good Technique

Coaches and sports medicine specialists tell us that correct technique minimizes wear and tear. Bad habits and poor technique practiced again and again erode the quality of the play and harm the body. Many experienced coaches can spot a poor motion likely to lead to problems down the road.

If you find your child complaining of chronic pain when performing a specific drill, ask the coach to check out his or her form. Sometimes a slight deviation has gone unnoticed, which can be easily corrected before more damage is done. A consultation with another experienced coach is sometimes a good idea as well. Good form usually leads to good outcomes and minimal pain.

I end this chapter with a promise and hope. Parents and young athletes—care for your health. Guard ankles, knees, and shoulders with unequaled passion. Aim to prevent injuries. Give time to heal when accidents occur. Focus at least some of your competitive drive toward care for yourself, so that in three decades, physical activities and sports can continue to be a positive part of your life and your child's life, too.

10

Self-Efficacy, the Mental Game, and Learning

"I've done this so many times, I can do it now."

NAGANO, Japan.—"Before I started," the seventeen-year-old Michelle Kwan said, "I heard people cheering and I thought, 'I'm in heaven.' People clapping, billions of people watching on TV and I'm skating. It's just me and the ice. When I'm on the ice, I don't think anybody can stop me." She had "butterflies" in the warm-up, but she put them to rest by thinking, "I've done this so many times, I can do it now. I've done everything possible. I've trained hard." "I kind of knocked some sense into myself."

—Steve Wilstein, Associated Press, February 1998

Open your sports page any day of the week, and you'll find intimate stories of self-assessment, agony, hope, heartbreak, and aspiration. Athletes' words often reflect amazing personal insight woven with powerful threads of self-awareness and cognitive self-appraisal. What they may leave out, their coaches, sportswriters, broadcasters, and others soon fill in.

"HOW DID YOU DO?"—METACOGNITION

Metacognition—thinking about thinking—can be a valuable skill for athletes to cultivate. Ask many young athletes, "How do you think you did?" and articulate kids quickly nail down physical and mental errors with scalpel-like readiness to excise performance problems. Kwan agreed with her coach's appraisal of a performance that ultimately snagged silver instead of gold at the Nagano Olympics. "In Philadelphia [at nationals], I was more free—it felt like I was flying," she said. "Here I was more cautious, like I was in my own world. I didn't let go. I'll have one more in 2002. I'll be twenty-one then. Who knows?"

The ability to respond to questions like "How did you do?" with candor and personal insight reflects maturity and psychological balance. When you encourage your child's thinking about thinking, you give your child license to step out of his or her current perspective and make changes in mental patterns. Many parents work long and hard to develop honest self-assessment in their child, and some parents apparently teach it better than others.

THE MENTAL GAME

Many icons in the world of sports, such as tennis star Billy Jean King, believe "more matches are won internally then externally." Yogi Berra similarly emphasized the powerful cognitive aspects of athletic performance: "Baseball is 90 percent physical and the other half is mental." While Yogi's math yields a personal investment of 140 percent—a sum many top athletes and their parents would support, by the way—most athletes share the view that thinking makes a tremendous difference in performance.

According to Olympic champion Mark Spitz, "During practice, performance is 90 percent physical and 10 percent mental. During competition, performance becomes 90 percent mental and only 10 percent physical ability." Spitz has taken the cognitive insights learned through athletic training and brought them to corporate boardrooms. Translating an athlete's winning discipline and self-regulation into winning corporate tactics, Spitz has become a much sought-after national and international motivational speaker.

Thinking Like a Winner

There is nothing like winning to teach someone how to think like a winner. Ask Charlie Jones, announcer and sportscaster for fifty years: "One of the most intriguing aspects of sports is that at the end of a contest (not unlike the end of a business day) you can look up and see exactly how you did. There's always a large scoreboard, and it tells you (and the world) whether you won or lost." Charlie pulled together from his experiences, conversations, and interviews with athletes a rich little book entitled *What Makes Winners Win: Thoughts and Reflections from Successful Athletes,* a superb compendium of quotes from winners and their coaches. A few samples:

> Every time I play, in my own mind I'm the favorite.
> —Tiger Woods, three-time U.S. Amateur champion,
>   1996 PGA Tour Rookie of the Year, and 1997 Masters champion

> Confidence is only born out of one thing—demonstrated ability. It is not born of anything else. You cannot dream up confidence. You cannot fabricate it. You cannot wish it. You have to accomplish it. Macho or swaggering kind of confidence many times is just a cover-up for lack of confidence. I think that genuine confidence is what you really seek for your team and your individual players. That only comes from demonstrated ability.
> —Bill Parcells, former head coach of the New York Giants,
>   the New England Patriots, and the New York Jets

As Bill Parcells knows, past performance is a powerful foundation, but if it were the sole determinant of future success, only winners would continue to be winners and all bets in sports would be on last year's champ. Athletes, coaches, parents, and bookies alike know there is more to success than simple past performance. Sports fans know that the excitement of big championships, heavy-duty rivalry, media coverage, television cameras, newspaper photographers, and even the presence of a visiting grandpa from Kansas also can affect a player's ability to perform.

Ask many athletes about their favorite moment in sports and they often tell you about a time when the pressure was on and they rose to the challenge. Steve McFarland, president of U.S. Diving, says, "The gift of a champion is the ability to compete under pressure, to give a peak performance at a peak moment." How do they do it?

Self-Efficacy Is the Key to Optimal Performance

Research supports the idea that a player's level of self-efficacy is the key determinant of athletic success. Interestingly, an athlete's level of perceived self-efficacy takes precedence over past performance. The more difficult the situation, the more important an individual's perceived self-efficacy to carry out the plan of action necessary to achieve the desired goal.

> Athletes of comparable abilities but different self-assurance do not perform at the same level. Gifted athletes plagued by self-doubts perform far below their potential, and less talented but highly self-assured athletes can outperform more talented competitors who distrust their capabilities. Many athletes with failed careers would be champions if they performed as well in contest as they did in training. Such discrepancies between capabilities and accomplishments underscore the influential contribution of efficacy beliefs to athletic adeptness. Competitive sports also reveal the fragility of perceived self-efficacy. A series of failures that can undermine belief in one's efficacy sends professional athletes into slumps. Because of self-misgivings, they do not execute their skills well even though they have perfected them and their very livelihood rests on their doing well.
> —Albert Bandura, *Self-Efficacy: The Exercise of Control,* 1997

When the going gets tough, the tough get going. More true than not, sports *can* build tough resilience. Many star athletes acknowledge, "I have lost more games than I've won and missed more shots than I've made." They believe learning to play in the face of loss is crucial to becoming successful. The numbers speak for themselves. When you look within any sport at any suitable measure, the accuracy is far below 100 percent. All athletes must learn to accommodate their error rate and balance it with their success rate.

No One Bats 1.000

Take a look at the following table. No one's batting 1.000. We have stadiums of fans cheering for home-run swings rousing from a 30 percent record. We have folks making two million dollars with 50 percent success rates. Our nation regularly celebrates sports performances in the 70 percent range, and sponsors snap up athletes with 60 percent accuracies. If these were scores on an academic exam, the athletes would be receiving an F, F, C-, and D, respectively.

Success Percentages Among Top Competitors in Various Sports

Baseball	National League Batting Average	
	Larry Walker, Col.	.363 = 36%
	American League Batting Average	
	Bernie Williams, N.Y.	.339 = 34%
Basketball*	NBA Field Goal Percentage	
	Shaquille O'Neal, L.A. Lakers	58%
	NBA Three-Point Field Goal Percentage	
	Dale Ellis, Sea.	46%
	NBA Field Goal Team Stats	
	L.A. Lakers	48.1%
	NCAA Men's Div. I Field Goal Percentage	
	Charles Jones, LIU-Brooklyn	45.3%
	NCAA Men's Div. I Three-Point Percentage	
	Jim Cantamessa, Sierra	56.4%
	NCAA Women's Div. I Field Goal Percentage	
	Myndee Larsen, So. Utah	72.4%
	NCAA Women's Div. I Three-Point Percentage	
	Kristi Green, Indiana	90.8%
Football—Passing	AFC Individual Leader	
	Mark Brunelle, JAX	60.7%
	NFC Individual Leader	
	S. Young, S.F.	67.7%
	College Division I-A	
	Cade McNown, UCLA	61.13%
	College Division I-AA	
	Ali Abrew, Cal Poly SLO	68.06%
	College Division II	
	Wilkie Perez, Glenville St.	65.8%
	College Division III	
	Bill Bochert, Mount Lion	69.8%
	Single Game Highs	
	Michigan	49.66%
National Hockey League	Save Percentage	
	Dominik Hasek, Buff.	93.2%
Men's Singles Tennis	Win Percentage, 1997	
	Pete Sampras	71%
Women's Singles Tennis	Win Percentage, 1997	
	Martina Hingis	93%

Men's Golf **	Average Number of Greens Reached in Reg. Play, 1997	
	Tom Lehman	72.7%
	Driving Accuracy, 1997	
	Allen Doyle	80.8%
Bowling	PBA Pinfalls	
	Walter Ray Williams, Jr.	74%
	Senior Pinfalls	
	Gary Dickinson	74%
	Professional Women's Bowling Association	
	Wendy Macpherson	71%

Sports Illustrated 1999 Sports Almanac
* No comparable stats for WNBA.
** No comparable stats for women and seniors.

TIP **In sports, no one bats 1.000.**
Helping kids learn to persevere in the face of errors and defeat makes a powerful mental framework for life.

The statistics presented above are by no means exhaustive, but were selected from the sports enthusiasts' popular bible, the *Sports Illustrated 1999 Sports Almanac*. It seems wherever you turn in sports, the top numbers are in the 50 to 70 percent range; even the very best athletes at the zeniths of physical performance must accommodate and adjust to regular errors and failure. As the parents of each of these athletes could tell you, every top performer worked long and hard to build up these admirable accomplishments.

God gave me this gift and He can take it away just as quick. I don't want to tempt Him by not practicing. There's nothing else I'd rather do than play golf . . . There's no such thing as a natural touch. Touch is something you create by hitting millions of golf balls.
—Lee Trevino, winner of two U.S. Opens,
two British Opens, and two PGA championships
As quoted in *What Makes Winners Win:*
Thoughts and Reflections from Successful Athletes
by Charlie Jones, 1997

Athletes must learn to deal with their own regular mistakes in arenas where excellence often hovers around 60 percent:

> I guess you could say I was an over-the-edge perfectionist when I started basketball in the seventh grade. My parents really wanted me to try out for the school team, and I knew the minute I walked onto the court that I was the worst in the gym. The other girls were dribbling, passing, shooting free throws while I stood there blushing at the word *lay-ups*.
>
> I still don't know why—maybe it was my really tall brother who was a junior center on the high school team—but the coach was really nice to me and stopped by to give me a few hints that first day. I was nearly in tears the whole time, but just plain faked it. After the tryout the coach called me over when my brother picked me up. He asked how I felt and I told him I'm used to doing well and this tryout made me feel awful. I kept trying, but I kept missing even the easy stuff. He gave me some advice that day that changed my life. He said, "You know in sports, you can't expect to shoot 100 percent. Even 90 percent is too much. No one does. You have to learn to let go a little. Start wherever you're at and just work little-by-little at improving. A+s here start if you can get your shots in."
>
> —University NCAA Div. I basketball player

Learning to accept mistakes, establish goals, and improve over past performance is a wonderful experience for perfectionist kids. It is also valuable for the lackadaisical athlete, too. Both ends of the spectrum benefit from sticking to hard tasks and building self-efficacy.

Self-Regulatory Skills

Coaches broadly call it discipline. Psychologists label it maturity. Psychologist Albert Bandura specifically defines it as self-regulatory efficacy. Parents call it a great blessing. If you have a kid, no matter what age, who does what he or she needs to do when it needs to be done, takes care of business for himself or herself including handling all the details required, you've witnessed self-regulatory efficacy in action, another powerful tool in the mental game of athletics. According to Bandura, efficacy here means being able to:

1. Diagnose task demands (what did the coaches need from you?),
2. Construct and evaluate alternative courses of action (assess options: should you play soccer, volleyball, or both?),

3. Set out a plan with proximal goals (for an overnight away game—write timeline, make lists with deadlines, pack bags early),

4. Create self-incentives (imagine the fun of juggling two teams and ready-made sets of friends),

5. Manage stress (pack fun CDs to listen to on the team bus).

Self-Ameliorative Skills

Self-ameliorative efficacy is based on an individual's belief that he or she has the means to manage his or her distressing thoughts or feelings. Stress is not disturbing when we believe we have means to relieve it. Kids can be taught stress-reducing techniques such as muscle relaxation, deep breathing, and exercise, but one mental key is knowing when to draw on that bag of tricks. Parents need to teach their kids how to recognize their own stress and cope as well as ways to mentally frame stressful events that reduce the negative stress power.

Positive Appraisal of Stress

Although popular culture says otherwise, stress and arousal are by no means necessarily unilaterally negative. When kids see stress only in negative terms, its effects may be more physically damaging and psychologically more debilitating. Teach your kid that some stress can be positive; even that perception can help ease the damage of the negative stress. "The same arousal is experienced as anxiety when athlete stressors are viewed as threats, but as being psyched up when they are seen as challenges," explains Albert Bandura.

Teach Calming Self-Talk

Learning to answer one's own fears with well-chosen words can break a mental downward spiral. Kwan and others tell of "talking some sense into themselves." "I did this in practice a hundred times. I know how to handle it. I'm ready to do it now."

Show Your Child How to Visualize

Athletes who visualize themselves performing the skill or task before the actual competition can enhance the quality of their performance. Perhaps the mental process helps marshal their abilities, particularly in times of greater stress or distraction. However, if your child visualizes a negative outcome, his or her performance may well suffer. Notably, all people are not equal visualizers, but it's a very learnable skill.

Encourage Your Child to Seek Social Support

Turning to your friends, family, and teammates in times of distress turns out to be a very positive method of coping. Young athletes who use social and emotional means of support in the face of stress are much less likely to turn to alcohol and drugs to help cope. For parents, this means you need to support your young athlete's availability for social comforting. If you can't be there, someone else should be. Make sure your child rides the team bus, especially after a heartbreaking loss. Let your kid get on the phone so teammates can talk each other through some tough times.

TIP   **Mental tricks for sports success:**
See threats as challenges, use calming self-talk, use visualization, and know social support helps.

Reinforced Self-Efficacy Breeds Success

Across the board, whether you're talking Little League or Olympic training camp, the kids who maintain a strong sense of their own ability to achieve goals set for themselves seem to have the best chance of coming back year after year. Athletes who believe something they can do matters, do it. Self-efficacy readies them to take on another challenge.

I MADE A COMMITMENT TO WORK TOWARD MY POTENTIAL

During the past year, I made a commitment to work toward my potential. I first began to take this mental attitude during lacrosse practices and matches. My hopes of playing varsity lacrosse as a freshman gave me the motivation to improve. I began to push myself harder than I ever thought possible, but the leaps and bounds that I was expecting to make did not happen. My level of play even dropped at some points. I talked to both my club and my school coaches. They both understood how frustrating my situation was, and they both identified the root of the problem as my way of thinking. When I had been pushing myself, I had been thinking negatively, hoping to get out of the slump. They both told me that I needed to focus on doing my best every day and improving on my past performances every time. It's not enough to come in first when we would run field drills, I needed to finish faster than *my* previous times, every time. I applied this new mental approach and my efforts were soon rewarded. My level of play rose very quickly, and when the cuts were made for varsity, I had been selected to play on the varsity lacrosse squad as a freshman. I went on to have one of my best seasons, in which I started the majority of the games. After seeing how rewarding my new-found way of thinking was, I began to apply it to school.

—High school lacrosse player

Self-efficacy techniques learned in sports may also translate to other areas of life. From research, we know that college athletes typically have higher average GPAs during their sports season than off season. Past performance, role models, physiological state, and encouragement work together to keep the mental ball rolling forward.

MENTAL MIND GAMES

Superstitious Behavior

The lucky sports bra, the never-washed-after-the-win jersey, even the ritualistic pre-game meal—we all know athletes who hold these totems as the source of their success. Ironically, believing in the value of these superstitions and performing them is a type of self-efficacy and may actually enhance success by supporting positive thinking. Don't get confused here. No lucky sports bra, dirty jersey, or special meal has ever won a game, but the young athlete's belief that he or she had control of something that mattered did. The self-efficacy belief wins for the kid.

Many folks develop superstitious behavior. UCLA coach John Wooden reportedly had a sequence of actions before every game that included sitting down, rolling up the game program, and slapping the program in his hand. The ritual lasted no more than twenty seconds. Most folks never noticed, but if you knew to watch for it, it happened every game. Would UCLA have lost if the ritual was skipped? Probably not, but if Coach Wooden believed he had let down the team, he might have skipped other valuable things he normally would have done.

Rosy Lenses/Cloudy Lenses

As I mentioned in chapter 8, it's easy for kids to fall into the belief that they make mistakes because of external factors but that other kids goof because they are intrinsically stupid. Parents can fall into the same trap: My kid makes mistakes because of bad lighting, poor health, lack of teamwork. Your kid makes mistakes because he intrinsically lacks the great genes my kid has. To avoid the parental fundamental attribution error (PFAE), parents and kids need an essential reality check. The kid or parent who always has an excuse is not only boring, but isn't facing what needs to be done, not to mention destroying team morale by blaming others.

Kids who can face their own errors squarely are kids who are ready to learn. The self-handicapping "Ooh, I didn't play well today because I hurt my back" or "I can't get any rebounds today because the coach is riding my case" protects them in the short run with excuses. If the excuses are accurate, good. They know the problem will be ready to go when it resolves. If the excuses are self-handicapping excuses, forget it. The youngster won't improve until he or she gets comfortable with facing down errors and becomes ready to learn tough lessons.

The Return of Eeyore: Depressive Realism

Unlike most folks' tendency to shower their memories of themselves with rosy glows, some people have very vivid, often accurate views of reality. No soft focus, no self-protection. They see themselves in lucid relief and see their failings just as clearly. As such, the truth can become the beginning of a downward spiral. Some studies cite a modest incidence of depressive realism, around 5 percent of adults, but I know of no studies on children and adolescents. Children who clearly see their mistakes but don't possess the efficacy to change them may be prone to this kind of depressed outlook.

The Mirror Loves Me: Self-Serving Bias

Ironically, the rosy glow some children see in their mental mirror may have some protective features. There seems to be a modest advantage for kids who remember things positively—termed *self-serving bias*. They don't dwell on personal mistakes, but use them as curriculum for new learning. Uncontrollable stuff fades from memory. Self-serving bias lets kids get over their errors faster and grow from them. Frankly, time spent blaming oneself and others does little good for anyone's development (though learning to appropriately accept responsibility does). Perhaps self-serving bias short-circuits negative thinking by simply allowing the child to forget the uncontrollable.

Kids who stay in sports (or any pursuit for that matter) seem to believe that what happens is within their control and is stable and predictable. Kids who drop out of a pursuit are more likely to feel that outcomes are variable, uncontrollable, and due to factors outside of them.

Learning from Experience

Do our kids learn from everything they encounter? Of course not! Selecting and screening what gets learned, optimizing opportunities to learn, and facilitating learning are all dynamic processes, useful for parents, coaches, teachers, and learners. The mental preparation of learning is essential to the young athlete's development. If your child has an experience that teaches him or her something new and of use in terms of lifelong development, it's a very *good* experience, whether or not it was a particularly *happy* one. My kids have often heard: "Experience is what you get when you don't get what you wanted."

Few of us set out to give our kids a whopper of a personal challenge. Most of us want our kids to have Super Coach incarnate, be on the all-star team winning all the games, playing in their favorite position, doing their very best. But consider for a moment the alternative. A lot more can be learned when the coach is mediocre—kids learn from the simple process of playing. Critiquing their own play; motivating themselves; figuring out how to make a team bond; how to build leadership skills; how to get what you need out of someone who is not skilled at teaching all can be unexpected bonus lessons. Losing a game or two, even losing all season can also become a learning experience about persistence and motivation in the face of defeat. Getting on a team of older skilled players may mean your kid sits on the bench, but gets to practice with the better players. "Riding the pine" humbles prideful players, and learning how to come in off the bench and play well is an important skill as valuable as most learnable physical techniques.

It may take some thinking, but you need to guide your children to learn from *every* experience. Learning isn't always fun. There are many lessons, some of them tough and some of them painful, but all of them useful. Once he or she has learned them, however, your kid will be better, smarter, and more resilient. It's your job to help your child make the most of the opportunity.

TIP   **Help your child grow personally:**
See every sports experience as a learning opportunity.

11

Role Models: Just Do It!

I started playing hockey when I was ten, but the turning point happened when I was an eighth grader and went to a special hockey camp in Orem, Utah. A junior from Judge Memorial High School was there and I remember watching him on the ice. The coach asked him to demonstrate different skills to our group. He seemed to be able to do everything well. He became my idol. Every time I really wanted to improve on something, I would think about him and ask myself, "How would he do this?"

Later, my dad took me to some professional hockey games and I saw Wayne Gretzky and Mario Lemieux play, but for a long time the immediate guy I looked up to was the older kid I saw at camp and at my high school.

—Luke Kelly, middle and high school ice hockey player,
Salt Lake City, Utah, 1999

Imagine if your child had to learn the intricate skills of his or her sport by trial and error alone. Just standing up on the skates could take hours to figure out, and smooth gliding would require inevitable innumerable falls and months of practice. Yet through a single demonstration—modeling—your child can learn multiple skills simultaneously.

HERO WORSHIP

A picture is worth a thousand words, and one live model may be better than a whole book of words. Parents may be gratified to learn that a majority of kids mention one or both of their parents as important role models. If you talk specifically to folks who have played sports, many quickly come to a story about their first sports role model. With admiration in their voices, the names they mention are not ones you'd recognize, rarely having made it further than the local or high school newspaper. Young athletes talk about Wayne Gretzky, Kerri Strug, Mark McGwire, or Karl Malone as inspirations, but many youngsters speak with similar admiration about their personal local hero.

Many young athletes I've interviewed mention coaches, but they also have a respected role model a little older than they are, often their same sex, similar in important ways, and regularly available for observation. The eighth-grade hockey player looks up to the high school junior who helps out with their team. The seventh-grade volleyball player looks up to a sophomore on varsity who was a counselor at the sport camp. The third-grade soccer player admires her sister who is three years older. The freshman looks up to the juniors and seniors on the team. Superstars may provide inspiration, but role models of assumed similarity give proximal guidance and motivation.

Hero worship of a skilled older kid serves four important functions for many budding young athletes. First, the learner sees that he or she shares certain valuable characteristics with the role model, which assures the observer that he or she has what it takes. Second, the model presents the desired skill(s) in a form scaled down and within reach of the observer. Third, the model is available for repeated live viewing. Fourth, the model performs within a familiar context similar to the performing context of the learner. The pro athlete playing in the Superdome on TV before an audience of millions is a long way from home for most kids. The local high school hero is a closer fit.

How important are these proximal role models for young athletes? Ask any person who played a sport as a high school freshman who the seniors were on his or her team. Most, even decades later, can cite names, dates, skill levels, and even spin out an enthusiastic story or two. We all seem to have our own collections of memorable "stars" in the plays of our own lives.

FAMILY MEMBERS AS ROLE MODELS

We all weave role models in and out of our lives, and most of us have several role models at any given time. Your kids probably have different role models for each sport and additional role models at school. Our role models change as our needs change, and seeking out new role models is an important and healthy activity supporting growth.

Interestingly, most people believe that "old" is about ten years older than they are now. So to the five-year-old, fifteen is old; to the fifteen-year-old, twenty-five is old. In studies, when people are asked to identify their main role model, they often select someone within a few years of their own age. Negative role models, people you don't want to be like, are often your same age with distinct characteristics you dislike.

Siblings As Role Models

Coaches I know say that the youngest in a family of athletes often starts out way ahead of others their age. They seem to be more "naturally" coordinated than kids from nonathletic backgrounds. It's possible that the "natural" coordination is more a function of available role models than innate gifts. Younger kids get to watch their brothers and sisters perform. Many younger siblings in athletic families spend the better part of toddlerhood and preschool hanging out and watching while big brother or big sister plays in a game or practice.

THREE NOMADS

All three of my girls play soccer now, but when they were younger and Corinn was in Division 5 at age 8, Kjersi was only 6 and Cailin was just a new baby.

Over the years, I have been team mom, assistant coach, team manager, coach, you name it. Cailin seemed to grow up knowing how to kick the soccer ball even when the ball was just a little shorter than she. Her sisters would get her out in the front yard and put her at goalie, then later, they would let her play the "field." Kjersi and Corinn got to be very good, and our weekends soon became one school or club or AYSO tournament after another.

The funny thing is, we were all so sure Cailin would be amazing when she started soccer herself. I said I would coach her team and the first practice was great! I used her to demonstrate each of the basic skills, and she was so good at doing everything that the other parents were pretty impressed by her. My buttons were popping and I told everyone she had learned from her sisters. We all figured the team would have a great season . . . that was until the first game. Cailin refused to go in. She stood, feet planted squarely under her shoulders, arms folded across her bright fuchsia jersey, and shaking her head. "NO!"

That was the way it went the first half of the season. I never pushed. Just said, "Okay!" I tried to talk to her at night or in the car, but she wasn't talking. I had her sisters, even my friends who knew her try. Nothing doing. She wasn't going into a game. Then the next practice would roll around and there she would be again, performing every drill, every skill just perfectly.

I never figured it out really until late in the season when we went to one of Kjersi's games. Cailin sat by me watching her sister play like I had never seen her do before. She usually doodled and socialized, scooted balls herself, but she had never really watched PLAYING like that. During her sister's next few games, she asked more and more questions about what to do. By the last game of the season, when I asked if she wanted to go in her own game, she nodded yes. I nearly fell over. She ran in from the side and took her position. Well, she got the ball and brought it halfway down the field. She looked around for someone to pass it to and everyone was still back trying to figure out where she went. She looked confused at me and I just laughed and yelled, "Keep going! You're a forward! Make a goal." We all stood in amazement as she flew off downfield, paused a loooong time to avoid offsides, then kicked it hard into the goal! She scored!

There has been no stopping her ever since.

—Jani Nomad, mother of three, Laguna Niguel, California, 1997

Parent Role Models

If you are Archie Manning and you have a son, role model theory explains how that son, Peyton Manning, would know more than most other kids his age and why he would look like a pro quarterback his first season out of college. Peyton had been doing a lot of observational learning long before he strapped on his pro helmet.

You don't need to be Archie Manning to your kid. The majority of successful athletes did not have a successful same-sport athlete for a mom or dad. What successful athletes often have are sport-savvy parents who learned to be appropriate supporters. If you were modestly successful in your sport, maybe some high school or college ball, you're already a pretty hard act to follow. Most kids of very successful athletes find their parents' shoes extremely big and often too hard to fill. It's a tougher road when you're little and think you have to shuffle up a mountain in mental size 14s. Everyone expects you to do so well. It's very common for these kids to try, see how far below their role model they are, get discouraged, and give up, long before they've really had a chance to begin.

Extended Family and Beyond

Grandparents, aunts, uncles, even distant cousins can become role models. My favorite parents seem to have a knack for drumming up just the right role model at the right time. If your child is in junior high, check out the local high school, community college, or university games. There will be windows in time when your young athlete will ask open questions best answered via exposure to the right role model.

TIP   Seek out positive role models for your young athlete.

Clever parents take advantages of opportunities. I watched with pride as a long line formed to get the autographed posters from the Stanford women's volleyball team. The players were seated in a long row, gold pens poised, and the line of kids, moms, dads, grandmas, grandpas, and a few college-age students wound all the way around the court. The line had an overrepresentation of nine- to thirteen-year-old girls watching and approaching the table of players with a mixture of awe and joy. I overheard one girl: "Mom! Mom! She saw me. She just gave me a wave. Did you see? Did you see? It's Katherine!" The player the mom and the daughter waved back to was my daughter. I couldn't help but smile. I remembered Katherine's words just before the match: "Sorry I can't go out to dinner with you right after the game. Tonight's poster night and it makes me feel so good when kids I've coached stop by to say hi." The good feeling seemed mutual, all the way around.

DISTANT MODELS

Somewhere along the line, as kids' skills improve, many kids get interested in seeing top performers in their sport. Kids still pick role models with some similar characteristics, namely gender, size, sport, and position. The quick, coordinated kid with a great arm picks quarterback Peyton Manning as his role model, not B. Smith from Buffalo, top quarterback sacker in the nation. The high school basketball player of modest height is more likely to pick John Stockton than Shaquille O'Neal as his role model.

Sports Heroes

Does your kid play baseball? How many baseball cards does he or she have? What are the stats of the players he or she admires most? I recently visited the local toy store and stood in awe admiring the wall of sports superstar collectibles. Nicely packaged five-inch figures proudly shooting free throws, catching footballs, swinging baseball bats, and jumping deftly shone back at me. Next to each detailed figure was a small card including height, weight, college, birthdate and place, player statistics, and a little box detailing recent highlight action.

It was a good minute of scanning before I realized there was not one single female athlete on this wall. I could have gone to three dozen toy stores and still not found a woman athlete. The teams on the back of the plastic blister cardboard card were all men's. As I turned away to leave, the candy pink Barbie doll section caught my eye. There—in all their glory—were multiple Barbies posed picture perfect still in a range of outfits from ball gowns to WHAT?—WNBA basketball uniforms. That same hourglass-shape, Barbie doll's friends Christie, Teresa, and Kira, all with perfect cone-shaped breasts, were wearing numbered basketball jerseys, satin shorts, and athletic shoes. A photo of the WNBA star, Rebecca Lobo, appeared in the lower corner of her respective basketball box. I looked for Rebecca's card of stats. No stats, but I learned her favorite foods, cartoons, colors, movies, actors, and basketball shots. Each Basketball Rebecca sports bendable knees and can "shoot and pass" (thanks to spring-loaded shoulders). Mattel says "Collect them all and coach your own team." Mattel, five Rebeccas? Perhaps we could draft Mia Hamm Soccer Barbie to play! Compared to the entire wall of male athlete action figures, a Basketball Rebecca Lobo and a Soccer Mia Hamm are truly better than nothing, but somehow the hourglass shape—with or without a sports bra—still gives a mixed role model message to young female athletes.

Great Resources for Gathering Information About Sports Heroes

Collecting baseball cards about real athletes is about action and role models. Learning what people have done celebrates their accomplishments and models active behavior. Of course, you don't have to become a toy collector or spend money to gather information, although the toy manufacturers would be glad if you did. Libraries have shelves of books full of vital information about past and present heroes. The Internet also features a number of sports sites, and many athletes have Web pages featuring information, photos, and upcoming events.

The true value rests in the time you spend with your child recognizing his or her admired hero's accomplishments. When you help your child gather information about sports role models, you foster cognitive and research skills, far surpassing in quality any dollar amount you could ever spend at a toy store—and you become the best kind of role model yourself.

PHYSICAL SKILLS AND ROLE MODELS

Watching a role model perform can offer the best type of observational learning:

KENT STEFFES: REACH-SWING-COLLAPSE

It was a gorgeous day at the Santa Monica Beach Club. All nine of the girls had parents who had donated money in the name of a school charity for their opportunity to have this small group lesson with Kent Steffes, Olympic beach volleyball champion. Most had played some volleyball for school and most had one or more years at the club level. All were eager for this special experience.

As one, they all turned to stare at Kent as he ambled up wearing OP wrap dark sunglasses, a navy Fila shirt, and beach shorts, looking more like a magazine model than the proficient volleyball athlete they all knew him to be. He grinned and tossed some beach volleyballs into their group. "Okay, I'm Kent. Who are you?" With the ease of a natural teacher, he took a moment with each of the girls to gather information, seeming to offer recognized names from their training and smiling at just the right time.

The first lesson began with a toss and spike. He demonstrated the approach, jump, and swing three times. Signaling their turn, he stood to the side and watched thoughtfully as they made their attempts. Nodding, he offered a few individual suggestions. Reach higher, jump sooner, good swing. One run-through later and he gathered them into a tight semicircle again. He demonstrated reaching high with his right hand, lifting his shoulder, then bringing his arm down fast as he collapsed his chest, adding these muscles to the powerful downward stroke. Shirt tossed to the side, he redemonstrated the muscles working as they added the needed power in the sand court. At last, he had one of the girls stretch her arm high. He faced her, reached for her hand, extended it, then demonstrated the swing-collapse combo. Pairing the girls up, he again demonstrated with one girl how to reach high, swing, and pull in, then helped the pairs practice the reach-swing-collapse sequence.

The next run-through went better. Two girls had made the adjustments and their shots made solid thunks as they hit deep court. "Great!" he grinned. "Come back and do that one more time. Everyone watch!" After everyone had repeated the drill, he gave one last demonstration himself, blasting the ball into the opponent's court, sending up a spray of sand.

—Shari Kuchenbecker, volleyball mom hat, summer of 1997

Observation provides much information, but not all observers "see" the same thing. Sitting nine girls down to watch an outside hitting demonstration didn't yield nine identical mental tapes nor end with nine perfect outside hits. Helping observers see the important distinctive features is a skill of a great coach. Naturally, the coach with a trained eye sees the components, extracts the most important, then points out the portions that need to be perfected in a learnable sequence.

Discriminative Modeling

John Wooden, winner of ten national championships at UCLA in twelve years, used *discriminative modeling* to teach his players. First,

Wooden demonstrated how to perform the skill correctly. Next, he would enact a player's faulty method. He would then go back, redemonstrate the skill correctly, pointing out physically and verbally what to watch for in the correct versus incorrect performance. Without any ridicule or insult, Coach Wooden used discriminative modeling to perfect technical skills: Here is the correct model. Here is what you're doing. Here is what you need to do right.

Can Kids Learn from Video Playback?

I, like many parents in sports, have filmed miles and miles of videotape of my three children in various games—volleyball, soccer, football, in-line skating. Most of the tapes are excellent dust collectors. Perhaps one day we'll watch them.

If you're like most parents, your videos are of little interest to your child. You really shouldn't try to force your child to watch nor presume to tell your child what to do to correct his or her play if you do watch. You are not your child's coach. Get out of his or her space.

Only one of my children begged me to film his games and he consistently watched these videos right after every game. TV controller in hand, he systematically played and replayed in slow motion portions of his swing, jump, and pass, which he wanted to improve—and improve he did. It wasn't something I could have forced. It came from him and I marveled. Keep the idea as an option, but don't force it.

Some coaches use video liberally for instruction. Many college teams and pro teams have weekly "films" where the coaches or assistant coaches point out specific things they want individual players or the team to work on. The research on this kind of modeling suggests that players learn very little from passively watching their mistakes. Players learn a lot more from guided observation, positive models, even positive models of their own play—computer spliced to show them practicing the correct technique. It makes sense. It is a positive behavior they themselves perform. You bet they learn it.

Do/Say Something Positive: Instant Mental Replays

THEN JUST DO IT!

I watched in horror as she went up to swing and power-blasted another ball out of bounds, third time in a row. I cringed.

Between games, I tried to offer a word of encouragement with "Forget what your brother said about your hitting." ("I hear you hit the ball harder than I do. Too bad it's out of the court." Big laugh.) I had seen the hurt look on her face. It was kind of like telling her NOT to think of a pink elephant. Nothing becomes quite as vivid as that pink elephant you're not supposed to think about. Same with the vivid "power-blast the ball out of bounds" image; it seemed to be broadcasting megavolumes on the big screen in her mind. "Just forget it" advice was lame, but I tried anyway.

She scrunched up her shoulders and walked away from me, tossing her towel into a heap at my feet. What did I know?

I rarely say anything, but a few minutes later, when her coach walked by, I found myself stumbling to explain the sibling conversation in the kitchen two days before. I fizzled and ended by saying, "I'm just 'Mom.'" Big brother was big brother! The coach's face brightened and he grinned. "I know what to do. Thanks for telling me."

The last half of the match began twenty minutes later. I could tell something was different immediately. She went up to block then passed a long one right on the money. Again, and again. The winning shot—when it came—power-blasted right into the opponent's ten-foot line. Her smile flashed as she pumped her fist and teammates came over to give her high fives.

I could barely wait until we got into the car for the ride home. So what happened?

Casual as always, she said "Oh, nothing." I prodded. "Well, Coach T asked me to count in my head. So I mentally started counting 1, 2, 3, 4, 5 . . . then all of a sudden, he says, 'WHAT'S YOUR NAME?' 'Karalyn!' I blurted back. He grinned. 'What happened to your counting?' Ahhh. Well. I told him I just answered his question. He said I was supposed to be counting in my head. Get it? Great huh!"

After several more questions and eventually asking the coach himself, it turns out he recognizes there are negative voices in everyone's head. When the voices get going, you can literally talk them away by saying something (out loud) that is positive. So if your negative inner voice worries about hitting the ball out of bounds, do/say something positive out loud like, "Come on! Let's pass this ball here" to overcome the voice. Then just do it!

— Shari Kuchenbecker, volleyball mom hat, club season 1999

Turhan Douglas, men's volleyball assistant coach at the University of Southern California, an accomplished athlete himself, knew about the detrimental effect of negative inner voices and vivid negative mental pictures. In Karalyn's case, both were envisioning her power blasting the ball out of the court—over and over. To stop the cycle of negative replays, Coach T gave her a physical demonstration to help her understand the mental versus physical performance. He then gave her a strategy—do/say something positive—to end the negative mental image. It works.

Behavior Leads Attitude

Behavior and attitude are tied together, mutually affecting each other. Positive behavior leads to a positive attitude. Negative behavior leads to negative attitude. If you try to change someone's attitude—"Gee, you're a great player, really," or "You can do it if you try," or my all-time favorite "You need better self-esteem; feel better about yourself"—you are barking up the wrong tree. Oftentimes, behavior is the horse and attitude is the cart. Get positive behavior going and attitude will follow.

Foot in the Door

The hardest part of changing is taking the first step. Getting a foot in the door, a well-known technique among sales folks, greases the initial move. If you want to change your child's attitude about something, get your foot in the door by changing just one small action. From that small start, the path may open.

SUGGESTED PARENT SCRIPT:
JUST WATCH ONE PRACTICE

"I know you don't feel like you have enough experience to try out for the high school team this year, but you really seemed to enjoy last year's ninth-grade team once you got started. Tell you what. Why don't you just go and watch one practice? There's one today at three-thirty and I could pick you up at the field after school at four forty-five. Of course, it really is up to you, but I don't want you to get a month into the season and be sorry you didn't even consider it. Just go look today for an hour and see what you feel like doing."

Again, a parent's job is never to push, but to make sure children keep paths open to them that potentially provide valuable experiences, build self-efficacy, and increase their understanding of themselves and the world.

> **TIP   Behavior leads attitude.**
> If you want your young athlete to do something new, try the foot-in-the-door technique.

MOTOR LEARNING AND BEHAVIOR

Researchers know that athletic performance requires much more than simply mastering mechanical actions. The invaluable use of role-modeling coupled with guided instruction speeds athletes' progress quicker than trial-and-error learning, live modeling, or video instruction alone. Building skills and true self-efficacy depends on reciprocal performance and feedback. As behaviorist B. F. Skinner first pointed out, whenever someone performs a behavior, four outcomes are possible: he or she can receive a positive (get a reward); experience no effect (extinction); receive an aversive (be punished); or have an aversive withheld. Of course, personal evaluation of these outcomes plays an important role in the effects, but in simplified form, Skinner called them reward I, extinction, punishment, and withholding punishment-reward II.

Reward I

When a young player kicks the soccer ball with the broad, strong portion of her foot, the ball efficiently lifts up and sails cleanly away. The kicker gets the immediate reward of seeing the excellent outcome of her kick, whether or not a coach, parent, or teammate says a thing. The intrinsic value of this reward is the surest, truest reward for behavior well done. The external rewards of praise, whistles, even applause come as an afterthought.

Internal and external rewards can work together in athletic training situations, particularly where the ideal behavior requires years to master. Coaches frequently point out and praise performances moving in the right direction. You may hear your child's coach say things like:

> "Good job, Jesse. Keep swinging! Lift your shoulder a little higher next time."
>
> "Nice shot on goal, Nan. Bring it up a little closer next time and try your angle shot."
>
> "Good catch! We'll work on your vertical jump in practice to give you that extra inch so you can get your fingers around the ball better."

Given the natural rewards for efforts well performed, it should be no surprise that coaches need not praise every correct effort. When the coach has too many players and essentially ignores your kid, your kid still improves via the intrinsic rewards for performing skills well, observational learning, and other naturally rewarding feedback associated with practicing and being a part of a team. Sharp coaches can reduce the time spent in trial-and-error learning by precisely identifying and praising the specific behaviors needed next in the young athlete's performance. Clever coaches even praise successive approximations, performances that are "on the way" but not quite there yet.

Extinction

Trial-and-error learning lets the newcomer to a sport try out variations in technique. When the behavior yields no results—receives no natural rewards and no praise—these behaviors just fade away. Kick a ball the wrong way, watch it fly off the field, and you quickly figure out what doesn't work.

Punishment

When the young bowler first goes to the lanes, a fair proportion of those first visits are devoted to "finding the right ball." Many young bowlers eagerly grasp the ball and hoist it up their chin, Don Carter style, only to watch the ball plummet rapidly from their too-weak fingers. Woe to the child whose socks are the only toe cover to cushion the heavy ball's fall. Dropping the too-heavy ball on your toes is a natural and inevitable punishment for hastily choosing and hoisting a ball too heavy for you to hold.

Removal of Punishment = Reward II

Any kid who has ever dropped a bowling ball on his or her bare toes quickly learns never to make that mistake again (that is, if you can talk them into coming back to the bowing alley at all). The new water-skier who manages to go into an eggbeater spin, knocking out his front teeth because he kept his legs stiff, learns to ski looser (that is, if you can talk him into ever getting into the water behind a boat again). The youngster who plays tennis with an older kid who delights in smashing the ball into the younger one's lightweight racquet, sending painful vibrations up her young arm, soon quits or switches to a heavier racquet to handle the power in the balls coming at her.

When intrinsic physical punishment is associated with an action, kids and adults rapidly learn to do what's needed to avoid the painful experience. Get a light ball and hold on to it. Ski looser-kneed. Use a heavier racquet. Wear your new hiking boots around the house until they are broken in.

ROLE MODELS CAN TEACH PAIN TOLERANCE, FOR BETTER OR WORSE

Going into and staying in sports requires a strong component of personal commitment on everyone's part—athletes, families, coaches, assistant coaches, administration. The participants say they'll do something and they do it, no matter what. All have been taught to respect the authorities' (coaches, refs, etc.) judgment. All participants learn mental and emotional discipline to override trivial physical problems.

Interestingly, watching role models tolerate pain helps individuals endure greater and greater levels of objective pain. This mentality is beset with the great potential for personal abuse. Kerri Strug's 1996 Olympic vault to land perfectly—albeit with a small one hop on a severe sprain—gave her instant hero status in our nation. Very few athletes didn't applaud her; they would have done the same had they been asked. The coach

says, "Do it." You do it! State championships have been won on broken ankles by athletes enduring excruciating pain. Championship baseball
games have been pitched and won despite a stress-fractured back. Rumors
of children playing for league championship with 102-degree fevers
emerge every so often. Most parents speak with a mixture of pride and re-
gret when they retell these stories of compliance in the face of personal
risk.

In 1998, with the nationwide heat wave, two Wichita Kansas high
school football players died after practicing in 100-degree heat. The au-
topsies of Matthew Whittredge, fifteen, and Robert Barrett, seventeen,
were consistent with heat-related causes of death. The specifics of each
child's tragic death, here and elsewhere, often find the child makes no obvious complaint or gives mixed signals about the severity of his or her distress.

While much of this book focuses on developing your child's self-
efficacy, please realize that our children depend on us as role models and
guides to appropriate and inappropriate behavior. If we, in all our self-
sacrificing righteousness, endure unreasonable pain, we are poor role
models. If we, in all our supposed wisdom, regularly reinforce our children for enduring unreasonable pain themselves, we are not teaching
them to care for themselves. We are rewarding them for not taking care of
themselves. If our athletic training programs regularly reward the short
run at the expense of long-term health, we are entrusting our children to
systematic abuse.

Parents who try to hold themselves up as perfect and praise obedience
to all authority, for the sake of obedience alone, teach their children a limited life strategy. In fact, rewarding compliance with all demands others
make on us—as people, as parents, as athletes—sells our children short
in learning crucial self-protective skills. Parents who blindly demand un-
questioning obedience of their children offer them up to athletic training
programs that may or may not be attending to their child's best interests.
Supremely compliant children are at risk in a world with real threats to
their well-being. Four decades of social psychology research has sought to
understand how the German people in the 1940s could turn their faces
to the side as Hitler and his army systematically exterminated a large proportion of the German Jewish population. Supremely compliant children
often become supremely compliant adults.

There are times in life when your children need your empowerment to appreciate personal freedom and understand disobedience is at times a reasonable choice. No adult, no coach, no authority figure—no matter how famous or powerful or prestigious—has a right to demand an individual's blind obedience. It could be as simple as speaking up for a new member of the team during team meetings or as important as attending to and noticing a teammate's bright red face during a drill, but young athletes who are cognizant of their behavior and concerned for the welfare of others speak up for themselves and others, creating a safer community of mutual support.

12

Athlete Spurts, Stalls, and Burnout: Parents' Job As Jock Supporters

4/15/87

Dear Diary,

Today the coach started me at PITCHER! It was so cool. Mom got a whole bunch of pictures. I did really great for the first five !!! innings, but I was getting tired by the end. Never struck anyone out. But coach said I did a good job and WE WON. BEAT the ugly North team 14 to 6. Cool, huh?

—Greyson, age ten, Little League pitcher

2/12/91

Dear Diary,

It happened again today. I just didn't want to get out of bed. Mom asked what was wrong and I told her my stomach hurt and my head and my shoulder. She let me go back to sleep until nine, then she made me get up to go to the doctor. This time Doctor Hew didn't stick the Q-tip down my throat and nearly kill me. He just sort of said, "Hmmmm hmmm hmmm," then he and my mom talked for a long time while I waited outside.

I had to go to school at eleven. That was okay 'cause it was nearly lunch and then it was only three hours until baseball practice started. I'm working on my fastball with Coach Q. He says I have a "natural talent."

—Greyson, age fourteen, junior varsity pitcher

3/11/92

Dear Diary,

Spent the game on the damn bench again. Last year, I pitched every inning, every game, and we won. Now, the varsity coach doesn't seem to know I exist. That idiot he has on the mound can't hit the side of a barn. If he would give me a chance, I would show him. Coach Q sure was better. I went to talk to him, but he wasn't in his office. Maybe I'll hunt him down tomorrow. I told Dad I was thinking of quitting the team but he said I should talk to Coach Q first.

Greyson, age fifteen, varsity baseball team

3/7/94

Dear Diary,

We beat the Cougars 9–8! Toughest team in the league! It's smooth sailing from here on out to STATE CHAMPIONSHIP. South hasn't won a state championship since 1983. When I struck out the Cougars' last guy, the team went crazy and poured water all over the coach and me, too.

Greyson, age seventeen, varsity baseball pitcher

2/5/95

Dear Diary,

This is even better than I thought. We went on our first road trip last week—flew to Boston then over to Trenton. We stayed in the Residence Inn. They have this great breakfast starting at 6:00 A.M., so we had the team meeting at the same time. I didn't get in the game, but my practice stats are improving. After we won, the coaches treated us to a movie.

Greyson, age eighteen, university baseball team

5/23/97

What's Up Diary,

It's been a while. I got a good write-up in the local paper and the school did an article with a half-page shot of me before the game. I sent it to Mom to put in her scrapbook.

Last week we had midterms and the team had to fly to D.C. for two games—one Friday night and one Sunday. Missed my Thursday afternoon classes and Professor M's exam was 30 percent of my grade. I took it on Monday, but sure didn't get enough studying in. The guy's notes I borrowed stunk so there was a lot of stuff I didn't know. The athlete advisor says to go talk to the prof if I'm really serious about applying to law school. My grades this semester need to be strong. LSAT is in November.

Greyson, age twenty, baseball pitcher and . . .

There are no prescribed flight plans that smoothly loft your child from nine-year-old pitcher with promise to scholarship college star and life-long success. Like Greyson, every young athlete has ups and downs, rapid spurts, backslides, and many stalls. Burnout can occur when emotional exhaustion significantly reduces the young athlete's personal sense of accomplishment.

SPURTS

Seemingly effortless athletic spurts forward happen for many reasons. At age nine, your kid may be faster, quicker, more coordinated than all the other kids on the team. Like Greyson, your kid may walk into a new sport and enjoy quick success. Spurts are great boosts to a kid's confidence and provide easy bonus points in performance; they may be due to one or more factors, some fleeting and some enduring.

Secrets of Athletic Performance Spurts

If your child experiences a rapid spurt forward in athletic performance, he or she may have:

1. Matured sooner than age mates.
   (Clue: Had a full head of hair at birth and cut adult teeth at four years of age.)
2. Genetic gifts reflecting years of contributive breeding for athletic prowess.
   (Clue: All family members for the last two generations have been members of the NBA and Mom was playing pregnant with the kid during the first WNBA game.)
3. Slow competition, so by comparison looks fabulous.
   (Clue: Most kids in league are younger, less mature.)
4. Early puberty and testosterone kicking in.
   (Clue: Your kid had more facial hair than some of the dads on the sidelines.)
5. Physical attributes ideal for the sport.
   (Clue: Team photo of your kid and the team resemble Jolly Green Giant and his little peas.)
6. Cognitive skills adapted to the particular game.

(Clue: You play chess every evening, honing your kid's competitive strategic thinking.)

7. More experience.

(Clue: Five years of participation trophies in the sport grace your mantle, and your kid is only eight years old.)

8. More drive.

(Clue: Your kid never sits still.)

9. Favored treatment on the team due to being the coach's pet.

(Clue: Your kid gets a lot of attention at every practice and never sits out.)

10. Benefited from the coach's positive expectations.

(Clue: Coach uses a lot of praise and the kids love to come to practice.)

11. Performed some instrumental behavior and built self-efficacy, contributing to an upward spiral.

(Clue: Your kid did something that made a difference in his performance; you read chapters 2 and 10 and believe in the importance of self-efficacy.)

12. All of the above.

(Clue: Everything sounds possible.)

13. Heretofore undiscovered factors contributing to success.

(Clue: Nothing really fits above; maybe it's a fluke or a gift.)

Other Boosts for Spurting Performance

Praise and Recognition

If you want to see a kid spurt forward, use genuine praise for effort. Enough has been said in preceding chapters, but an honest positive word really greases motivational wheels.

Knowledge of Results and Goals

When kids get feedback about their performances, often the simple feedback itself provides a benchmark that they can use for setting goals. Letting the young athlete set personal performance goals can be an excellent mechanism, not only for improving performance, but for reducing the chances of stalls and burnout during training.

Home Field Advantage

Home field advantage is not a myth. Home field advantage may boost success by 6 to 20 percent or more, depending on the age, level, and sport. Players feeling comfortable at home is a plus. It cues the learning that occurred during home field practice, and the home crowd is a bonus, too. Away sites have their own distractions, not the least of which are site peculiarities (e.g., lighting, floor flexibility) and more fans rooting for the opposing team. Cheering and praise make the athlete try harder—ask any cheerleader or avid stadium fan.

Eustress

Kids who thrive on live performances enjoy the positive stimulation termed *eustress*. For these kids, the excitement of performing invigorates them and translates as positive stress they love. Some kids don't. Kids in sports who feed off of the crowd, the so-called "gamers," seem to love the process of playing and will marshal their eustress to win.

Self-Efficacy and Spurts

If the spurt is a physiological by-product (extra tall/short; early maturation) rather than anything your child has done, you're wise to silently enjoy the spurt while it lasts. Since your child's positive sense of self-efficacy contributes strongly to performance, particularly in tough situations, such bonuses have psychological benefits. Your kid may figure it out. Maybe not. Meanwhile, just smile.

Performance spurts provide the most potential learning when the contributing factor is something the young athlete *actively* does. If your child puts in an extra hour of practice and plays better in the next game, point it out. If he attends summer camp and his play improves the next year, recognize the value of the effort. If added years of play give your child knowledge of field strategy, laud the value of experience. Research supports the unequaled importance of emphasizing effort over natural gifts.

STALLS

Flip over every cause of a spurt, and you have a potential cause for stalling. Genetics program some kids to be taller or shorter or have earlier or later puberty, each advantageous or disadvantageous depending on the sport. An absence of athletes in the family may reflect the role of genes and environment. Some of your child's individual characteristics—style of thinking, experience, and energy level—can also contribute to a stall, not to mention unique aspects of the coach and team.

Temporary Stalls and Developing Skills

As many youngsters learn in the process of growing, some things change, while other parts just don't hang together quite as well for a while. Growing bodies mean ongoing adjustment of skills. The two-handed backstroke in tennis—a wonderful choice for the smaller, less physical child—can become a handicap to the larger youngster with the muscles and skeletal structure to support a more versatile single-handed backhand. Similarly, the snowplow in downhill skiing can be a great starting position, building inner and outer quad muscles while controlling downhill speed and motion. While the snowplow is appropriate at one time in development, it eventually needs to be discarded for stem christie and parallel ski maneuvers to develop enjoyable advanced proficiency. The process takes time and effort. Many athletes go through a slump as they start putting their skills back together again at a newer, higher level. They describe feeling incompetent while they struggle:

"EVERY TIME I WORK ON SOMETHING, MY GAME FALLS APART FOR A WHILE"

"The coach has me changing my free shot form. I thought I was a good shooter, but this coach says I need to make some important adjustments. I understand what they want me to do, but since I'm not doing what I know how to do and I can't yet do what I'm trying to do, I just look like an idiot. I haven't had decent percentages in three weeks. It's so frustrating."
                              —University freshman, NCAA women's basketball team

Some young athletes find sudden shifts downward in the competition hierarchy emotionally discouraging. To these youngsters, the lowered achievement relative to others in their league can undermine confidence and effort while others ride out the discrepancies without much fuss.

THE TEAM PEANUT

He always has been the peanut on every team. It didn't matter if it was third-grade basketball or fifth-grade soccer and now ninth-grade football, he always manages to be the peanut. He knows it, but it sure doesn't bother his play. He can run faster and do that side maneuver thing a lot easier than the bigger guys. We've never really even talked about it much. He is who he is and I love his attitude. The coaches do too! He plays a lot more than some of the other kids almost twice his size. It may not last. I mean, the NFL won't be knocking on our door, but he has a good time being a member of the team and I wouldn't trade him for the world. He has taught me and my husband so much about how far a good attitude can take anyone.

—Mother of three, oldest is a ninth grade football team member, 1998.

Your Child's Frustration with His or Her Own Performance

If your child complains to you about his or her performance or shows other signs belittling his or her ability, then parental action may be in order. Does he or she seem personally frustrated? Anxious before games or practice? Have you seen a sudden surge in nail-biting, short-tempered outbursts, or extra forgetfulness? Does she or he blame everyone else for losses? Has he or she asked you or the coach for some extra help? Frustration can take many forms. Some children are at one extreme, fuming and storming with no clue that frustration fuels their fires, and other kids quickly see and label their problem. Watch for these clues:

1. General Irritability

Two hours before a game, Lane would start to fume. His jersey was lost. His stick wasn't where it was supposed to be. His underwear (!) had wrinkles. Driving to the game, he would say he hated his team, his coach, even the dumb sport. So it went for three weeks. I just listened. Uh huh. Uh huh. He wanted to quit. It wasn't until the Atlanta game that I got any clue. The same pre-game fuming and raging, but when we got to the field, I just shut the car door and cried. Funny thing was, he strapped on his stuff and he played fabulously. His team won 10–0, first win ever. Buoyed by the win, on the way home, Lane finally started explaining how frustrated he was on J.V. All his friends were on varsity and this team needed more help than he could give them, but today, well, it finally fell into place. The coach had told him he was needed on J.V. (there were three seniors on the varsity in his position), but so far, he felt like he was hitting his head against the wall. Today, he guessed he was so damn fed up that he just started giving directions on the field to tell these younger guys what to do if they wanted to win. By golly, it worked.

He finally took the leadership position he was supposed to hold and his directions made all the difference. His frustration vanished in the space of one game.

—Mother of three-sport junior in high school, 1999

2. Well-Articulated Skill/Training Deficit

I was about twelve or so and I was in this one swim club. It was pretty good and we did pretty well. My times were improving, but meet after meet, I would look over at this other club that always seemed to win—Santa Clara Swim Club. I asked my dad and he looked into it. I wanted to be on that club. I wanted to win.

—Mark Spitz, winner of nine Olympic gold medals, reflecting on his early training

Supporting Self-Efficacy During a Stall

When your concerned child experiences stalls and asks for some advice, offer logical explanations focused on maintaining self-efficacy. By helping your child understand the possible causes both within and beyond his or her control, you may short-circuit the self-defeating tendency for kids to believe that nothing they do matters.

Secrets of Athletic Performance Stalls

During a performance development stall, your kid may have:

1. Matured slower than age mates.

(Clue: At seven, your kid had to have several baby teeth pulled and has no body hair at the age of thirteen.)

What to say: Tell your child about family members who similarly were slow to mature, but turned out fine. Don't be tempted to make up a fake cousin who went from baby fuzz at thirteen to a full beard at fourteen. Truth is always best.

2. No physical prowess.

(Clue: No family members played sports, own any piece of athletic equipment, or see ESPN as a life-line necessity.)

What to say: Have a candid discussion about how everyone is different. Point out positively the skills and interests of near and distant family members and note that your child's own skills may be in athletics or in new, unexplored areas. Time and effort will tell and make a difference. Point out the extra learning kids from athletic families may have done in the past, but that is in the past; effort and the future are up to them. You and your child may find it interesting that among male intercollegiate athletes, 24 percent had a dad active in sports and 7 percent had a mom. Among female intercollegiate athletes, 21 percent had a dad and 15.5 percent had a mom (Sage, 1980).

3. Fast competition, so your kid looks slow by comparison.
   (Clue: Most kids in the league are older, more mature).

What to say: Discuss age as an important contributor to kids' sports. Let your child know that evens everything out. You might let them know that some savvy athlete parents hold their kid as long as possible in a lower division to *reduce* the competition.

4. Early puberty and testosterone kicking in.
   (Clue: Your child has significantly maturing secondary sex characteristics—breasts, etc.—while others have late puberty and slowed growth.)

What to say: Discuss the natural course of development for everyone. What is natural is best, and it's important to respect and trust the body's own timeline.

5. Physical attributes challenging for sport.
   (Clue: After seeing *Peter Pan,* Cathy Rigby is your child's role model. Your kid already is twice as tall and twice as heavy; may knock head on the uneven bars due to excessive height.)

What to say: Stand the both of you in front of the mirror. Discuss the fact that doctors don't know for sure how tall anyone will be, but that your child is likely to be taller than most gymnasts. You can do a little positive press for sports where height is an advantage, perhaps even visit a local basketball game.

6. Cognitive skills particularly ill-suited to competition.
   (Clue: Your child's empathy causes them to stop midfield and run back to help up a player from the other team she just

knocked over. Cooperation chats seem to sink in better than "Kill the competition" chalk talks.)

What to say: Discuss cooperative and competitive styles of behavior. Within a team, both cooperation and competition are required. Respect your child's inclinations. Some children want to learn to become more competitive, and to a degree it is beneficial. Some children are too competitive, and sports competition puts them over the aggressive edge. Addressing the balance of cooperation and competition within his or her personal goals will help your child understand and respect individual differences. You need to respect these differences and help your child find comfortable environments in which to thrive.

7. More experience.

(Clue: Your child's five years of participation make the current team look bad. Your child has little motivation to improve and does not seem to be trying anymore.)

What to say: Many coaches note that kids play to the competition. If your child feels frustrated, explain the obvious lack of competition within the team. Remind him of working and improving. If it doesn't bother your child, why is it bothering you?

8. More drive.

(Clue: Your kid not only doesn't sit still, he can't slow down long enough to listen to the coach's instructions.)

What to say: If your child (or his coach) mentions that he's got a high energy level, but little ability to listen productively, a stall in development is often due to an uncoachable package of behaviors. Discuss the importance of listening and respect for coaches and teachers who work on your child's behalf.

9. Being the coach's pet.

(Clue: Teammates may *dislike* your kid because they judge unfair treatment an undeserved bonus. By the way, it is.)

What to say: If your child feels social pressure and complains, discuss respect for the coach's opinions (positive and negative). Go back and read chapter 6. Have a self-efficacy discussion and see what your child decides could help. Encourage your child to see other players and become more supportive of them.

10. Suffered from coach's negative expectations.

(Clue: Coach uses a lot of criticism, little praise, and your kid hates to practice.)

What to say: Begin a self-efficacy-building dialogue. What can your child do to improve what is happening? Listen to their solutions. Support self-efficacious choices.

11. Experienced deteriorating self-efficacy and skill loss in a downward spiral.

(Clue: Your kid becomes convinced that nothing she does makes a difference. You must have skipped chapters 2, 8, 10, and 11; everyone needs to read a positive coaching, optimism, or technical skills book.)

What to say: Begin a dialogue about alternative actions they could try to rebuild skills. Remind them of successful experiences from their past.

12. All of the above.
(Everything sounds on target.)

13. Heretofore undiscovered factors contributing to dismal performance.
(Nothing fits, keep looking.)

Caution: Intervene *Only* If Your Athlete Is Troubled

Parents take note. Your first job is to be certain that your child—not you—is the one bothered by his or her performance. If your child seems comfortable with his or her experience, keep your nose out of it. Why are you trying to butt in? Not only will you throw your child's self-efficacy off balance, but you may do more harm than good.

Sustaining Self-Efficacy Through Goal Setting

When frustrations with performance come into question, it may be time to have a heart-to-heart talk with your child about goals. That doesn't mean you sit down and lay out a set of goals you feel are appropriate for your child. That means you ask your child to describe his or her own goals.

Distant vs. Immediate Goals

We know that kids often spontaneously set goals for themselves. When asked about their athletic goals, many kids are quick to respond with broad statements like, "I want to be on the U.S. Olympic team." "I want to be just like Kobe Bryant." "I want to play for the Raiders when I grow up." "I want to make varsity as a freshman!" Obviously, such goals are distant and very grand. While distant goals provide inspiration, most kids succeed faster with nearer, day-to-day, immediate goals of intermediate challenge—not too easy and not too hard.

SUGGESTED PARENT SCRIPT:
HOW YOU CAN HELP YOUR CHILD SET MEANINGFUL, DOABLE GOALS

KID: "I want to be Kobe Bryant."

PARENT: "What does Kobe Bryant do that you admire?"

KID: "Make a gazillion dollars and get on TV all the time."

PARENT: "Is that all? 'Cause if you want to make a gazillion dollars that is a different question than becoming a good basketball player."

KID: "I know. He gets a lot of chicks, too."

PARENT: "So, what do you think you want to learn to do better?"

KID: "Dribble well down court and make a lay-up. It's my money shot, but in games I keep getting called for traveling and I get the ball stolen too often, too."

PARENT: "Okay. Dribbling and lay-ups both improve with practice. Why don't you start with one or the other. Which do you think is more important to you right now?"

KID: "Dribbling. Not traveling and getting the ball stolen in games. Coach took me out after three travels and four steals in the second quarter of the last game."

PARENT: "Okay. Let's work on traveling first. How many travels do you think are okay per quarter?"

KID: "None! Just kidding—maybe one is okay since I'm almost at three now."

PARENT: "Okay. So, what can you do to get better?"

KID: "I could get to practice early and work on my hands. Maybe I could ask the assistant coach to help. He offered to shadow

me last week and I was so mad at myself after the game, I just
blew him off. Should I ask him if he could give me some dribbling pointers after practice on Friday?"
PARENT: "Good plan."

Well-defined, doable tasks facilitate performance improvement better
than nebulous, grand, overwhelming goals. When your child sets lofty
goals a decade away, frustration often results, so you may need to help
them sort out a path ahead. One huge step can be daunting, but little
steps, one at a time, become manageable.

TIP   **When appropriate, help your child establish goals that are:**
1. well defined
   (specific behaviors—usually defined in numbers to increase or decrease)
2. of intermediate challenge
   (not too hard, not too easy).

Step by Doable Step

The principle works for young players as well as elite athletes competing for spots on the Olympic teams. Lofty goals serve as inspiration, but
the persistent commitment to immediate subgoals, logically sequenced,
leads to success, step by doable step. Olympic swimmer John Naber assessed what he would have to do to win a gold medal. He figured he would
have to shave four seconds off the best hundred-meter backstroke time he
had ever accomplished. Discussing his plan, he said, "It's a substantial
chunk. But because it's a goal, now I can decisively figure out how I can
attack that." He broke his stratospheric goal into smaller, achievable steps
and built his training program around each subgoal, leading up to his
gold-medal performance in 1976.

In volleyball, the first team to get fifteen points wins the game. The
first team to win three games out of five wins the match. Coach Gerry
Gregory, USA National Team Member and head volleyball coach at Azusa
Pacific University, established for his team three smaller goals within the
fifteen-point goal—first to five points, first to ten points, push the last five
points to total fifteen and win. By giving his players small, immediate
goals all leading step by doable step to the larger goal, he knew progress
would move more certainly forward. The same principle works in football

with the ten-yard progress in four downs, breaking the hundred-yard field into ten-yard bites. In golf, players know par on each hole and can shoot for par, then compare hole by hole how their play is going—above par, below par, on the money. In fact, examine most sports and you will see immediate goals and guidelines, focusing participants each step of the way.

Parents, please watch yourself during the goal exploration and setting process. It is very easy to push *your* ideas and goals on your child. Remind yourself to listen first, last, and in the middle. Many lofty-goaled parents find themselves stumbling into disappointed self-reflection when they ask their child's goals. Don't be let down if your child says, "Get to the snack truck before the other kids so they don't sell out of Ring Dings" or "Avoid having to ride home in car pool with John's stinky baby brother." It really is okay.

Short-Circuiting Stalls by Building Self-Efficacy

Once your child has clarified where he or she wants to go and what he or she wants to do, it might be worthwhile to discuss normal frustration resulting from discrepancies between goals and skills. Your help setting appropriately challenging goals will bring your child numerous small successes in the short run and contribute to long-term progress.

Record Keeping

Empower your kids to keep their own records and monitor their own progress. If you become the record keeper, you hold the numbers and the success or failure, and in so doing, undermine an important aspect of your child's self-efficacy. You can ask what your budding athlete most wants to improve, figure out the numbers needed and how the kid can gather the stats wanted. Let your child be in charge of his or her method as well as the number collection. Teaching your child to draw a simple bar chart puts that kid in charge of his or her improvement. The chart doesn't have to be fancy, just a day-to-day record of the information. Show your young record keeper how to draw two lines: one going across to stand for time and one going vertically to stand for the number of behaviors (e.g., ball steals).

Don't Become the Statistics Sheriff

Psychologically, you need to stay in the parent as child-advocate ("I'm proud of you for who you are") role. It is far better to be your kid's cheer-

Sample Chart: Greg's Steals During a Game

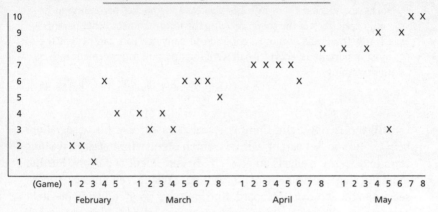

	(Game) 1 2 3 4 5	1 2 3 4 5 6 7 8	1 2 3 4 5 6 7 8	1 2 3 4 5 6 7 8
	February	March	April	May

leader for performance effort, no matter what the numbers. Given many young athletes' tendency to be self-critical, it's your job to recall the one great shot, the one fabulous pass, the one great steal that punctures your kid's negative self-critical evaluations. In balance, a positive self-serving bias (propped up with your support) can help kids move on after mistakes and keep playing confidently.

Win/Lose—Good/Bad—Black/White: Judgmental Thinking

It's easy to fall into some common traps as you ease your child toward self-efficacy in sports. Putting the main focus on winning is one of the biggest, easiest traps of all.

TWO-POCKET PARENTS

Let me share with you an experience I had while umpiring a youth T-ball league. The league was designed to be a noncompetitive recreational league, and umpires were told to emphasize fun and skill improvement while de-emphasizing the importance of winning. We were told to let the children swing until they made solid contact and to allow as many children as possible to score (scoring appeared to be the most enjoyable aspect of the game for most players). We were also told not to keep score, thereby reinforcing the notion that winning was not important. The children rarely asked who was winning until parents, against our wishes, began bringing scorebooks. During a game, after a parents' meeting in which we banned the scorebooks, I found a parent picking up rocks and placing them into his pockets (one pocket per team) so he could keep track of the score, relaying the information to other parents! Clearly, there was nothing I could do to convince this parent that the most important aspects of T-ball were fun and skill improvement rather than winning.

—Daniel Wann, *Sport Psychology,* 1997, pp. 52–53

If Wann is right, and there is research to support his observations, being a "two-pocket parent" with the emphasis on winning can have long-term undermining effects on your child's enjoyment of playing. Furthermore, personal development as well as athletic self-efficacy become second to the score on the board. Knowing that your child will inevitably encounter stalls and spurts prepares you for reality. No kid has smooth sailing. Yours won't either, but at the end of any competition, sports enthusiasts declare a winner and a loser. Black/white. Successful/unsuccessful. Good/bad. Reality is more complicated. In most competitions, the separation between the winner and loser represents only a few points, often determined in the last few minutes of play. Are the players or teams so different?

Win/lose thinking lets people simplify hours of personal effort (practice time aside) and talent into a single qualitative judgment. This reductionistic thinking presents a serious threat to developing youngsters. Parents' statements can inadvertently feed polarized evaluations. "That was the best game you have ever played." "Your game was perfect." "That was the finest baseball I have ever seen." "You were the best player on the team again!"

Best. Finest. Greatest. Highest. Largest. Most. Richest. Strongest. Toughest.

Worst. Laziest. Lousiest. Lowest. Smallest. Least. Poorest. Weakest. Softest.

"*Est*" thinking invades sports. All or nothing. Of course, you *know* there are shades of gray between black and white, but kids don't necessarily appreciate this fact. I once tried to explain this to a parent on the sidelines. As I talked, he became increasingly worried he might have hurt his daughter's development with his harsh judgments. Finally, as I closed with a flourish about the importance of being positive, he seemed to suddenly brighten and at last said,

"I get it. I shouldn't have told her she was the worst on the team. I should have said, 'Jennifer is positively the worst!' Then I could explain how she could beat Holly and be the best if she only tried."
—Shari Kuchenbecker, curmudgeon trainer hat, 1997

I got an F as a teacher. The fact of the matter is, everyone learning makes mistakes. Performances are rarely best or worst ever. I worked on the dad for another hour that day and the rest of the school year, and eventually he did seem to soften. Less judgment. Less good/bad. More support for development.

Mental Gym Bag of Stall-Proof Athletic Equipment

Through ups and downs, you can help your young athlete become increasingly "stall-proof" as he or she gathers a mental gym bag of things to do when performance doesn't match expectations. Increased practice time, reading a skill manual, taking an extra lesson, seeing a live pro demonstration, attending a technique camp, and watching video footage with guidance can put the brakes on a performance slide. Such behaviors also enhance your child's personal self-efficacy.

BURNOUT

Sports Should Not Be All Work and No Play

Whether your child is simply sampling from the cafeteria of life experiences or has world-class athlete dreams, the quality of play and fun in sports experiences is precious. In a high school newspaper, Jack Schneider, 1998 guest columnist and two-year varsity baseball player with eight years' baseball experience, wrote:

Sunday morning and the last place on earth where I want to be at 8 A.M. is Monterey Park. But I feel that it's my duty. So, I drag my weary body out of bed at 6:30, throw down some breakfast and jump in the car. It seems like this has been happening to me too much lately. My sport has become like a second job, and between it and school, I'm killing myself.

Justin Berkman is at the gym until 9 every night. Gabe Goldstein gets home at 7. The entire baseball team is supposed to be in year-round training. And this goes all year long. As athletes, we have to be dedicated, but to what degree? At what point does a sport actually become a job? Many high school athletes claim that they "just want to play in college." But why? Is it really worth the tremendous strain of trying to live on just a few hours' sleep and a constricted social life?

I'm not saying that I have the answers to any of these questions, because I too continue to ruin my life because of my love for my sport. Love for my sport. That's something I haven't heard for a while. I remember when that was the real reason we all played: that and the fact that our parents had signed us up for the league. But even Little League can be too competitive. I still remember crying every time I struck out, and then going to the batting cages after the game to practice. About a week ago, I saw something really beautiful. It was about 7 P.M. and getting dark, when a big green station wagon pulled into the parking lot at Mar Vista Park. A man about 40, in a suit and tie, stepped out, accompanied by a jumpy youngster, probably about 6. They walked around to the back of the car and began to unload their gear. It took two trips to get all their stuff out onto the grass but finally the chore was complete and the fun began. Although it was getting dark, the boy and his father proceeded to play baseball, basketball, football, Frisbee, soccer, and tag for the next hour as I watched in amazement. The weren't practicing, or even concentrating on one sport. But they were having fun.

Take a month off (if your sport is not in season), and give yourself a break from training, club teams, weekend practices, and the gym. If you can't take a month, try a week, or a day. Do things you haven't done in a while. Finish all your homework. Get some sleep. Watch TV. Go out and play a sport that you're not particularly good at with some others of equal talent, and have fun. Take some time off, and when you come back, return to a sport, not a job.

—Jack Schneider, *Brentwood Flyer,*
Los Angeles, October 29, 1997, p. 15

Spurts and stalls are inevitable aspects of sports performance, but burnout becomes a likely outcome when the emotional drains regularly exceed the rewards. Young Mr. Schneider is right. Watching the dad and the kid have fun reminds us all of the value of enjoyment. No matter how skilled or trained or professionally successful someone is, if the process is not enjoyable, something needs to be changed.

QUITTING

According to old athlete dogma, there is nothing worse than a quitter.

CAROLINA CAPER HAS ANOTHER VILLAIN

Carolina Panther quarterback Kerry Collins made a mistake. Had he assaulted his girlfriend, been caught driving drunk to work, or failed a drug test . . . All right, that's not so bad in the world of professional football—when can you get ready for the next game, my man.

Collins did something worse by athletic standards—he quit.

At least that's the Panthers' story and they're sticking with it, so downright indignant that they quit on Collins, cut him, and got nothing for a franchise quarterback. That will teach him.

"If I saw him walking down the street, just the sight of him would [tick] me off," said Warren Sapp, Tampa Bay Buccaneer defensive lineman. "Forever noted he is the first pick [in Carolina history] and the first quitter in the NFL."

—T. J. Simers, *Los Angeles Times,* October 17, 1998, p. D5

In the world of sports, casual onlookers might get the feeling that *quit* is the worst four-letter word utterable. *Quit* and a true athlete are not spoken of in the same breath. So when popular sports hero Michael Jordan gave the statement on Thursday, January 14, 1999, that "this is a perfect time for me to walk away from the game. I'm at peace with that," headlines in the major papers of the nation played do-si-do with their thesauruses to find ways to say it without using the four-letter epithet.

We listened to Jordan's words: "Mentally, I'm exhausted. Physically, I feel great." Fans from towns across America chided his decision to leave when he was playing so well, but few could bring themselves to label him a quitter. The fact of the matter is, just as he brought dignity to the game of basketball, Jordan gave dignity to quitting. Quitting is, at times, an individual's best choice.

Most sports participants quit one or more sports at some time. If you're doing your job, your athletically and nonathletically talented kids will have multiple experiences and sports to pick from, eventually quitting the less suitable. Even the supremely successful quit eventually. The *why* and the *how* become the important aspects; the *when* is simply a matter of time.

When to Quit

It is time to quit when your child says, "I don't want to play anymore." When the available lessons have been learned and the joy in the process has dwindled to meager returns on the effort required, your child will let you know. As Yogi Berra says, "When you come to a fork in the road, take it."

Use natural endings as times for reassessment. The start and end of seasons—before teams are chosen and team commitments are in place—offer obvious opportunities to explore commitments and goals. If your child is wavering at all, avoid pushing him or her into starting a season anew. With the exception of injuries, if your child wavers in the midseason, reinforce commitments until season end. Sort out where the stalling motivation is coming from and work on building personal self-efficacy. Letting a child quit because his "fun" is sagging does a disservice to the child's abilities and teaches him a very poor lesson. Sticking to commitments, once in season, is a part of living up to a promise. However, you'll have to judge each situation individually and carefully. Never sell your child's potential to learn a tough lesson short, but avoid compromising your child's overall development because of some generalized rule. There are exceptions to every rule, and your child's well-being in the long run is the most important.

> **TIP**   **"I don't want to play anymore."**
> When the joy is gone, injuries hurt, other time demands pull, many kids leave organized youth sports.

Why: Good Reasons to Quit

If you ask folks who've quit a sport why, they often say, "It wasn't fun anymore." One articulate youngster wrote:

My sport does not thrill me anymore. I no longer care who wins or loses. Practices are a chore. My shoulder hurts all the time and the doctor says it will only get worse with continued activity. I am at a very different place in my life than I was two, five, or ten years ago, but I am still playing the same dumb game. Who cares anymore. There is a difference between quitting and choosing self-preservation. I do not want to be selfish, but I just don't know if I can muster the energy necessary to continue. My team will be fine without me. I know that. I resent that my stubbornness and sense of duty have caused me to give over a significant portion of my life, my most valuable gift and commodity, to a cause that no longer interests me. When I picture myself in a position of having left, I imagine an immense sense of relief and peace. The thought of having my winter, spring, summer, and fall free to do whatever I want to do makes me giddy.

—University water polo player, 1997

In recent research completed at Loyola Marymount University by Carla Workman, Stacie Stern, Cindy Weglarz, and Melissa Fields, the best reasons sixth-grade and college kids cite for quitting a sport are similar and range from injuries down to friends:

1. Injuries (74.2%)
2. Schoolwork (72%)
3. Illness (50%)
4. Family conflicts (47.7%)
5. Cost to play (36.4%)
6. Moving (34.1%)
7. Time (30.3%)
8. Kicked off a team (22.7%)
9. Another sport (22%)
10. Friends (8.3%)

Every one of these general reasons are legitimate reasons to quit; in addition, there are a host of unmentioned unique individual reasons with personal stories behind each. Stanford psychologist Albert Bandura's research documents other common reasons for quitting, which include disappointments in achievement, inadequate reward for efforts, too much pressure to win, and poor coaching. Add to that list mismatching personal skills, abilities, interests, and other competing opportunities for time.

QUITTING IS *NOT* FAILING

From Tuesday to Tuesday, in one week, the words were hard for my son to hear. "Quitting is *not* failing."

Sitting on the wooden bleachers at Hardy Field at the U., I looked down at the drill in progress and could see the fine lines around the young players' eyes as they looked up at the assistant coach throwing fast balls—sixty miles per hour—at them. First one direction then another. Crouch; run forward; look over your shoulder, move to the ball; receive the pass. Again and again.

I watched my son's eyes closely. The surgery on his left knee last March had been a quote-unquote "success." The three tiny scars healed well, and six months of rehab, including three times a week physical therapy, swimming every day the last two months, and weight training at the gym, supposedly had done the job. But the eyes told another story. Crinkles of pain at the corners of each eye cupped as he made the first jump. A lunge for a short pass and his face told no lies. No one else seemed to notice, but I knew him too well. He was hurting badly.

Sitting on the lawn after practice ended, two huge bags of ice Saran-wrapped to his once-bony kneecaps, he sat and stared at the watermelons where his knees used to be.

"Quitting is not failing! You have to make the choice that is the healthy one for your body in the long run. You need to protect yourself." He knew cartilage didn't regrow. He knew he hurt because the cartilage cushion in his knees was gone. The doctor had explained that his once smooth, easy-sliding cartilage was like a shag carpet. They had shaved all the shag off they could. He was down to bone on bone. Of course it hurt. "So stop!"

"NO!!" His eyes flashed up at me. "You need to support my decision. I won't let the team down." I watched as his jaw jutted forward and his eyes clouded with a combination of pain and sadness.

Hopefully, I asked, "What about the anti-inflammatory medicine you took last year?"

"No!" Dead end. The doctor had said he might hurt his stomach at the high doses he needed. He didn't need a bleeding ulcer on top of sore knees. He needed to figure it out, he explained.

I know.

I sat, reaching one hand toward one of his painful swollen knees and prayed to know what to say. I sighed. "Quitting is not failing. Sometimes it is the beginning of a new success."

Five visits to a specialist later, he worked out a program of personal training and self-monitoring. Deciding to become the team manager was easy, and I will forever love his coach for giving him the option. He felt a lot better about quitting.

—Mother of college football player turned team manager

Sports psychologist Daniel Wann wholeheartedly supports the positive value in quitting a sport. Nonetheless, he notes, most decisions to quit include a moderate degree of negative feelings, stress, or disappoint-ment. How parents handle the decision to quit can mediate the disap-pointment.

You may find yourself holding your child's hand as the doctor rolls him into an operating room for knee surgery and wonder why you ever signed him up for football in the first place. You may watch your child struggle to stay awake as she finishes her history assignment after three hours of soccer practice and wonder why she continues to play. The an-swer should be straightforward: because your child loves playing. But the time may come when the play no longer brings happiness and the avail-able paths dwindle. The day comes when you ask, "Why are you playing?" and the answer comes back, "I don't know." Now is the time when the conversation must turn to quitting.

Your child needs to make the final decisions about his or her time, choices, talents, and interests. You can guide and advise, but you cannot make this decision for your young athlete.

How to Quit

When it is clear that the athlete is ready to stop and the reasons behind the decision are solid, quitting with dignity is important, whether it in-volves Michael Jordan, Wayne Gretzky, or twelve-year-old Timmy up the street. Parents can build their child's integrity by supporting the positive process and the gains. Using the simple mnemonic, when it is time to move on, they need to go on to a new PLACE.

Praise positive growth through participation (friends, skills, self-efficacy, etc.);

Logical reasons for quitting should be emphasized;

Applaud those who coached and supported your child during partici-pation;

Cherish the rich memories;

Embrace the future and the new paths opening as this door closes.

As tempting as it may be, avoid sour grapes. As a child moves on, many kids and parents want to announce to the world the negative, awful, terri-ble thing that led to this departure. Pinpointing "terrible coaching," the "poor organization," the "favoritism of other players," even the "politics" must make some folks feel better, but it's not in the best interests of your child. The best and the only reason to quit is because it is the right choice for your child. Period. Most decisions have many, many small supports, and pinpointing only one misses the true complexity of most well-thought-out choices.

Parents should remember the value in playing and value in quitting, both right at different times in their child's life. As the PLACE in their child's life changes, support the value and integrity of the time invested and growth afforded through participation.

TIP **Quitting with dignity is important.**

As kids move on to a new place in their lives, remember to Praise the positive growth through sports, emphasize Logical reasons to quit, Applaud those who coached and supported, Cherish memories, and Embrace the future and new paths opening.

Your child will have many junctures and choices. As a parent, your guidance will be important in helping him or her make the right choices and frame the past positively. In so doing, you will be providing a better springboard for the next opportunity.

13

Turning Girls and Boys into Great People Through Athletics

I clapped the portable phone shut and experienced a swollen heart, lump in my throat, moist eyes, and disorienting light-headedness. What might be undiagnosable to eminent M.D.s was vividly clear to me. I had an acute onset of a classic syndrome: PRIDE. Kristy was going to be fine. She had gotten up her courage to speak to the coach and now she knew what she needed to do. She was going to be better than fine. She was taking care of it herself. Excellent.

It had been a good week. A friend's twelve-year-old son had been struggling. A strict teacher's scathing criticisms were undermining him; he had rebounded daily at home with temper tantrums and pouting. David's mom knew he needed something else in his life to build him up, teach social skills, buoy and counterbalance his classroom experiences. Sports seemed to be an alternative. He was already on a Little League team, but she had added after-school tennis lessons with the beloved school P.E. coach, bought Rollerblades, and enrolled him in a park league basketball team with a supportive friend-of-the-family coach. The plan was working. He was again eager to go to school in the morning and seemed to be learning what he needed to learn. A recent parent-teacher conference reaffirmed that he generally was handling himself better, staying in his seat, and doing his work. Excellent.

—Shari Kuchenbecker, Ph.D., psychologist's hat, 1998

Pride and emotional fulfillment. You won't find them listed in the DSM-IV or in any prestigious medical textbook, but I regularly find them among the players, parents, coaches, and staff associated with youth sports. Girls and boys alike are learning important lessons through participation.

Kristy's and David's stories are not unusual. Sports provide wonderful learning opportunities for our girls-into-women and our boys-into-men. Both are developing personal self-efficacy; building physical skills; learning to handle competition; and enjoying the camaraderie of teamwork. They are learning to turn aggression into teamwork; reach out to one another; cooperate; communicate; share support and friendship; sacrifice individual glory for team success; welcome the emotional sustenance provided by one another; and more. You'll see winning celebrations of joy and mutual comfort in loss among boys *and* girls. The lessons and opportunities available in sports are not and should not be discriminated by sex.

GIRLS AND BOYS ALIKE NEED SOCIAL COMPETENCE TO ACHIEVE THEIR POTENTIAL

With two daughters and one son, I've seen the rapid emergence of women's athletic opportunities since Title IX's passage in 1972. The more I've watched, the more lessons in progress I've witnessed and the clearer the dual learning in progress emerges. UCLA's Natalie Williams developed amazing physical and competitive skills and became the first woman to win All-American honors in basketball and volleyball in the same season. The young men in the stands bowing in unison with mock exaltation at her performance showed respect for a woman's athletic skills. Girls *and boys* flocked to meet the U.S. women's soccer team following their World Cup victory in July 1999. Grade school, high school, college age folks, and beyond exuberantly cheering for female and male athletes alike teaches everyone something—boys and girls, cheerers and athletes.

BOYS AND GIRLS BOTH LEARN THROUGH ATHLETICS

Every baby announcement begins with "It's a Girl!" or "It's a Boy!" With this proud pronouncement, many parents believe (right or wrong) that they have a handle on their child's future. Unsuspecting parents in one study were shown a photo of an infant named Larry; they then proudly and confidently proclaimed him to be "large-featured, robust, strong, and alert." When the same photo baby was renamed Laura, parents assuredly described her as "fine-featured, small, delicate, and soft." Same baby. Different names. Different sex. Different expectations.

Different sets of expectations for boys and girls gleaned from living in our culture may grant parents a measure of calming certainty as they watch the unfolding of their child's individual skills and talents, but this certainty may come at a tremendous individual cost to "Larrys" as well as "Lauras." According to statistics, girls are more likely to be overprotected and lack self-confidence, while boys are more likely to have trouble with impulse control, aggression, and appropriate social interactions. Sports participation potentially offers both Laura and Larry some of what they need.

GREAT EXPECTATIONS

How much do parents' expectations influence their behavior with their children? The answer probably varies from parent to parent and child to child. According to gender researcher Eleanor Maccoby at Stanford University, dads generally play more physically with boys than girls and are more likely than moms to want to "toughen up" their sons. Power assertion over sons and efforts not to show weakness or signs of effeminacy seemingly concern many dads. While mothers tend to be more even-handed from their children's early infancy on, they nonetheless spend twice as much time talking with their female infants and daughters, particularly about feelings and emotional responses, compared to how they talk to their sons. When asked to attribute feelings to ambiguously depicted children, moms and dads alike are both more likely to see boys as angry and girls as fearful. Parents are also more likely to describe boys as "high-spirited" and active while girls are seen as more relaxed and calm.

Notably, parents' attributions reflect their *expectations,* not necessarily real or substantial differences. Scientists recognize, across a number of psychological measures, that boys and girls are remarkably similar. Physiologically, boys and girls also have large areas of overlap. However, in general, young boys tend to have higher metabolic levels, higher activity levels in group play, greater arousability in challenging and teasing situations, more dominance hierarchy play, less ability to control themselves, and more modest language facility. In contrast, girls have lower metabolic rates, calmer play, less participation in hierarchy and dominance play, more emotional arousal to fearful video sequences, greater ability to self-regulate behavior, and more language at an earlier age. On many measures of maturation, boys take longer to develop. Thus, both sets of gender differences may be mediated by the fact that girls are simply more physiologically mature at the same chronological age.

When kids reach the age of three, many girls show a preference for same-sex peers. At about the age of four, the same-sex peer preference occurs among boys. Moreover, girls' and boys' group play tends to be substantially different in form and content. Boys play in large groups four times as often as girls. Boys' group play characteristically includes a lot of rough and tumble interactions and good-natured one-upmanship. Dominance hierarchies are established early among grade-school boys, with as much as half of their play time devoted to direct competition. The top male (alpha male) often emerges through a series of challenges, "strong-arming" and "shouldering their way" to the top of the heap. Boys tend to play more aggressively than girls. Girls tend to play in smaller groups of two or three children; typically, less than 1 percent of their activities are competitive, with leadership based on verbal persuasion and bargaining. Leadership thus emerges among girls based on interaction skills rather than physical dominance.

The bottom line emerges. Many girls play with girls and many boys play with boys from about the age of four on. When asked why, girls often explain that "the boys don't play fair," "the boys don't know how to take turns," or "the boys play dumb games." The quality and content of girls' play emerges as different and becomes quantitatively divergent. While researchers believe that the same-sex groupings are not imposed on the children by teachers—they rather appear to be self-selected—schools can make a difference. In traditional classrooms when kids have a free choice, they form same-sex groupings 70 percent of the time, compared to only 41 percent of the time in open schools.

YOUTH SPORTS AS A POTENTIAL FORCE

For several years, I have enjoyed the privilege of coordinating trophies in my AYSO region and have also helped with team photography:

AYSO PICTURE DAY

On picture day that year, the girls' Division 6 (now U-8) went first: Road Runners, Blue Jays, Raspberries, Quick Silver, Bodacious Babes, and so on.

The seven- and eight-year-old Road Runner girls trooped up. I told them to form a line from shortest to tallest. The entire process took about two minutes as they checked one another's heights, then fell into place without much fuss or bother. One small shift was needed (a girl thought she was shorter than the girl ahead of her, but the reverse was true). The girls stood in line chatting, rearranging their shirts and fixing their own and one another's hair. Bobby pins and clips were shared. When it was time to move to the chosen photo location in a nearby arbor, they walked eagerly to the midpoint. The group was then divided so that the two tallest girls were on either end fading on into the middle with the four smallest girls kneeling down in the center. The coach and assistant coach happily took their places on either end by the two tallest girls. In twelve minutes flat, we'd taken three team photos and the entire series of individual photos.

The second team to arrive was a boy's team, The Avengers (followed that day by other boys' teams named Scorpions, Terminators, Killer Bees, Death Rays, and the like). The seven- and eight-year-old Avengers informed me as they arrived that they were the championship team. I was surprised. It was only October and playoffs were not for a month and a half. I explained they needed to form a line from shortest to tallest. I knew I was in trouble when two were adamant that it had to be tallest to shortest. Fine. The next seven minutes were spent arguing and comparing to a hair's breadth who was taller and who was shorter. Boys stretched their necks, straightened their torsos, and stood back to back, nose to nose, recruiting friends to judge the various height competitions. Finally, I had to settle two disputes, but the boys eventually formed the line . . . sort of. The next five minutes brought a plethora of butt pokes, knee dips from behind, hair pulls, and side tweaks. Not one kid seemed to wonder about his hairdo or shirt, but several fell into small heaps of two or three tussling about for a few minutes before returning to vertical positions. At one point, the whole line nearly fell over like a set of dominos when a big middle kid suddenly leaned backward and forward to clear himself more space, knocking the kids on either side on down the line.

When it came time to move into the arbor, I asked the boys, as I had the girls, "Please walk in line to the big circle midline in front of the camera." Well, I wonder if I really said, "On your mark, get set, go!" because what happened next was fourteen boys shot from the starting gate to race to the line, each trying to beat *anyone* else. Of course the tallest-to-shortest line had to be reconstructed, and the separation, at the boys' insistence, went with the tallest boys in the middle fading to shorter at the sides; four boys reluctantly took their spots kneeling on the ground in front. Two seemed to have had lots of experience with this position, however, and quickly demanded to share the privilege of holding the soccer ball in the photograph's center. The six-to-nine inches the boys in line preferred to leave between one another was substantially less than the average foot or so the girls chose and probably reflected an ideal opportunity for the inevitable rough-and-tumble play that emerged. The photographer shot seven pictures. During the first shot, several boys moved at the last second. Picture two included one kid making an Alfred E. Neuman finger-in-ears, tongue-out display. The coach reprimanded the kids, and they seemed to shape up for photos three and four, but the boys in front dropped the ball. Photos five and six included at least one with rabbit ears, and photo seven may have made it. Exhausted, the photographer then started to do the singles as the boys broke line. More jabbing, teasing, falling, and general mischief followed. Twenty-five minutes later, the boys charged out to the field, again battling against anyone in the near vicinity for the position at the front of the group.

—Shari Kuchenbecker, AYSO Pacific Palisades trophy chairman hat, 1996

The general mischief and activity levels among the boys' compared to the girls' groups are consistent with a number of experimental and naturalistic investigations. Boys and girls play differently, and the kids themselves recognize the different styles. Maccoby concludes, "I have argued that the reduction of contact between the sexes during middle childhood is a social phenomenon that protects girls from male dominance and coercion. When girls live their lives primarily within adult-monitored structures (the family, the classroom) or in all-girl groups, they are free to develop social and academic competencies in accord with their individual interests and talents. For boys, the situation is different. We have no reason to believe that contact with girls threatens the development of their individual competencies (scholastic abilities, musical talents, and so on) in any way. But having settings in which they operate outside the sphere of influence from either adults or girls allows them to work out the complexities of male-male relationships: maintaining individual status among male peers while at the same time becoming part of a cohesive male group that can hold its own in competition with other male collectives."

As I poured through Maccoby's impressive volume *Two Sexes: Growing Up Apart, Coming Together* (1998), I found myself asking adamant questions in the margins. "How about girls in sports?" I exclaimed in scrawling letters to Maccoby's comments that "boys' social contacts with each other tend to occur as by-products of their joint activities. Indeed, boys tend to choose friends on the basis of similarity in activity interests (such as love of baseball), while girls choose more on the basis of personality compatibilities (Erwin, 1985)." While Erwin's observations may have been accurate in 1985, the last fifteen years' influence and women's sports seemed important to recognize. I thought about my own athletic daughters' circles of female friends, all selected through junior high and high school primarily from their various sports teams. I pondered their even larger collection of male friends, most of whom were athletes as well. Was this the case for girls fifteen years ago? I *knew* we needed new research.

Maccoby mentions, "In recent years, schools have offered much more in the way of active sports programs for girls, and although sports have not become as pervasive and absorbing an activity for girls as for boys, they now do provide a major focus of interest for a substantial subgroup of girls. (It is notable, however, that after the first few years of grade school, participant sports activities are almost entirely sex-segregated.)" The word *subgroup* seemed an underestimation of the one in three high school women who plays sports and the fact that women now constitute 36 percent to 40 percent of all high school and college athletes.

In my multiple hats as researcher, university teacher, and soccer and volleyball mom to girls and a boy, I know that the sports playing fields are ripe for gender studies. Has anyone ventured onto the playing field to watch a Division 7 (U-6) coeducational AYSO soccer game with gender questions in mind? Has a research team visited grade-school playgrounds to see fourth-grade girls lining up with the boys to play handball? Has anyone received funding to learn about the kind of self-efficacy a girl has to develop to join an all-boys football team at the ninth-grade level? Had they watched some girls play horse with the boys in tenth grade because they like the challenge the boys offered? How many researchers have seen a girls' team take on a boys' team and clobber them at soccer or volleyball, especially at the fifth- and sixth-grade level, when the girls—most already full swing in their growth spurt—outsize the boys? How many have ever watched open gym at their university where coed teams play competitively? Where had the researchers been that they could overlook this undercurrent in gender relations? When girls choose to play with boys, they—like all players—play to the level of the competition and improve. Girls and girls' teams who choose to play with the boys often have substantial skills and earn a lot of respect from their male competitors. Self-efficacy abounds, and simple generalizations about boys and girls as two very different sexes begin to blur.

WOMEN IN SPORTS AND TITLE IX

The pragmatic facts emerge. There are many girls and boys who follow the current sex-stereotyped norms, but there are growing numbers of individuals violating these expectations. Women's sports may offer a window onto cultural change in progress. Indeed, according to a recent study by the National Council for Research on Women, a consortium of research institutes and universities, more girls are participating in a wider range of sports and exercise than ever before: 2.2 million women are now involved in high school athletics (compared to the 3.5 million men), more than two and a quarter times the number of women in 1971.

Unisex Is Not the Goal

I know of no parents who watch their daughter compete and wish she were a boy. Accepting our daughters and sons as people who also play sports includes acknowledging obvious sex differences.

It's only been recently that height on women has been seen as a general advantage. In the past, tall girls were often treated with banal social niceties and told, "You should be a model." Now *there's* a challenging career choice. Girls with any meat on their bones or muscles that refused to be starved away simply slumped as short as possible, wore dark colors, and bought flat shoes. Most tall girls, certainly big and tall girls, were often made to feel awful. As we move into the twenty-first century, tall girls in tall sports are not shunned; they are respected and sought after. Why did it take so long?

The kind of musculature that graces Martina Navratilova's physique is also gaining acceptance. Martina used her natural endowment as the foundation for strength-building and fitness, creating a cross-training program for herself long before it was fashionable. The "ripped" physique she achieved not only gave her tremendous physical dominance in play, it blew her graceful competition out of the water. I am proud to see young girls cultivating stronger muscles over anorexic matchstick limbs.

Title IX

As most know, in 1972, Congress passed Title IX as part of an education amendment that states, "No person in the United States shall, on the basis of sex . . . be subjected to discrimination under any educational program or activity receiving federal assistance." Buoyed by the legislation, Donna Lopiano, who oversaw women's sports at the University of Texas, sat at a 1972 coaches' meeting across the table from the male coaches' stronghold, which included legendary football coach Darrell Royal. "We asked for half the athletic budget. The guys almost fell off their chairs." However, half the funds did not instantly flow into women's programs, not at UT or at any NCAA school for that matter. Betsy Alden, president of the National Association of Collegiate Women Athletic Administrators, summarized the twenty-five-year history of Title IX. "Back in 1972, a federal law was passed and people stuck their heads in the sand and ignored it." While the Title IX legislation seems to offer a fair shake, the gains have been achieved slowly through the unrelenting efforts of several hardworking individuals *and* a number of lawsuits to bring the changes about. The fact of the matter is, institutions have not jumped at the chance to hand over half of the dollar pie to the women. Quite the contrary, economics have been hotly argued and a fair distribution has yet to be achieved.

According to research completed by the Womens Sport's Foundation, in the 1995–96 school year, among NCAA Division 1-A schools, 65 percent of the scholarship dollars went to men and only 35 percent to women. In terms of overall expenditures, 78 percent of the dollars were spent on the men's programs and only 22 percent on women's programs. Combining total scholarships and expenditure dollars, women's sports earned just shy of 26 percent to men's 74 percent. In NCAA Division I-AA schools, the proportion of men's to women's scholarships was 64 percent to 36 percent. Overall expenditures were modestly more equitable with 68 percent of the funds going for men and 32 percent for women, yielding total scholarship plus expenditure dollar amounts at 34.5 percent for women compared to men's allotment of 65.5 percent.

In a 1997 *New York Times* interview with Marcia Chambers, Mr. Cedric W. Dempsey, NCAA executive director advised, "We must keep pressure on these institutions to address the need [of gender equality]." The NCAA requires all schools across divisions to present a plan toward gender equality if a school is to retain certification. The Office of Civil Rights also has power to enforce compliance, but investigations are time-consuming and no school has ever lost federal funds for noncompliance. Despite a modest amount of public awareness, evaluation of compliance and efforts toward equality include qualitative judgments difficult to investigate thoroughly, much less envision and mandate. As parents, if we want our daughters to get a fair shake on the athletic field, we must continue to fight for more equitable distribution of these funds and institutional resources.

A Tough Road Ahead for Women

Researchers know that women are twice as likely as men to suffer from mild depressions and major depressive disorders. Susan Nolan-Hoeksema (1998) at the University of Michigan notes that depression rates peak among fifteen- to twenty-four-year-olds, and women's overall depression rate hovers around 7.5 percent for all women, to men's 3 percent. Research by Alexander Astin and Linda J. Sax, director of the thirty-third annual survey from UCLA's Higher Education Research Institute, shows that freshmen college women are five times as likely to feel anxious as men, frequently feeling "overwhelmed by all I have to do." College women are working much harder than the men and feeling more stress, while more of their male counterparts report "having a good time."

Opportunities for women in sports may provide beneficial experiences that counter the cultural tendencies and women's compromised psychological health. Nike's ads share some of the most-publicized research in psychology.

If you let me play
  I will like myself more
I will have more self-confidence
  I will suffer less depression
I will be 60% less likely to get breast cancer
  I will be more likely to leave a man who beats me
I will be less likely to get pregnant before I want to
  I will learn what it means to be strong.
If you let me play sports.
                    —Nike ad campaign, 1997–99

Athletics Help Girls Overcome the "Guy-Superiority Stereotype"

Research on the subtle cultural messages and beliefs our daughters and sons experience can sometimes best be understood through the eyes of individuals. As one female fifteen-year-old two-sport, club, and school athlete explains:

Basically, young female athletes grow up in this world where we may have been brainwashed into thinking guys are so much more naturally talented than we are. What makes my experience with athletics so phenomenally valuable is that I have been able to overcome that guy-superiority stereotype.

When you see yourself performing things on the field or in a gym that other people admire, your confidence level goes up. I have learned to be organized, because I had to. You gain an overall view of life that you just wouldn't see if you didn't have the opportunity to learn these important things.

I think a lot of it is possible for me because of the team. On the team level, we are able to work together, build friendships, and I think our communications (better than guys) on the field increase the intensity as well as the success of our play.

                    —Carly Katona, age fifteen, Harvard-Westlake School,
                    Studio City, California, 1998

By becoming self-efficacious, by being physically active, by increasing healthy behaviors, women learn to be stronger in some of the ways in which men have long been trained.

ROLE MODELS AND OPPORTUNITIES FOR GIRLS IN SPORTS

Alice Coachman grew up in Albany, Georgia. "It all started when my great-great-grandmother took me along on her walks. I'd skip and run ahead as fast I could." She got a kick out of displaying her athletic skills and competing with the boys. "We'd jump and play softball, and they'd say, 'We can beat you,' and I'd say, 'You just try!' " A half a century ago, Alice Coachman became the first African-American woman to win an Olympic track and field gold medal. She went on to become a physical education teacher, raise two children, and found the Alice Coachman Track and Field Foundation to support young African-American athletes.

Rhonda Windham, former USC star athlete and general manager of the WNBA's Sparks, notes, "We are the product of Title IX. We would not be here if it wasn't for the opportunities . . . the scholarships we received to play in college. My mother told me in fourth grade that she wanted me to go to college but that I'd have to get a scholarship. Basketball was my best chance. That was something I could strive for because I knew it existed."

Donna Lopiano also credits Title IX. "I don't think people realize that over the last twenty-five years, the basic nature of the American woman has changed. It has become acceptable for girls to play sports because the legislation has created a generation of moms and dads who believe their daughters can get an athletic scholarship to a university." Realistic or not, the dangling scholarship carrots have been powerfully motivating to get parents of girls into the gyms and fields supporting their daughters' play.

In actuality, it is impossible to prove that Title IX caused the changes in our culture. More likely, the legislation reflected an overall shift in our economy and culture toward men and women equally sharing a number of opportunities and burdens because of economic demand. Beyond providing opportunities, Title IX and athletic participation does provide a kind of schooling that was once only available to young men and that may be crucial for women to compete and succeed in the workplace.

There's a lot of gamesmanship here [in the business world]. Business is much like a game, and there's always a person who is ahead, the winners and the losers, and the concept of "a team"—who's going to carry the ball on a project and who's going to follow up. I think all of this is really

tough for women to understand. I don't think every man working for a corporation has a clear sense of the game either, but I do think that, in general, women haven't been exposed to it as much.
—Beth Milwid, *Working with Men: Professional Women Talk About Power, Sexuality and Ethics,* 1990, p. 139

While Beth Milwid, I, and others in our parent generation rarely had the opportunities to learn competitive strategies and steel personal competitive skills, the young women who are now emerging through athletics do.

THE SCIENCE BOWL CONTEST

Every spring, the Los Angeles schools come together at the Department of Water and Power for the annual Science Bowl Competition. Schools, private and public alike, send their academically successful students to compete for honors and the opportunity to represent the area in the regional, then national competition.

As I looked around the large granite-floored area of bright, attentive students and their supportive parents, I listened as the format and rules of the Science Bowl were clearly laid out. There were to be a series of competitions between pairs of teams. The competitions would each earn points for the teams, last thirty minutes in various small rooms in the building, and culminate in a semifinal and final round with a side "Land Yacht Contest" in the cafeteria. Winners of the final-round competition would represent the region, and the Land Yacht winning team would earn four hundred dollars for their school.

I glanced over at my daughter. Blond, five feet, ten inches, wearing a peach shirt and Levis. She slouched in the chair and twiddled with some odd straw found on the floor as the speaker continued. To a naïve observer, she did not appear to be listening, but I knew her. If asked at any given moment, she could recite the last few paragraphs of the speech all the while continuing to create more straw rings or stars. More deceiving was her athletic training. She had played volleyball for six years, basketball for five. Her volleyball school team had won two state championships and her club team lounged in the gold division of Southern California. She knew how to compete. She knew how to win, and she hated to lose . . . anything.

After heading off to the first room for her team's competition, I knew this was going to be a really interesting day. The four fellows and my daughter were a tight band as they trooped into the room, and I watched my daughter "size up" the competition. She took a seat near the front of the fifteen-foot executive table, casually resumed her chatter with the boys, then quickly secured her long blond hair in a ponytail and got down to business. Elbows propped in front of her, she glanced across at the opponents. Not long into the first round, she was whipping out answers with her teammates and helping the team make decisions about whose answer was likely correct. She was dubbed captain of the round.

Six minutes before the clock ran out—in the middle of a response opportunity—she spread her arms across the chests of the fellows on either side before they could answer suddenly and said, "Stop! Don't answer yet." The Physics Master looked puzzled, and Computer Guru dropped his jaw. She smiled prettily. "We want to run out the clock. Fewer questions to answer and we're ahead." A laugh. So it went in the rest of the paired competitions. She was the de facto competition expert for the group. None of her fellow (literally) Science Bowl team members played sports. She did. She knew about clocks and time and scores when the final buzzer blared.

The Land Yacht contest proved to be the high point of the team's day. Given an assignment (build a Land Yacht that moves) and an array of odd materials, her team worked together, designed, built, and won the competition! She still laughs about the great time they had working as a team and the pride they shared when their school was presented with the check for four hundred dollars that their team had earned with their Land Yacht!

—Shari Kuchenbecker, mother of L.A. Science Bowl team member hat, 1996

SOCIAL COMPETENCY PREDICTS FUTURE SUCCESS

Spectators celebrate—whether the player is male or female—watching a skilled individual perform. Participation in sports can build skills and self-efficacy, but what can kids learn through sports that will permit them to stay in sports if they so desire, and, more importantly, what can they learn to help them be successful in life?

In current longitudinal research, Stanford's Albert Bandura and R. Woods find children's social skills at third grade predict academic success in eighth grade, outshining even third-grade academic success as a predictor. Furthermore, UCLA's Norma Feshbach, Sy Feshbach, and I found that six-year-old children with high empathy scores who were predicted to fail academically not only did *not* fail, but went on to academic success. Apparently, social skills, including empathic responsiveness, are important assets.

> **TIP** Social skills are tremendously important for success in the
> classroom, on the playing field, and in life.

The conclusion is obvious. We want to raise our children to be competent—within athletic institutions, educational institutions, and beyond.
Parents who help their children work on the following modest list of social competency skills will help their kids flourish and chart their own
courses within the social groups and institutions defining their progress.

Social Competency Skills

I. Social Abilities

1. Get and maintain the attention of adults in socially acceptable
ways (stand close, ask questions in pleasant voice, smile, tell information)

Gregory, six, looking into the soccer coach's bag of equipment,
finds bright orange cones. "Coach T, what is this?" (No response.)
"Coach T, is this a roadwork thing?" (Coach explains that they could
be used for roadwork, big ones sometimes are.) "You've never
brought these before. Do we get to use these in practice today?"
(Coach responds in the affirmative and explains they will try dribbling in and out of cones to improve their footwork.)

2. Use adults as resources (verbal request, demand, or physical
demonstration of need)

Betti, seven, upon receiving her new team shirt, repeatedly tries
to pull it on over her ponytail. Unsuccessful, she goes to her coach,
leaning forward with her head and ponytail trapped in the collar and
in a muffled voice says, "I can't get it over my ponytail." The coach
lifts the neck rim over the elastic. She stretches her arms into the
sleeves and pops her head through with a "Thank you, Coach," then
runs off to join the team.

3. Express both affection and hostility to adults with appropriate
verbal and physical means

When a favorite adult enters the area, Sally, twelve, catches her
eye and smiles broadly.

When the assistant coach asks Bobby, seven, to join the team
running around the field, Bobby falls back limply and says he can't.
Coach encourages him to stand up; he reluctantly rises but melts
back onto the grass. Coach asks a few questions this hot summer day

and Bobby says he feels like a leaf on a plant in the desert. Coach tosses him a water bottle. He sits and drinks slowly as the drill goes on. A few minutes later, smiling, he trots over and joins the team.

4. Lead and follow peers (suggest actions; direct and guide others; set oneself up as a model; other times, chose to imitate others, depending on the situation)

Kelly's eighth-grade team is lackadaisically walking into the gym. Kelly says, "Let's run in yelling and screaming. Let 'em know we're here to PLAY!" She revs up the team with smiles and laughter, then runs full steam ahead into the crowded gym with the team following, mirroring her lead.

Sara complains, "This section of the volleyball warm-up routine looks lame. I think we should move two together, then three, then four, then they can fade off at the left—four, three, two, then one." "Good idea!" says Kelly. The team practices for the next thirty minutes on the new maneuver, which they integrate with the pregame warm-up.

5. Express both affection and hostility appropriately to peers (physical and verbal communication)

Mark waits patiently in line while the coach goes to his car to get the money to pay for the ice cream at the truck. J.T. arrives late and trots up to his friend standing in front of Mark, butting into line. Mark speaks up immediately and matter-of-factly says, "J.T., no cuts." J.T. looks away and pretends he doesn't hear. Mark says a little louder and looks him in the eyes, "J.T., you know there are no cuts allowed on our team." J.T. sheepishly gives a half grin and shrugs his shoulders as he moves to the back of the line.

Just as the whistle blows, Mark bounds into the air waving his arms, runs diagonally with a mock Indian war whoop across the field to bear-hug the forward who just made the last goal. Five, then twelve team members pile on, celebrating in a rolling heap of arms and legs.

6. Compete with peers (interpersonal competition)

The coach tells the kids that they have to run back and forth between the lines, each time going one line farther until the final lap, when they clock in. Kristi moves to the head of the group as usual, but slips on the first turn. She pushes harder during the next three laps to regain her position in the lead.

7. Praise oneself and show pride in one's accomplishments

After winning the team competition again, Kristi plops down in a folding chair with a little self-satisfied smile on her bright red face. One of her friends ruffles her ponytail. "Good job! I almost beat you this time, though." Kristi smiles broadly. Her teammate didn't see her slip and Kristi doesn't mention it—just laughs a good-natured chortle.

8. Get involved in adult role-playing

Michael and the team are hanging out. The coach is late. After lounging around for a few minutes, Michael takes a book (pretend clipboard) from the table, puts on a whistle, then strides to the front of the group. "Okay," he says in a voice imitating the coach's, "today we really have to work on our passing." Someone in the back of the group asks if he means gas passing, to the delight of everyone. Pseudo-coach Michael pretends not to hear. He assigns some kids to go get balls, some to set up nets, some to bring in the water, then tells them to work in pairs for the next ten minutes. The "business" is carried off with assorted waistband adjustments (just like the coach), neck twitches (just like the coach), and crotch readjustments (just for the laughs). Twenty minutes later when the coach arrives, his practice is in full swing and Michael hands over his mock clipboard and whistle with a smug smile.

II. Nonsocial Abilities

1. Language competence (vocabulary, grammar, articulation, and extensive expressed language)

Walter was helping out with the ninth-grade football game of reserves. Having recently been moved into the quarterback position on the junior varsity team, he had received a clipboard along with the assistant coaches and proceeded with their instructions to the team. Quietly standing with his clipboard at his side, he watched over the group while the coaches spoke. Some of the kids were horsing around. Called on it, they "listened up," but had already missed some important information. When they got onto the field, Walter stayed in their vicinity and repeated the plan with elaboration. He translated some instructions into other words. Kids would come and ask questions—"Does the coach mean . . ."—which Walter answered.

2. Intellectual competence

a. Ability to sense dissonance or note discrepancies

Holly listened as the coach explained what the team was supposed to do right after the first at-bat. He told the girls about gathering up their equipment, then started to move on to another subject. Holly raised her hand. She reviewed what he said, then elaborated: "Does this mean that Kim, Christina, and I are supposed to gather the equipment up if we were the last three at-bats, or do you mean the first three in the line-up are supposed to do it?"

b. Ability to anticipate consequences, effects, sequences

Whitney listened as the coach described the next two games before the season end. He explained the other teams' win/loss records, then closed with a spiel for them to play hard and win the next two. Whitney raised her hand and pointed out that if the number-three team beat the number-one team, giving them one more loss than they had, then wouldn't that mean they were number one in the win/loss record? The coach smiled brightly and seemed pleased with this observation for a good five seconds, but then sobered and said, "Yes, but we can't count on them losing, we can only depend on ourselves to give it our best every game."

c. Ability to deal with abstractions (numbers, letters, rules)

The coach explained the rules for playing. If anyone missed practice, they would not start. If anyone didn't follow instructions, they would not play the next quarter. If anyone roughhoused or became a danger to themselves or someone else, they would not play the next game and might even be out for the season. Mary looked concerned. She had missed practice on Wednesday for a doctor's appointment. Did that mean she wouldn't start?

d. Ability to take the perspective of others (how things look to another person, both emotionally and mentally)

The kids lined up for the distribution of the treats. A mom held a large Tupperware container containing many brightly decorated Halloween cupcakes with plastic pumpkins, witches, and ghosts atop. Kimberly, six, noticed a child behind her looking at the box with a sad look. "Don't worry. There are plenty for everyone!"

e. Ability to make interesting associations

Coach suggested to the Pee Wee football team members that they practice running in a wedge. Sam pipes in, "You mean like a piece of pie?" Geoff says, "Sort of, but more like you see the birds in the sky flying south." Paul makes the analogy physical and adds, "More like hammering a triangle of metal into wood to split it. We want to split their defense."

3. Executive abilities

   a. Ability to plan and carry out multistep activities (self-directed activities children set up for themselves)

Sports offer tremendous opportunities to plan and carry out sequenced activities including personal preparation of sports bag, drink, snack, and necessary equipment up through personal-time budgeting and management needed to attend away tournaments while completing necessary schoolwork by deadlines. Not surprisingly, these skills do not emerge full-blown as the child leaves for college. They develop gradually through opportunities to practice, integrate, and juggle increasingly more difficult obligations.

   b. Ability to select and organize material and/or people to solve problems (flexible thinking; recognition of unusual uses of some people or equipment)

Diana, eleven, put the finishing touches on her sport bag as she added the second PowerBar with a flourish. Today, right after school, she had coed football practice. At 4:45, AYSO soccer practice started and went until 6:00, then she had arranged to go to her friend's house to finish their project researching D.C.'s Museum of Science and Technology. She started to zip the bag shut, then went and got one more water bottle from the cupboard and filled it—just in case the team mom forgot to bring their water bottles to soccer.

4. Attention abilities: dual focus (doing two things at once or in rapid alternation; talking while doing something else; monitoring distant events while performing immediate tasks)

Jason, fourteen, kept watching the coach instructing the next older team practicing at the other end of the ice, all the while performing the puck-passing drill in progress. His gaze darted back and forth rapidly, focusing in when it was his turn, then switching to the distant practice as soon as his immediate obligation was completed. The older kids' coach was demonstrating some swift direction-change maneuvers his team had not learned yet, and he was eager to learn.

THE CENTURY AHEAD

As we begin the twenty-first century, it's difficult to have perspective on the cultural and economic changes in progress in athletics. On the positive side, we know that many young American women are gaining athletic and academic stature, but many studies also show that girls are now also smoking, drinking, and using drugs as often as boys. They tell us girls are stressed. Physical aggression among women has been rising for the last three decades, and women's imprisonment has tripled since 1985 to almost sixty thousand, while men's has doubled to a staggering half million. Women's sports are not the cause nor the panacea for these changes, but I believe the self-efficacy sports helps develop can make a crucial difference among those who participate.

"Making the U.S. Olympic hockey team is one of the greatest experiences of my life," said Jenny Schmidgall. At eighteen years of age, she was the second-youngest player to be a part of the 1998 Winter Olympics team. "In eighth grade, I first heard there would be women's hockey in the Olympics. By tenth grade, I dreamed of making the team, and I never stopped believing I could play at that level. Even though I was playing boys' bantams in ninth grade and JV the next year, I couldn't wait to get to the park to play pond hockey. How often? Every day, of course!" (Jack Blatherwick, *Let's Play Hockey,* 1/2/98).

Whether your daughter is a tentative first-timer on the soccer field or, like Jenny Schmidgall, chomping at the bit to compete with the boys' teams and aspiring to the top of the U.S. Olympic competition, the range of needs is wide. Whether your son is struggling in school or, like Wayne Gretzky or Michael Jordan, rising as a gentleman through the ranks of his sport, his range of needs is also wide.

Men and women are both being asked to learn new roles and assume new duties. I see great promise for the future already unfolding. The magazines *Women's Sports & Fitness* and *Sports Illustrated Women/Sport* enjoy increasing popularity, reflecting health-conscious women's interest in current information. Women's Sports Foundation has a Community Action Program (CAP) in seventy-nine communities dedicated to increasing sports and fitness opportunities for all girls and women. You can call toll-free to find out about activities available in your area (800-227-3988). A Title IX sports catalog out of Emeryville, California, arrived at my house last week. Inspired and created by and for women, it features real women like Chris, Dana, and Theresa boating, in-line skating, mountain biking, and coaching lacrosse. Lillian, thirty-seven, is featured in jogging clothes by the ocean. Some of the women wear their wrinkles as proudly as their pregnant tummies in featured maternity pants and shorts.

No one can predict what gender roles will be in the next fifty years, but change is in progress, and Eleanor Maccoby's insights provide much for parents of both sons and daughters to consider:

> Within this framework, wide variation is possible, ranging from an exact division of child-care functions between the two parents, to a strong division of labor in which one parent does most of the child care and the other most of the out-of-home earning of economic support for the family. Our social institutions should be geared to this diversity so as to permit maximum flexibility for families to arrive at the division of child-care responsibilities that best suits their individual circumstances.
>
> There are many reasons to continue to press for greater male involvement with children, but the father role can involve different functions from the mother role while nevertheless being highly important in the lives of children . . .
>
> Most modern Western societies have already adopted a variety of policies aimed at enhancing the ability of working parents to care for children (parental leave; subsidized daycare; child-support payments from noncustodial parents). When properly implemented, these policies help redress the imbalance between mothers and fathers who differ in their investment in child care. It seems to me axiomatic that public investment in such programs is eminently justified, on the grounds that anything that eases the pressures on parents and enables them to foster their children's healthy development will redound to the benefit of society as a whole. In the end there is no reason to expect that men and women will want to make exactly the same choices about the way they invest their time. But there is every reason to work toward equity in power and resources, so as to make each sex's choices as free as possible.
> —Maccoby, *Two Sexes*, 1998, pp. 313–14

Women and men are as complementary as two halves of a circle; change for women necessitates change among men. Embracing change with a positive, flexible attitude is a valuable prescription for lifelong happiness according to the Max Planck Institute. Nurturing our sons and daughters to recognize gender issues and be prepared with a range of responsive adaptive skills increases their chances of succeeding no matter what challenges life puts in their paths.

> **TIP**   **Our sons and daughters deserve equal shots at personal fulfillment.**
>
> Parents should watch out for their own as well as institutional and cultural limitations.

"Big Boys Don't Cry," "Women Are Pussies," "Guys Are Better Than Women"

I think most parents want their daughters and sons to have equal shots at personal fulfillment as they share a culture in transition. Necessarily, some cultural yokes are being cast off, while others are being rewhittled. Certainly the Title IX funds need to be equitably shared, and continued pressure from athletes and parents on institutions to achieve this equity is important.

However, it's also important to set aside stereotypes that limit individuals solely on the basis of gender. A modicum of "toughening up" of young boys works fine for some and might be a good idea for some girls as well. Further, limiting some boys from crying may rob them of their feelings, but limiting some girls may give them a handle on who they can become once their feelings don't give them a daily roller-coaster ride. Ideally, with judgment and care, parents should be able to support children's development as individuals without making decisions based on arbitrary cultural expectations. As dynamic forces dictate, adaptability for both sexes may be the key to making the next century successful.

14

College Scholarships: Academic Success + Athletic Excellence + Balance

Extra energy electrified the air as our throng of parents and spectators moved into the arena. We *knew* recruiters were in the crowd. Big ones! NCAA Division I! Pac 10! Big 10! ECA! Central Collegiate! SEC! WAC! Ivy League, too!

Parents' eyes darted furtively across unknown faces then zeroed in on the telltale signs. Recruiters tend to look a lot alike. They often wear a standard uniform: collared polo shirt with the university logo on the left breast; khakis or dark slacks (only a few wear warm-ups); a soft briefcase (holding important papers); new athletic shoes (Nikes, Reeboks, or Asics, depending on who sponsors their team), but the biggest giveaway is their *presence*.

Recruiting coaches define power in the world of young athletes—and they know it. They've got the money. Full rides: tuition, room and board, and book allowance. Partial rides: free food, shoes, travel, even health coverage. All in the recruiter roulette giveaway sweepstakes.

A recruiting coach may be offering individual young athletes scholarship packages each worth upward of $150,000 over four years, with the added bonus of a B.A. or B.S. degree at the end. For a few athletes, college becomes a springboard to a professional athletic career; for most others, athletics open the door to valuable educational choices. For all athletic scholarship students, playing sports offers a tax-free education and a ticket (albeit with pros and cons) to a bright future.

ATHLETIC SCHOLARSHIPS

Most parents have heard about athletic scholarships, and in polls, as many as 50 percent of parents mention them as a primary motivation for kids' sports participation. I suspect there isn't a parent of a serious young athlete who hasn't had the prospect of a college scholarship dance regularly across his or her imagination—he or she's just too nervous or savvy to talk about it. As college costs have increased 200 to 300 percent in the last fifteen years, many parents feel that jockeying their child into scholarship position is essential.

Reality Check: Only 1 in 190

Many colleges and universities offer scholarships, but the numbers aren't in your favor. Currently, there are about ten thousand scholarships available for women and twenty thousand available for men in the approximately eight hundred NCAA Division I and II schools. Division III schools, including some of the most prestigious Ivies, do not offer athletic scholarships. When the statistics were compiled by a group of *Los Angeles Times* staff writers in 1995, with 3.5 million boys and 2.2 million girls playing high school sports, the chance of one kid getting one of these NCAA Division I or II college scholarships comes out to about 1 in 190.

TIP   The chance of a young athlete getting a collegiate scholarship is about 1 in 190.

Luckily, in addition to the NCAA, there are two other associations in charge of scholarships for young athletes, the National Association of Intercollegiate Athletics (NAIA) and the National Junior College Athletic Association (NJCAA). All of the organizations work on behalf of student athletes and institutions to assure professional recruiting methods and equitable distribution of scholarship funds to student athletes. The total athletic scholarships including additional sources at non-NCAA institutions improves an individual athlete's chances modestly, and as you will see later in the chapter, a range of athletic talents can receive scholarship support.

Playing the Odds

Many parents want to know how to increase their child's chances of being one of the successful scholarship winners. There are a number of books on the subject. Most give some guidelines and outline the minimum requirements for eligibility. Most also provide cross-listings by sport and school, with coaches' names, phone numbers, and addresses. Association phone numbers as well as conferences' main offices are handy references as well. Nothing will replace the time you and your young athlete put into exploring the different alternatives. The best guidebooks provide you with information about colleges and universities you may not have considered before. The few well-known bumper-sticker schools for any sport get inundated by interested kids and their parents, but a range of excellent but lesser-known institutions are available and deserve consideration. A good match between your kid's academic interests, athletic talents, personal aspirations, and school's offerings becomes more likely with more options. The guidelines presented here are just a beginning.

WHAT IT TAKES TO GET A SCHOLARSHIP

Athletic Skills

Cream of the Crop
Across the nation, at the top of every sport, a thin cream of the athletic crop gets the attention of the recruiters early on. The best kids in each sport may be identified as young as thirteen to fifteen, and in some sports, it's even younger. Competition at the national level is fierce.

If your kid is one of this small elite group in his or her sport, you probably already know it. Recruiters start knocking on doors and schmoozing the parents as soon as they can. Bushels of college announcements, brochures, and entreating personal letters from college coaches start arriving sometime during the kid's sophomore year of high school. For yucks, some coaches even send letters of interest to newborn sons and daughters of gifted athletes, just to be the first recruiting foot in the door.

Although recruiting rules vary from year to year, currently coaches may not speak to a young athlete until after July 1 preceding their sophomore year of high school. After July 1 preceding their junior year, coaches may send only one letter to which the young athlete may respond. E-mail correspondence during that year is unlimited, as are contacts by currently enrolled student-athletes, but phone calls and personal visits are forbidden. After July 1 preceding the kid's senior year, a coach may contact and give a National Letter of Intent to athletes of his or her scholarship choice. The purpose behind this limitation is to restrict inundation of young athletes. The NCAA has a forty-three-page single-spaced section of its 1998–1999 manual devoted to recruiting principles and rules. Check with your club coach, high school coach, and/or the NCAA (800-545-5201) to learn the specific rules for your kid's sport; violations can mean losing eligibility—for both your kid and the recruiting program.

The Next Tier

Just below the handful of cream-of-the-crop athletes rests a small pool of excellent athletic talent. Most of these kids participate in national competitions and have tremendous success at the regional level. College coaches know kids from this pool will likely succeed quickly at the college level and are always eager to take a look at kids with this competitive experience.

At this level, club coaches or trainers often write to the college coach about the interested athlete, but families and the young athlete themselves are encouraged to take the initiative as well. Most coaches are happy to learn about a young athlete who has a strong interest in their school. Recruiting can be a very depressing process, with numerous athletes ignoring early bids from all but the biggest school names, so the kid with a clearly identified choice reduces the coach's uncertainty and increases the chances that his or her recruiting efforts will be rewarded.

Great Local Young Athletes

These kids may enjoy recognition on the state level and have tremendous local success in their sport. College recruiters love to learn about them and eagerly accept letters from current coaches, parents, and especially the young athletes themselves. When a youngster and his or her family are truly interested in a particular school or conference, contacting the coach sooner than later is a really good idea. While there are rigid restrictions on coaches and programs, young athletes may initiate contact freely as early as freshman year. Let manners, respect, and common sense be your guidelines. Find out what the coaches would like to see and follow through. Sometimes a good-quality video, even one Grandpa made, may be okay. Taking your kid on a personal visit to a school and adding a moment to drop by the athletic department can give your kid an advantage. Not only does your kid get to know the school better, but the face-to-face contact helps the coach remember your kid's profile better. *Always* remember to send notes of thanks for a coach's time.

In reality, many of the college scholarships end up going to the local young athletic heroes and heroines. The competition for the funding is still tough, and consideration includes a range of factors, not the least of which are grades and personality.

Academic Preparation and Grades

The primary purpose of attending college is to get an education. Sometimes, parents of young athletes get so caught up in recruiting and playing sports that they seem to forget the fundamental value of a college education. The foundation of a good education requires past educational experiences, motivation, and evidence of academic competence. If your youngster doesn't have these things in place, the pursuit of a scholarship, much less higher education, is really pointless.

Athletes who want to play for a NCAA Division I or II school should register with the NCAA Eligibility Clearinghouse. The standards set out for athletes' initial eligibility were designed to increase the chances of success in college for recruited athletes through a combination of rigorous core curriculum classes and GPA, cofactored with the ACT or SAT scores. Minimum requirements are: high school graduation; a grade point average of at least 2.0 (on a 4.0 scale); and a sum of at least 68 on the ACT or combined score of 820 on the SAT. Early registration is encouraged, ideally as soon as your kid decides he or she wants to play in college, but not before the junior-year grades are on their official high school transcript. Registration gives the recruiters important information for making recruiting decisions.

Simply put, coaches don't have time to waste on a youngster who cannot make it into their school. The clearinghouse decreases the chances of disappointing a young athlete and his or her family down the road. To register, simply call the NCAA Clearinghouse and request a copy of the registration materials or obtain copies from the high school counselor. The NCAA Clearinghouse phone number is (319) 337-1492.

The NCAA registration package will include:

1. Brochure from the NCAA
2. Request for $18.00 registration fee (unless waived) before September 1 of freshman college year, or, $25.00 registration fee after September 1 of freshman college year
3. Student release form
4. Transcript request: Athletes need to give it to their school registrar. It will need the high school's official seal. Most high school transcripts include official SAT/ACT test scores. If yours does not, arrange to have the scores sent to the NCAA Clearinghouse. Pink and yellow copies of the student release form go to the graduating high school and a copy of the student release form to the schools of interest.

The standards for Division I schools are the toughest, with Division II schools next, and so on down the line. Notably, many students qualify for the NCAA I and II schools but choose to play in NAIA and NJCAA schools. Financial aid may be offered to individuals enrolling in NCAA Division III schools, but will be based solely on financial need and not as a function of athletic performance.

NCAA Division I
Most high school counselors are aware of the NCAA core curriculum and GPA/SAT/ACT requirements, but parents should double-check with the schools and their kids. If any questions arise about curriculum content and grade eligibility, better to learn about them early and fill in any deficits before it's too late.
Core curriculum for Division I:

• High school graduation
• Completed basic curriculum including thirteen academic courses:
     four years of English
     two years of math (algebra and geometry, or one year of higher level math with geometry as a prerequisite)
     two years of social science
     two years of natural or physical science (including one lab class if available)
     one additional course from above
     two additional academic courses (any of the above plus language, computer science, or philosophy)

GPA Cofactored with the SAT or ACT Score
(Qualifier Index) for Division I NCAA Schools

Core GPA	SAT Score (Verbal + Math)	ACT Score
2.5 and above	820	68
2.475	830	69
2.45	840–850	70
2.425	860	71
2	860	72
2.375	870	73
2.35	880	74
2.325	890	75
2.3	900	76
2.275	910	77
2.25	920	78
2.2	930	79
2.175	940	80
2.15	950	80
2.125	960	81
2.1	970	82
2.075	980	83
2.05	990	84
2.025	1000	85
2	1010	86

NCAA Division II

The qualifier checklist for a Division II school includes a dual curriculum and standardized test score, but the standards for the Division II are modestly lighter, including:

- Completed basic curriculum with thirteen academic courses
    three years of English
    two years of math
    two years of social science
    two years of natural or physical science (including one lab class if available)
    two additional courses from the above
    two additional academic courses (any of the above plus language, computer science, or philosophy)

- Combined score on the SAT verbal and math section of 820 (recentered scores) or a 68 on the ACT.

Are the GPA/SAT/ACT Combinations Fair?

Parents, student athletes, even college coaches have been known to debate the utility of the standards as set forth by the NCAA Division I and II. In fact, the ability of standardized tests such as the SAT and ACT to reflect and predict a student's functional ability accurately has been hotly debated in educational circles for nearly three decades. Research shows that a student's SAT scores explain only 16 to 25 percent of how college freshman grades turn out. A lot more goes into getting good grades as a college freshman than the SAT can account for. Particularly for ethnic minority students, bilingual, and culturally different students and all kids who worry about their score, the SAT emerges as a limited tool for predicting future classroom performance. A kid who wants to do well, has social skills to optimally utilize the school's resources, and works hard has a great chance of succeeding at anything, including college.

At the present time, as the NCAA and educational institutions struggle to discover fair, simple methods of sorting applicants, the SAT remains the standard test of choice. For a variety of reasons, some students tend to score higher on the ACT; thus, taking both tests increases an athlete's chances of getting the target score. If your young athlete typically performs in the bottom tenth of the population on standardized, multiple choice tests like the SAT, get your kid additional SAT/ACT tutorial support. Courses, books, computer programs, even specialized tutors can all enhance a student's performance. Until something better comes along, parents are advised to work around the SAT hurdle. The same practical approach applies to grades. When your child's grades fluctuate or fall below the desirable level, encourage your child to get help from the teachers of the problem subjects or utilize the support services at your school. Although specific subject tutors can be helpful, the cost can be high and the benefit only as good as the tutor.

Personality

On top of a youngster's athletic performance level, academic skills, high school grades, and SAT/ACT scores, the final leg of scholarship determination is personality. Coaches like nice, positive, coachable kids. When coaches are in a position to select from a range of talent and scores, a positive personality is invaluable. From observation, the most heavily recruited scholarship recipients are almost always great kids. Many a fine young athlete, however, no matter how great his or her grades or SAT/ACT profiles, will be overlooked if there is a substantiated hint of attitude.

Coaches don't need hot shots. Coaches don't want to fund ego trips. Coaches don't even want to chat with a kid who is rumored to be a troublemaker on a team. A coach has to spend three hours a day in practice for the next four years with the kid. Game days and travel time, plus team recreation, all add to that tally. The last thing *any* coach in his or her right mind would do is fund a brat for four years.

TIP   **Coaches recruit nice kids.**

Many parents, impressed with their kid's supposed amazing physical talent, have permitted their family "star" to get away with prima donna behavior. Some families even confess they have provided the red carpet treatment at home. Shame on you, Mom and Dad. A coach has no such need. Remember, a coach has no blinders, and with a team of kids, one brat can be a nightmare. When push comes to shove, nice kids get the invites hands down. Simply put, your child needs manners. For guidelines, check out Burton White's social competency list with sport story applications in chapter 13.

COLLEGE RECRUITING

Watching recruiters watch young athletes can be educational for parents. I have been at a number of national tournament sites where recruiters were making the rounds. At lower competition levels, I am amazed at the number of coaches who come in to watch the warm-ups, but leave a few minutes after play begins. A few will stay longer, but most believe they are quite capable of making a quick, solid judgment, then moving on. Each coach watches for characteristic movements and somehow—within a sport—a shared recognition of excellence emerges. Of course, individuals have special qualities they seek, but many recruiters *see* many of the same things, and most seem to agree about certain athletic habits that "can easily be fixed" and others that serve as an athletic death sentence. Some youngsters never get a second look and others catch coaches' eyes immediately.

Are Club Programs Necessary?

In the competitive arena of youth athletics, it's not surprising that many parents wonder about the importance of playing club. In a 1997 special report to the *Los Angeles Times* on the race for scholarships, *Times* staff writers interviewed UCLA women's basketball coach Pam Walker. Walker noted, "When I was a high school coach, I didn't want to admit [what a big role club coaches play]. But now that I am on the other side, I have to admit [club teams] are a necessary evil. I would say 90 percent of recruiting is done during the summer."

In light of the NCAA's special recruiting limits to protect young athletes during the school year, school season for all sports falls in the dead period of junior year. According to the NCAA rules, however, the month of July is open and, as such, is a time for many club tournaments and national competitions where college coaches make it a point to check out new talent. Moreover, good high school teams may have one top-notch player, but club teams pull together several excellent kids. When club teams compete against one another, coaches can review a fair portion of the top talent in the nation in just a couple of days at the annual junior national championships. AAU events for women include the annual girls' basketball national competition and the annual soccer national championships, to name only a few. Women's volleyball has tournaments at U.C. Davis every summer and junior nationals held the week before the men's volleyball junior nationals at various sites around the nation. Boys' basketball has a number of tournaments, as do most of the individual sports, including tennis and golf. Even the rifle association has a junior national championship competition.

Lisa Love, USC women's volleyball coach, confirms that "the majority of national recruiting is done at the club level." Many families in many sports feel the year-around exposure is essential to earn a college scholarship.

Many parents brand the club fees as money well spent—*after* receiving the scholarship for the full ride to college—but most parents know it's a gamble at best. Club participation does not lock up a scholarship, it just gives your child a better chance. Almost all parents know that the large majority of club players receive no scholarship, but they make the effort anyway.

Summer Camps

Many universities offer summer camps for different sports run by the coach or program director interested in recruiting young athletes. The camps are often staffed by aspiring coaches and by scholarship athletes currently enrolled in the program. The camps offer special skills training for the youngsters, but, more importantly, they provide a terrific way for the recruiting coaches to get a look at talent coming down the pike. Not only does attendance at the camp indicate parents' interest in the university's program, but parents pay for the opportunity to have their kid see and be seen by the program. Not surprisingly, the camps often concentrate on the prime ages for identifying early talent in the sport. Savvy parents often swap the names of hot camps and get the applications going by mid-April. Many of the top programs have full camps by the start of May.

Personal Coaching

When kids enroll in a school or club program, each child can receive only a small proportion of the coaching staff's attention. As the season progresses, dynamics and team needs may leave a kid with floundering skills losing a starting line-up position. Smart parents who have been around for a while often see the problem in the making. Enter the personal trainer or specialty coach who works one-on-one with the young athlete and can often zero in on the skill in trouble. Over a series of sessions (sometimes as much as fifty dollars per half-hour lesson), the skill starts to take shape again.

Personal coaching is becoming big business. Former minor league baseball player Nez Balelo and high school coach Bryan Maloney purchased the West Coast Baseball School in 1988. In ten years' time, the school has expanded to six locations with twenty-two instructors and a clientele of more than one thousand young baseball players annually. The individualized attention can move a young athlete's skill up a notch. A sharp-eyed specialty coach can quickly diagnose and set about remediating a sloppy habit or poor technique. When the next school or club season rolls around, the young athlete has an extra measure of spit and polish on his or her play that gives them a sparkling competitive edge.

Internet Recruiting

There are currently three major on-line data collection agencies: On-line Scouting, All-Sport Recruiting, and SportsPiks. Each relies on whoever enters the information to be accurate and fair. NCAA Divisions II and III, the NAIA, and the NJCAA are most likely to use the Internet resources. Only the nonrevenue sports in Division I take advantage of the information, and women's sports are more likely to do searches as well. Title IX may be at work here, as schools eager to comply with NCAA equitable distribution rules hunt for viable women recipients of their available scholarship money.

Bill Rassmussen, founder of ESPN, launched SportsPiks, the newest on-line database service, in the fall of 1996. His goal was to help high school athletes and college recruiters get together. Through the database hook-ups, 2,400 programs at 1,800 colleges can access a youngster's personal profile for as little as thirty to fifty dollars per athlete. Kids can learn who has accessed their profiles, and coaches can contact the young athletes via e-mail. Profiles can be updated through the course of the registered year, and young athletes can initiate contact with coaches who have inspected their information.

Professional Recruiting Services

Many sports have a seen a handful of self-designated professional recruiting services emerge in the last decade. For a modest fee, the service scouts the talent in an area, compiles an information sheet, then sends the information to colleges. Fees for athletes range from $200 up to $1,800, including a video with a kid's personal greeting filmed at their home gym or field, then duplicated and mailed to prospective athletic programs with scholarship opportunities.

As with the on-line registration, validity of the information is the issue for most colleges. Realistically, a paid recruiting service cannot push all of its young clients as equally skilled and equally likely to succeed at the college level. While some athletes and their families have been pleased, especially those without the resources to travel from one coast to the other making personal school visits, many lament the cost and the fact that they didn't take advantage of the service adequately. As with all these opportunities, the overarching message must be *caveat emptor.*

BIG MONEY IN ATHLETICS

At some private universities, the tuition, fees, and books average out to $33,000 per athlete per year. According to statistics compiled by the Women's Sports Foundation, at many private universities, Division I-A football potentially controls as much as $2,805,000 across eighty-five possible annual scholarships. Division I-A men's basketball at these same private institutions runs as much as $429,000, with thirteen scholarships plus expenses annually. State university coaches, with reduced tuition costs, average about half the annual value in scholarship sums, a still substantial $1.5 million for football and quarter of a million dollars for basketball, with comparably large expense budgets at both private and public institutions. Football and men's basketball coaches are rumored to be the power lords in most university athletic departments—biggest offices, best facilities, newest equipment, fattest slice of the athletic pie.

Total university athletic budgets can be very high—staggering in fact. Based on a survey of 767 NCAA Division I–III schools in 1995–96 compiled by the Women's Sports Foundation, scholarships that year totaled more than $566 million and operating expenditures exceeded $556 million, for a combined total of $1.122 billion flowing through the participating athletic departments.

Financial Aid Awards

There are three major associations that oversee college athletic awards:

1. National Collegiate Athletic Association (NCAA)
     Division I-A (usually schools with major football and basketball programs)
     Division I-AA (schools usually have major basketball but smaller football programs)

Division I-AAA (schools that have major basketball but no
football programs)
Division II
Division III
2. National Association of Intercollegiate Athletics (NAIA)
3. National Junior College Athletic Association (NJCAA)

NCAA

The NCAA, best known and largest of the three associations, commands the biggest numbers. It takes a 500-page manual for Division I and
additional ones for Division II and III to specify and define regulations and
laws guiding actions and spending within each institution. In the NCAA,
financial support for different sports is based on two criteria: *head count*
and *equivalencies*. Head count literally is the number of students receiving financial support. Head count sports include football (Div. I-A, Div. I-
AA), men's basketball, ice hockey, and women's basketball, gymnastics,
tennis, and volleyball.

The head count method limits a school's chance to "stack" one team
with, say, forty scholarship gymnasts compared to most other schools'
twelve. A stacked school would win all the competition between schools,
thus the head count rule. Equivalency sports let athletic departments
hand out, for example, 12.6 lacrosse scholarships to men. The department
can give all 12 to twelve different players with one 0.6 funded player or
give twenty-four players half scholarships and one athlete a 1.6 remainder
to total the 12.6 equivalency.

HEAD COUNT SPORTS

Each student athlete receiving aid, independent of dollar amount, is
tabulated as one *counter*. Head count sports include:

- Division I-A football—Annual limit of eighty-five players during
  academic year, with a yearly limit of twenty-five *initial counters*
  (athletes registering for the first time at an institution). By limiting
  both the number of scholarships and initial counters (Div. I football
  only), an institution is restricted and can bring in no more than
  twenty-five new scholarship athletes in one season.
- Division I-AA football—Annual limit of eighty-five counters with
  thirty initial counters during the 1999–2000 year, with financial aid
  awards (*equivalencies*) limited to sixty-three.

- Men's basketball—twelve counters
- Men's ice hockey—annual limit of thirty counters and eighteen financial equivalencies
- Women's basketball—fifteen counters
- Women's gymnastics—twelve counters
- Women's tennis—eight counters
- Women's volleyball—twelve counters

EQUIVALENCY SPORTS

• Division I Men's Sports	Total number of scholarships permitted per school
Baseball	11.7
Cross-country/track	12.6
Fencing	4.5
Golf	4.5
Gymnastics	6.3
Ice hockey	18.0
Lacrosse	12.6
Rifle	3.6
Skiing	6.3
Soccer	9.9
Swimming	9.9
Tennis	4.5
Volleyball	4.5
Water polo	4.5
Wrestling	9.9

• Division I Women's Sports	
Archery	5.0
Badminton	6.0
Bowling	5.0
Crew	20.0
Cross-country/track	18.0
Fencing	5.0
Field hockey	12.0
Golf	6.0
Ice hockey	18.0
Lacrosse	12.0
Skiing	7.0
Soccer	12.0
Softball	12.0
Squash	5.0
Swimming	14.0

Synchronized swimming	5.0
Team handball	10.0
Water polo	8.0

• Division II Men's Sports

Baseball	9.0
Basketball	10.0
Cross-country/track	12.6
Fencing	4.5
Golf	3.6
Gymnastics	5.4
Ice hockey	13.5
Lacrosse	10.8
Rifle	3.6
Skiing	6.3
Soccer	9.0
Swimming	8.1
Tennis	4.5
Volleyball	4.5
Water polo	4.5
Wrestling	9.0

• Division II Women's Sports

Archery	5.0
Badminton	8.0
Basketball	10.0
Bowling	5.0
Crew	20.0
Cross-country/track	12.6
Fencing	4.5
Field hockey	6.3
Golf	5.4
Gymnastics	6.0
Ice hockey	18.0
Lacrosse	9.9
Skiing	6.3
Soccer	9.9
Softball	7.2
Squash	9.0
Swimming	8.1
Synchronized swimming	5.0
Team handball	12.0
Tennis	6.0

Volleyball	8.0
Water polo	8.0

Through the combination of head counters and equivalencies, the NCAA has attempted to equalize the funding for men and women to assist schools in their efforts to comply with Title IX. The numbers are challenging to work out because of the heavy manpower (no pun intended) required in football. There just isn't an equivalent women's sport with those kinds of numbers; thus, at schools with football teams, the other men's sports typically have relatively fewer scholarships than women's in the same sport. By my best calculations at the Division I level, there are still about 11.3 more scholarships for men than women, and the system permits much greater funding for men, again greasing football's appetite. Bottom line: men get a bigger share of the pie. If you are concerned about inadequate Title IX enforcement, write to the Office of Civil Rights:

> Norma Cantu, Director
> Office for Civil Rights, U.S. Dept. of Education
> 330 C Street, SW
> Room 5000
> Washington DC 20202

The Women's Sports Foundation has a sample letter at its Web site, http://www.WomensSportsFoundation.org.

NAIA

According to Darren David at the National Association of Intercollegiate Athletics, NAIA includes schools from the American Mideast, American Midwest, California Pacific, Cascade, Central Atlantic, Chicagoland Collegiate, Eastern Intercollegiate, Florida Sun, Frontier, Georgia Athletic, Golden State, Gulf Coast, Heart of America, Heart of Texas, Kansas Collegiate, Kentucky Intercollegiate, Keystone-Empire, Main Athletic, Mayflower, Mid-Central, Mid-South, Midlands Collegiate, Midwest Classic, Nebraska-Iowa Athletic, North Dakota, Red River, Sooner, South Dakota-Iowa, Tennessee-Virginia, Tran South, Upper Midwest, and Wolverine-Hoosier.

As with the NCAA, there are upper limits for athletic aid, specifically capping money not to exceed the cost of tuition, mandatory fees, books and supplies, and room and board. For schools with in-state and out-of-state tuition, the extra dollar amount is added to the overall aid limit. All institutionally managed or controlled financial aid, exclusive of Pell grants, state grants, SEO grants, and loans not controlled by the institution, is subject to the regulation. The total cost of the education in dollar amounts is used to determine the total financial aid per sport with number limits per sport, including:

Sport	Scholarships
Baseball	12
Basketball (Div. I)	11
Basketball (Div. II)	6
Cross country	5
Football	33
Golf	5
Soccer	12
Softball	10
Swimming/diving	8
Tennis	5
Track and Field	12
Volleyball	8
Wrestling	8

NJCAA

The National Junior College Athletic Association (NJCAA) also has a supervisory program to regulate scholarships per sport per season:

Sport	Scholarships
Men's/women's cross-country	30
Men's/women's cross-country (Div. II)	30 (tuition, fees, and books)
Men's spring baseball (Div. I)	24
Men's spring baseball (Div. II)	24 (tuition, fees, and books)
Men's basketball	16
Men's basketball (Div. II)	16 (tuition, fees, and books)
Women's basketball	16
Men's/women's bowling	8
Women's field hockey	18
Football	85
Men's golf (Div. I)	8

Men's golf (Div. II)	8 (tuition, fees, and books)
Men's ice hockey	16
Men's lacrosse	14
Marathon	30
Men's soccer	18
Women's soccer	18
Women's fast-pitch softball	20
Women's slow-pitch softball	20
Men's/women's swimming	15
Men's tennis (Div. II)	9 (tuition, fees, and books)
Women's tennis (Div. II)	8 (tuition, fees, and books)
Indoor track and field	30
Outdoor track and field	30
Women's volleyball	14
Men's wrestling	16

PROS AND CONS OF GETTING AN ATHLETIC SCHOLARSHIP

A college scholarship brings obvious financial rewards, honor, and the clear status as a valued athlete. In terms of the dollar amount, a freshman athlete at a private university actually garners a comparable amount to a player on the WNBA in 1999. Although most parents are quick to recognize the obvious advantages of a scholarship, few actually have a clear understanding of what it means for their child. There are four things you might consider before pushing your child down the scholarship route.

TIP There are pros and cons to college athletic scholarships. It's a job. The job has pressure. Athletics limit other college life opportunities. It's a job that can be lost. After college, what?

First, becoming a scholarship athlete is identical to having a job. Moreover, for many sports, it's a *year-round* job. Preseason, season, postseason often include twelve months of workouts, weight training, and conditioning. On a daily basis, sports usually require two to three hours of work. Even if it's the start of finals week, team obligations come first. Classes must be scheduled around the team practice times, and a host of extracurricular school events must be passed by as the young athlete attends to the demands of his or her "job."

During the sport's competitive season, the time demands usually double or more. Game days are a complete black-out. Pre-game meetings, pre-game meal, warm-up, game play, post-game debrief, and early lights-out are mandatory. If it is an away tournament, add two travel days, one on each side of the competition. Most students must notify their faculty of missed classes for the purposes of athletic competition and then make arrangements to get the notes and materials. (Note, not all note takers are created equal, and a substantial proportion of academic information simply cannot be recaptured even with a professional note taker. Even tape-recorded lectures miss the writing on the board, overheads, and visual demonstrations. Naturally, student performance on examinations suffers, as do grades.)

Second, the programs and coaches granting scholarships have invested their time and professional reputations in having a successful program. They want to win. Their personal future often depends on fielding the most competitive team for the college or university, and that means the social niceties of "everyone plays" and "let's make sure everyone feels good about themselves" no longer have much of a place. Players at the collegiate level need to have professional attitudes and excellent personal adjustment to the professional standards needed for optimal team performance. The kids who play have a big responsibility and the kids who don't do, too. All contribute to the team morale and a disgruntled bench drains needed team energy. Two clever coaches honor the nonstarters, calling them the "machine team" and credit them for playing hard and keeping the starters on their toes.

Third, the heavy athletic constraints on students' lives substantially affect their college experience. Some majors cannot be chosen (afternoon hard science labs conflict with afternoon team practices). Some programs cannot be attended (overseas foreign study programs take players away during the season). Some intellectual opportunities of the university environment—speakers, concerts, plays, political debates, even other sports events—will be forever missed.

Fourth, when scholarships are awarded, they are usually given on an annual renewable basis. There are no four-year guarantees. If an athlete is injured, loses favor with the coach, or develops personal problems compromising his or her ability to contribute to the team, they may very well lose their scholarship. Student athletes need to earn their keep, day after day, week after week, scholarship year after scholarship year.

We know from other research that holding down part-time jobs usually compromises GPAs as well as available personal leisure time. Phoooey on leisure, think many parents, but I heartily disagree. Students need a balance in their lives. Many young athletes find themselves working from dawn to dawn with few breaks. Not uncommonly, sleep hours are sacrificed as youngsters struggle to maintain personal performance standards in their sport *and* in their classes. Often, there are just not enough hours to go around. In the end, many funded athletes end up fulfilling their team responsibilities first, and academic responsibilities get deferred as long as possible. Sometimes, kids just run out of time.

Most college athletes feel that their overall GPA could have been better were it not for the year-around athletic time demands. Hardly a modest worry. When it comes time to apply to graduate, professional, law, or medical school, the graduate programs may give a tiny bonus to the athlete's possibly diminished GPA, but it is not a bankable boost. Grades, standardized test scores, work experience, and recommendations from faculty are going to count for them just as everyone else.

SILVER LININGS TO THE SCHOLARSHIP AND UNSCHOLARSHIPED CLOUDS

With the numbers of kids playing sports in high school, it should be evident that most youngsters do not go on to play competitively at the collegiate level. Most kids discover other paths and other activities competing for their time, but the time invested in sports was not wasted. Not only did your child learn valuable lessons, build self-efficacy, and perfect personal discipline, the hours you and your child spent sharing sports time has yielded treasured memories to last a lifetime.

If the anticipated college recruiting doesn't emerge or if your child makes it clear he or she isn't interested in playing in college, parents and kids alike should feel gratified in knowing that sports participation strengthened their college application anyway. Sports participation provides a lot for a young kid's development, and college admissions committees look very favorably on high school applicants whose past record reflects time invested in athletics. Busy high school kids with good grades are likely to become busy, successful college students.

As parents who have had children win scholarships to colleges and prestigious universities know, there is a tremendous sense of satisfaction and personal accomplishment that comes from earning valuable honor through scholarship recognition. The glory is not without a cost. As you pore over the information and try to help your child sort out possible alternatives, it may be somewhat reassuring to realize that continued athletic participation does not have to end with a yea or nay scholarship bid.

TIP For the 189 unscholarshiped kids out of 190, sports participation can still go on! Walking on, intramurals, open gym, rec facilities, personal work-outs, pick-up games, and being active just for fun can last a life-time.

Walking On

Admitted students have the possibility of "walking on" to the college's team. While walk-ons receive no tuition, room/board, or fees, they do have the chance to continue to play. Many walk-ons receive an array of special opportunities including free food, free travel, free shoes, and free uniforms. Down the road, some walk-ons eventually earn a funded scholarship through their consistent dedication and contribution to the team, but don't count on it. The chance to play should be the primary motivation.

Intramurals

All universities and colleges have thriving intramural programs. Adaptable to the student's academic schedule, the competition can provide fun recreation without seriously denting the academic work.

Open Gym and Workout Facilities

Most colleges and universities also have workout facilities, training rooms, and open gym time, which provide additional flexible playing and exercise opportunities. Beautiful gymnasiums set up for basketball and volleyball; squash, handball, and racquetball courts; weight rooms with people on staff to assist; and some of the latest specialty workout machines are available on many college and university campuses. Best of all, use of these facilities is free, included as a part of your son's or daughter's student registration.

With the many organized and nonorganized sports paths available, and with lifelong health the ultimate goal, help your young athlete keep the big picture in mind and make good decisions, not the least of which is maintaining healthy, active habits with or without the time demands and the pressures of scholarship athletic participation.

15

Fun, Perspective, and Other Mysteries

Long ago, I learned that my personal tendencies toward voyeurism and my deep longings to be a fly on the wall could both be well served as either a psychologist or a car pool driver. I've been amazed how much I've learned as a chauffeur. Fact of the matter is, I love listening to kids, and the things they have to teach are immeasurably enriching. Now, if nature has given me any gifts, it may be my two very big ears. I am working on learning how to turn them backward, like donkeys and horses can, to better collect sound, but for now, I must rely on highly motivated listening.

Here is one of the first and last secrets I want to share. Driving car pool is tremendous fun. Kids make me laugh. Their wonderful, fresh-hatched, wet, wobbly, and wise views of our often silly world refresh my love of life. I have no hard scientific data to support this, but the kids and teams who survive athletics and thrive seem to share one special attribute—a tremendous a sense of humor, about themselves, with one another, and with life in general.

One of kids' favorite pastimes from junior high on is roasting their parents. Most of us know we are a half a bubble off from our kids' world, but those of you who don't realize this basic fact of life provide some of the best fodder for their cannons. Here is an sample of parent-roasting conversations I've overheard from the driver's seat:

I always know where my mom is in the crowd. Just as I go up to shoot the free throw I hear her out in the bleachers [he feigns an instant Mama-imitation-falsetto, covers his eyes with his hands]: "OH NO! Heeee's going to miiiiiss!

—High school sophomore, basketball player

Did you guys see my dad standing on the side when the ref made that call? He got bright red and started hopping up and down on one foot. Hop, hop, hop. With his potbelly jiggling, he looked like Rumplestiltskin. I thought I was going to bust a gut laughing at him.

—Sixth-grade basketball player

You know, I like this all-day tournament gig. I never get this much attention at home. First, my dad goes and gets two In-and-Out Burgers for me, then my mom starts worrying if I'm thirsty. I say, "Yeah!" so my mom runs out to the car, gets the Gatorade powder, fills the bottle with powder and drinking fountain water, and I can see her over by the wall shaking it like a mariachi bandleader. Bet she hasn't moved that fast since high school. Then she sends my little sister over with the newly made Gatorade bottle . . . so I just kept drinking it and sending Sis back for another refill, again and again. It cracked me up to have the two of them on the Gatorade merry-go-round and my little sister all buzzing and acting so important. After, Mark said he thought a real Clydesdale was in the men's locker room john. I peed like Niagara Falls . . . and I couldn't stop laughing.

—High school junior, two-sport athlete

Coaches also come in for their share of roasting. The irony here is that the kids often seem to enjoy scorching the coaches they love the most. Of course, kids roast one another, often making astute and occasionally painful observations. Within the context of a team, many kids learn to take and dish out a bit of roasting. In my observations, this round-robin humor rarely becomes inappropriately hurtful, but the potential is there. The usual plan is to retell stories at someone's expense, role-play the main character's starring role with exaggeration, and bring everyone to belly laughs within minutes. Ironically, some personal lessons seem to be taught to one another in this good-humored, "we're all in this together" way. Joking can be used to pull some kids back in from the extremes of behavior. Through roasting, a tight, cohesive social group emerges, learning from one another how to do better and feel better. The kids who join in poking fun at themselves—imitating their own errors—often have an extra shot at popularity through their ability to see themselves as others see them. The self-roasters seem to ease tensions by laughing at their own errors and getting on with the game.

OOOPS, WRONG BASKET

It was sixth-grade basketball at a very small private school, mostly renowned for its brains rather than athletic prowess. We are not talking NBA. We are talking hairless, mostly prepubertal players. In the beginning, the team with more library types than jocks would get onto the court and simply get their athletic behinds kicked.

Well, for once, the small troop of well-worn warriors was *ahead* on the scoreboard. They all were deliriously happy, and the coach put in a particularly beloved classmate for the last few minutes. Josh looked thrilled just to be in the game, so when the ball came squarely into his hands, he grinned like someone had just given him the best birthday present in the world. From the corner of his eye, he spotted the wide-open basket, pivoted, and took off dribbling, careful not to travel, gloriously arrived, and made a (relatively) smooth lay-up shot. He turned, arms raised to his team, the crowd smiling broadly.

He seemed to take us all in—standing mouths agape—as momentary confusion registered on his face. A kid from the other end of the court gently broke the news: "Wrong basket, Josh!"

His eyebrows shot up, but the grin never left his eyes as his mouth rounded out in consternation. "Oh, I'm sorry, guys!" He pantomimed his basket-making shot again, then said in mock horror, "Wrong basket!?" With aplomb far beyond his years, genuinely sorry, he loped back sheepishly to his teammates, who were eagerly awaiting to award high fives anyway. One of the guys found the whole scene so funny, he was weak-kneed on the court, laughing so hard they had to hold play for two minutes. All the while the worn warriors celebrated the beauty of Josh's basket, and Josh thrice re-enacted his glorious shot to everyone's redoubled laughter.

> —Shari Kuchenbecker, spectating mom hat,
> observing Josh Bauer and the Mirman School basketball team, 1993

I get a kick when laughter erupts from a player or a coach spontaneously celebrating an unexpected silly moment. I love to watch the spread of smiles on kids' faces. The awkward shimmy of a normally skilled athlete looking looser than a hula dancer in the back of a '57 Chevy can be acted and re-enacted for everyone's delight. The macho kid taking a big swing at a ball, only to see the jackhammer swing transformed into an air waffle, becomes a great joke, if the kid thinks to work the angle or good-naturedly lets someone work it for him.

TIP   Savvy kids celebrate fun and savvy parents do, too.

SAVVY KIDS SPONTANEOUSLY CELEBRATE FUN

One year, I walked into a junior national championship five-day tourna-ment flowing with the crowd of mostly six-foot, two-inch plus guys and their similarly double extra large tall parents to see a team of spiky-haired guys going the other way down the escalator. One had turquoise blue hair, another pumpkin orange, one Barbie pink, and two banana yellow. A skunk-striped fellow and his rainbow-haired companion brought up the rear. I never did watch the Skittles (as my thirteen-year-old daughter dubbed them) play a game; watching them live was fun enough. They seemed to wear smiles wherever they went. Maybe they were just reflect-ing the smiles people like me gave to them.

And then there are girls' teams who create special hairdos from beauty parlor hell as recreational decoration. Most girls in sports have perfected the slicked-back ponytail and create this sleek, no-frills hairdo in twenty seconds flat. For fun, some teams decide the business-as-usual ponytail simply doesn't fill the bill. They proudly sport big grins and their impossi-bly small braids jutting scrudiwumpus all over their heads or poky pig-tails and waterfalls crazily akimbo seeming to tell the teams they compete with that they are having fun. Hairdos, crazy striped socks, irreverently patterned shorts, and even teeny-tiny team T-shirts can underscore kids' right to enjoy playing.

GREAT COACHES NURTURE FUN

Talk to coaches (especially the great ones) and you will find many have a therapeutic bag of fun stuff they pull out whenever the mood needs a little lightening. Dick and Debbie Held, currently commissioner of region 69

AYSO, as parents have coached their three kids' teams for seventeen years and could be role models to us all. From their spontaneous parades and slumber parties to the infamous Nancy Kerrigan Look-Alike contest, prizes included, their teams consistently hit 10 on the FUN Index . . . and a lot of little kids have grown into fine people through their time with the Helds. Nurturing fun is fun.

Goofy Practice Day

Everyone on the team wears the most outrageous, funny outfit to practice they can find. Award prizes for the goofiest, silliest, and ugliest.

Celebrate Anything

When the team is losing, have all team members celebrate every teeny tiny good thing done by yelling in their loudest voice: "Bravo! Pip pip! Good show!" Bonus points if your team can simulate a British accent. Or have everyone run to the corner of the court, whooping up a wild storm of cheers and praise when a score is finally made.

Team Toenail Celebration Game Day

When the team is in a midseason lull, have a toenail celebration competition. Arrive early for the pre-game meeting. Start out with a team-member lineup—all pairs of feet in a single row—and invite in a beloved trio (preferably good-looking, well-loved fellow students of the opposite sex) to pick the winning pair of feet. Have prizes for the "happiest toenails on Earth," "most school spirited toes," and "most likely to succeed toes."

When the coach pays for the prizes him- or herself, it adds extra zippy fun to the festivities. Goofy prizes are even better. I know of one coach who proudly presented the award of the day, a carton of dairy cream with a gold sticker on it for the season's "best ball cream!" I know for a fact the carton (now emptied and carefully rinsed) still sits on the kid's dresser.

Win and I'll . . .

It's easy to slip into a pattern where practice and games become drudgery. *Any* change of pace, any alteration from the schedule can be a huge boost to everyone's mood, coaches included. Do anything different, and people will be happier. Treat the team to ice cream, a movie, a back-rub, or cancel the next practice. Get creative. One very proper coach, as he reached midlife and truly began to blossom, promised his team he would get his ear pierced if they finished in the top eight at the tournament. They did and he did, much to the delight of absolutely everyone, including parents. Jeff, you're amazing. Coaches, be careful what you promise. Your team will hold you to it.

KEEPING PERSPECTIVE AS A PARENT

Sports are fundamentally recreation. Why is that so easy to forget? The car pool drives or post-game parties roasting everyone might sear some people's ears, but when taken in context, the good times blossom to ce-ment friendships and enrich lives. I have to agree with the kids. Parents and coaches are really funny. We can take ourselves so seriously and get all bent out of shape over little stuff. Our personal lack of athletic training or overabundance of team memories from back in the Dark Ages make us say and do things our kids find hysterical. Good thing they have one an-other to laugh with.

Parents and kids alike can suffer from tension buildup. Not surpris-ingly, tense parents feed tense kids, and tense parents can feed on one an-other. I've been through some seasons when the uptight feelings on the team were so high, I started clenching up two days before a game just to be in shape for the parent tension-fest on the sidelines.

One season, we had a particularly noisy, bossy row of parents yelling at the kids: "Get the ball, Ginger! Come on!" "Here comes the forward. Get on her!" Even the refs and other coaches became fair game for verbal as-sessment. The tension was rising precipitously by March in a December-to-July season. We were sure to kill off a few of the middle-aged parents from high blood pressure if not murder one if we didn't find a way to ease some of the stress. One day the parent collective nearly mobbed the hap-less mother who had let her eleven-year-old daughter go to a slumber party the night before. Didn't she know that her daughter needed her sleep to be able to do her part on the team?

A plan was definitely needed. It was the coach, Rick Citron, who finally pulled it together. "Okay," Coach announced, "we need a parent/kid soccer game. Next practice, kids on the sidelines. Parents on the field playing."

When we got to the field on the appointed day, the kids lounged on the side feigning concern for our well-being, offering Gatorade, and prodding to be sure we drank enough water. One wiseacre kid even commented about her mom's party the night before, which delayed her bedtime. "She just won't be herself without her sleep," she quipped.

The first kick was a soft wuss skidding across the grass in my neighborhood. I ran like the dickens, almost doing what I was supposed to do. Back and forth, chase, run, dribble, watch your "man."

Five minutes into the running, I was doing triple-time breathing. If you've ever played soccer for the first time at any parental age, you will realize that I am hedging on the boundary of outrageous bragging because I am telling you I was still running and sort of talking ten minutes into the game. Some of my aged teammates were barely crawling. Moreover, my Brownian motion energetic movement still had not brought me within two feet of the ball.

Best of all, however, were the kids. Their imitations of us as parents gave us all new perspective. Not only was it darn hard to "get to the ball," but, "Hey, Michele. Stay on your man!" was a trip as well. Her man, a middle-aged dad, was prostrate in the grass, gasping for breath between fits of exhausted laughter.

PITA Parents

Talk to a coach who has been around for a while and you will soon get around to the topic of parents. Some are great. Some help. Some shag balls. Some make phone calls. Some make a coach's job a lot smoother. Coaches love these parents . . . and their kids tend to be pretty terrific, too.

And then there are the *other* parents. Some of the most complicated emotions and intense rage in sports come from parents who've lost all perspective. These are PITA parents: Pain In The Ass parents. Every coach knows about them. Every principal, school director, athletic director, and headmaster can give you a list. Some can give you a Rolodex file of PITA parents.

In each instance, the problem invariably comes from differing opinions (parent on the one hand, coach on the other) about the child's ability or present development (there's a difference). Since sports are played out in public, all our insecurities as parents are on parade. We don't want our children to look bad; on the other hand, we don't want to see them on the bench. We want them to be in position to take the shot that wins the game, but we don't want them to miss it. We like the fawning and the adulation that accompany athletic success in this culture these days, and we can seduce ourselves in a nanosecond into thinking that All-America honors and rich college scholarships are just another successful season away.

> Let me emphasize that there's nothing wrong with dreaming and there's certainly nothing wrong with working hard to achieve a dream, but reality does intrude. Of all the well-coordinated, well-coached winning student performers I have known over the years, I have seen few truly gifted athletes. I have known vastly more truly smart kids, and I honestly think there's a greater likelihood of kids' being bright than of their being athletic.
>
> —Thomas Hudnut, headmaster of Harvard-Westlake School, September 1998

Through sports, we have a multitude of golden opportunities to show ourselves at our best. As parents, we have the chance to model mature responses and grown-up behavior. We can show our children how to be socially respectful and an integral part of a community. Think about it. You probably spend most of your time doing most of your stuff at work with your coworkers. Your children never see you. Your leadership, respect, and kindness to others are visible to those with whom you work, but invisible to your children. Trust me, your genes will not pass on these qualities. In sports, however, children are in the same space and time with their parents, sharing common interactions with other parents, kids, and the coaches. How you as a parent behave is very important. Your style becomes your child's unwritten playbook.

Clearly trash-talking, ref-bashing, bitching behind coaches' backs, moaning about playing time, hassling officials, nudging program directors, even gloating over victories or wailing over losses as "unfair" are pretty sorry behaviors. PITA parents get such a reputation that coaches will swap stories about them in the same breath as they discuss a kid's athletic skills. Coaches warn one another. Junior high coaches warn high school coaches. High school coaches tell club coaches. Club coaches and high school coaches alert college and university coaches. College and university coaches high sign Olympic training coaches and professional coaches. And the media gets the picture, too.

TIP	Don't be a PITA parent.

Long story short, your behavior as a parent can be a tremendous detriment to your child's advancement if you get labeled as a PITA parent. A kid has to be twice as spectacular for a coach to want to take the kid *and* their PITA parent(s) on board.

CONFESSIONS OF A PITA PARENT

We were pretty naïve with our oldest daughter. She was so good so young and coaches were coming out of the woodwork to ask her to play for their club. We all ate it up. Maybe it went to our heads a little. We went with this really aggressive coach who called every day for three weeks and just acted like he knew everything. He had been around awhile and seemed to have a lot of connections. She was only thirteen at the time, so we believed it when he painted pictures of college scholarship bids from across the nation by the time she was a sophomore. Well, partway into the season, he wasn't playing her very much, and when she was on the court, he would yell at her. I went and complained. He was the one who wanted her on the club. Why wasn't she on the court more? He told me and my husband she was a little lazy and not trying up to her potential. That that was life. If she wanted to play, she had to work. We didn't believe him. I knew she was trying. She sure was crying every night on the way home. I started complaining to him after every game and called at least twice a week to "discuss" her progress. I worked on him for a good two months and ended up so mad one day that I just took her out of the practice and we never went back. Well, when the next club season rolled around, there were few coaches interested in her, and to those that were, I had to do a lot of explaining. Finally, one guy seemed to understand what had happened and was eager to have her on his team. We had a pretty good start to the season. That coach was pretty good, but the team didn't win many games. He just couldn't pull it together, and my daughter was carrying the team in competitions. I let it slip to a few of the parents, and pretty soon, the coach was giving me the evil eye at every practice. I think he was relieved when our no-win season was over. We sure were glad, too. Well, here we are at the start of junior year, and she tried out for all the clubs and couldn't get a bid from one. Her school team had won state, for god's sake. What the hell was the matter with these coaches, I remember thinking.

Finally, after I had called a bunch of times, one coach had a girl drop out, and they needed someone in her position. They took her. That fall, she went on two recruiting trips to pretty good schools, but then we never heard a word. It was the middle of her freshman year at our local college before someone, a woman coach we knew from our younger daughter's team, clued me in. I had earned myself a hell of a reputation among the coaches and had hurt my daughter's athletic career. If I wanted my younger daughter to have a chance, I had damn well better learn to keep my mouth shut.

—Mother of two athletes, five years apart

All right. So you can't fix all the parents in your kid's school. You can't even tidy up the parents on your kid's team. But you can fix yourself and perhaps work on your spouse as well. If you believe in your kid, you have done your job. Show him or her how to work hard, play with dignity, warm the bench with grace, accept possible inequities, speak honestly and appropriately, keep your mouth shut when you should, speak up when necessary, and your kid will be ahead and winning the most important game going.

TIP   If you believe in your kid, whoever he or she is and is meant to become, and you've done the very best you can, your kid is a real winner . . . and so are you.

MOMENTUM AND OTHER MYSTERIES

Many questions remain, such as what creates team momentum and how might we better develop our kids through sports participation? Might we tackle some of our thorny social ills via youth athletic organizations? How can we facilitate cooperation, empathy, and sharing? How can boys and girls grow up apart and come together more smoothly? How can we adults, hamstrung by our own limited upbringing, support an egalitarian world fairly? How can we help kids find the joy in giving? If social psychologists are right, and I believe they are, some of the greatest support for world peace comes through sharing a common goal. The Olympics bring athletes and their families from around the world together, reaffirming to us all that we are all more alike than we are different.

A brief note traveled the Internet and showed up in my e-mail:

> A few years ago at the Seattle Special Olympics, nine contestants, all physically or mentally disabled, assembled at the starting line for the hundred-yard dash. At the gun they all started out, not exactly in a dash, but with the relish to run the race to the finish and win.
>
> All, that is, except one boy, who stumbled on the asphalt, tumbled over a couple of times, and began to cry. The other eight heard the boy cry. They slowed down and paused. They all turned around and went back. Every one of them.
>
> One girl with Down's syndrome bent down and kissed him and said, "This will make it better."
>
> Then all nine linked arms and walked together to the finish line.
>
> Everyone in the stadium stood, and the cheering went on for several minutes. People who were there are still telling the story. Why?
>
> Because deep down we know this one thing:
>
> What matters in this life is more than winning for ourselves.
>
> What truly matters in this life is helping others win, even if it means slowing down and changing our course.
>
> —Author unknown, first ten lines submitted as "Author Unknown" by
>   Bob French and reprinted in *Chicken Soup for the Soul #3* and
>   *Condensed Chicken Soup for the Soul* (1996), Health
>   Communications, Inc., Deerfield Beach, Florida.

To paraphrase Crosby, Stills, Nash, and Young, we who are on the road, driving our kids to sports practices and athletic competitions, need a reminder to teach our children well. The joy comes in the process, not the destination, and there is a lot to learn along the way.

So I will end this here with one last hope.

I challenge parents and coaches to remember our goals as adults in our society. Recall our obligations to develop our children as participants and leaders to take their places in the future. Encourage real winners as people. I ask us all to rise to the challenge.

Epilogue: The Van

I watched as it slowly rode up the ramp of the tow truck, a cumbersome old, ugly blue van. How many times had I sworn at it? How many times had I cursed its too-tiny transmission as I chugged up yet another street. How often had I reveled in the hearty laughter and giggles coming from the seats behind me? How many times had I regretted the poor visibility? How often had we all sung "Baby Beluga" in off-key family harmony? Too many times . . . and not enough.

Good bye, Ugly Blue Van.

Good bye, Soccer Mom.

No more Christmas tree excursions with three eager young faces full of anticipation for Santa's arrival. No more spilled orange soda from 7-Eleven, flowing riverlike down the center aisle, seeping silently into the what-once-was blue carpet. I miss you already, and the years and the memories you hold. I say a prayer for the Make-a-Wish Foundation and hope some of the happiness we shared within you comes to the new owners.

I remember five muddy soccer players diving out of the storm, clumps of mud haphazardly shaken off out the door. I remember eight volleyball players celebrating a particularly delicious victory one night on the way home singing "Ninety-nine Bottles of Beer on the Wall." What did fifteen- and sixteen-year-olds know about beer and walls anyway?

Images of five bicycles riding nobly atop the van on the trip to Mammoth, Aerobat kites stacked up against the back window, the heap of Rollerblades, wrist and knee guards . . . all ghost-like memories as I say the final good-bye.

Good-bye, Ugly Blue Van. Good-bye, car pool. I did love you and the joy we shared when my children were small. Oh, what I would give to have those days back now.

APPENDIX A

Youth Athletic Organization Harassment Policy

Youth athletic organizations are committed to providing individual growth opportunities based on mutual respect and appropriate to age and developmental levels. The experience with a youth athletic organization is to be free from harassment of any type, including verbal, physical, visual, or sexual harassment. Harassment of a participant by a coach, referee, administrator, other participant, parent, parents of other participants, or other personnel associated with the youth athletic organization is prohibited.

Allegations of harassment will be treated seriously, promptly, and confidentially. An allegation of harassment shall not, in and of itself, presuppose wrongdoing. A thorough procedure for review and investigation outlined below will be completed step by step to give due process to all individuals involved. False or frivolous charges will be referred to appropriate authorities and subject to legal recourse. Notably, verified actions of harassment will result in appropriate disciplinary actions up to and including dismissal, referrals to state agencies, and other courses of action to assure the safety and well-being of the youth participating in the youth athletic organization.

Harassment includes any and all treatment that violates the rights of the developing individual. Positive environments are free of discrimination due to, but not limited to, the individual's sex, race, creed, color, national origin, ancestry, medical condition, sexual orientation, or physical disability. Harassment potentially occurs in many forms including:

> VISUAL HARASSMENT: any visual stimulation that portrays a negative, inflammatory, derogatory message, whether written, drawn, cartooned, or gestured.

Examples: cartoon depicting an athlete's race as negative, "flicking off"

VERBAL HARASSMENT: any statements or words including "jokes" that convey negative or derogatory messages directed toward or concerning another person.

Examples: ethnic jokes, racial slurs, statements suggesting mental disability: "You're a retard." "You can't slide tackle. Girls never can." "You play ball like a pussy."

PHYSICAL HARASSMENT: any physical contact that impedes normal movement, including intimidating stance, blocking movements, feigned or real blows, assaults, or touching that is unwanted or inappropriate behavior with a child.

Examples: shoving a player, hitting a player, pushing a player onto a bench, looming over a player, physically halting exit or entrance

SEXUAL HARASSMENT: any sexual approaches, suggestions for sexual contact, demands or requests for sexual favors, or any verbal or physical action implying sexual activity. Trusting relationships between caregivers, coaches, parents, and adults necessarily do not include any actions or innuendoes of action regarding contacts of a sexual nature.

Examples:

1. Sexual advances, including touching on the breast area of a developing girl; patting the butt of a player in a lingering or fondling fashion; fitting the cup to a developing boy with manipulation of the genitals

2. Exhibiting adult genitalia to children

3. Showing objects with sexually suggestive gestures or remarks

4. Telling jokes with derogatory or sexually loaded content

5. Threatening negative consequences if information is told to other players, parents, or administration

RESPONSIBILITY OF A YOUTH ATHLETIC ORGANIZATION

It is the responsibility of a youth athletic organization to establish and maintain a policy covering all forms of harassment. A governing review body should be put in place that meets regularly to evaluate problems, assess new information on the appropriate developmental needs of participating youth, implement responsive policy changes to better support the youth players, and act in an appropriate supervisory manner to assure quality experiences for all participants.

To these ends:

1. Establish a harassment policy committee of members from the community

2. Educate participants, parents, coaches, referees, administrators, and all personnel affiliated with the youth athletic organization of the policy mandates

3. Establish methods to ensure vigilance over the policy implementation

4. Engage in the active, ongoing dialogues toward the development of ever-improving educational environments free from harassment, intimidation, and discrimination

PARENTS' AND PARTICIPANTS' RESPONSIBILITIES

Positive development must be the shared goal of the parents and the youth athletic organization. Toward this goal, the developing child must be empowered with knowledge of personal rights and integrity of body space. Respect for the individual's personal space is at the crux of mutually respectful peer-peer relationships, child-adult relationships, and adult-adult relationships. Mature perspective about the developing child's needs is founded in empathy and tempered by wisdom with an eye to long-term maturation. The child's needs must take precedence over the adult's.

Youth athletic participants can be taught fundamentals of the nonharassment policy though the Golden Rule. By reminding the child "Do unto others as you would have others do unto you," you will be laying the foundations for appropriate, positive learning experiences.

Youth athletic participants must

1. choose prosocial actions contributing to a positive learning experience for her/himself and others;

2. omit any actions (verbal or physical) that may harm personal psychological or physical growth or the growth of others;

3. use self-efficacious methods to deter others who would injure or harm, including verbal statements such as "I don't like what you're saying. It is not okay to call me a wop. I am Italian."

4. notify immediately an adult (parent or authority) when self-initiated methods are not successful;

5. be responsive to the complaints of others regarding inadvertent harassing statements. Verbal apologies are appropriate ("I'm sorry. I didn't mean to offend you."). Ceasing the harassing or perceived harassing behavior immediately is mandatory.

Parents of youth athletic participants must

1. encourage prosocial actions by themselves and their players that contribute to a positive learning experience. Parents are the role model of appropriate behavior, and selecting positive actions (cheering for players' efforts) versus negative actions (criticizing failures, booing) is essential;

2. eliminate negative verbalizations or actions from their athletic-field behavior that may harm the psychological or physical growth of the developing child. Support eliminating negative behaviors from the child;

3. support self-efficacy. Teach your child to use their words and handle problems for themselves. Engage in dialogues with your child to monitor and assess problems in the making. Encourage thinking and plans of action for the child to take to resolve problems for themselves;

4. have knowledge of when it is appropriate to step in on the behalf of a developing child. Know when and how to notify appropriate authorities when a problem emerges you cannot resolve appropriately;

5. participate in parent groups to help develop consciousness of nonharassment policies and behaviors that facilitate cooperative, prosocial activities in developing youth.

COMPLAINT AND REVIEW PROCEDURE FOR YOUTH ATHLETIC ORGANIZATIONS

Procedure for filing a report must include six steps:

1. The youth (or adult acting on his or her behalf) should verbally or in writing tell (or attempt to tell) the harassment perpetrator that the harassing actions are unacceptable.

2. The youth should tell a parent, coach, assistant coach, or other adult not involved in the perpetration about the harassing actions.

3. The entrusted adult should approach the alleged perpetrator with information of the concern and explain the problem. If compliance with cease-and-desist requests are not achieved, a written complaint form must be completed.

4. The entrusted adult should support and monitor the youth activities in relation to the alleged harassing individual.

5. Formal investigation will include a meeting with the alleged harassing individual, a meeting with witnesses of harassment, and a review committee process to determine other sources of information that should be pursued.

6. All facts gathered will be presented to the harassment policy committee of the youth athletic organization for final evaluation. Appropriate actions will then be taken up to and including educational training, disciplinary limitations, or dismissal. Follow-through services will be recommended, including notification of appropriate state and federal social service agencies. Within the power of the youth athletic organization, based on the employment or terms of volunteer participation, due process will be pursued to completion.

Materials gathered in the course of the fact gathering should be retained by the youth athletic organization for ten years. Database storage of incidents that end in a disciplinary action should be maintained to serve as a resource for the organization and other youth organizations.

Appendix B

Sports Proactive Information Formative Feedback Inventory

Division & Team Number:_____

TEAM NAME:_____

Coach:_____

Dear (Organization Name) Family,

- Our (Organization) encourages development of the young athlete through positive coaching.
- Our (volunteer) coaches are offered annual training and we have adopted a program of formative evaluation to monitor and provide support for our coaching staff.
  At the start of the season, parents and coaches are reminded of the (Organization) mission in youth athletics. The (Organization) wants to:
    1) encourage parents' positive support of young players at practices and games, and
    2) recognize coaches who successfully fulfill (Organization) goals for individual and team development.
- Please take a few minutes as the parent of an (Organization) player to complete this short questionnaire and mail it to your (Organization) Office address listed below. ALL RESPONSES ARE CONFIDENTIAL, but information and summaries may be used for educational and/or professional development programs to help improve the quality of the coaching provided.
- If you have any questions or concerns, please contact your coach, division head, commissioner, or regional office at: (555) *phone number* or National (Organization) at (800) *phone number.*

Rank each of the following statements using a scale of 1 (disagree) to 7 (agree). *Circle your choice.*

(Organization) COACH

    a. Encouraged sportsmanship   disagree 1 2 3 4 5 6 7 agree

    b. Increased the player's enjoyment of (sport)   disagree 1 2 3 4 5 6 7 agree

    c. Distributed playing time fairly   disagree 1 2 3 4 5 6 7 agree

    d. Used praise to encourage skill development disagree 1 2 3 4 5 6 7 agree

    e. Conducted valuable practice sessions   disagree 1 2 3 4 5 6 7 agree

    f. Gave constructive feedback during games   disagree 1 2 3 4 5 6 7 agree

    g. Handled losing and difficult situations well disagree 1 2 3 4 5 6 7 agree

    h. Handled winning well   disagree 1 2 3 4 5 6 7 agree

    i. Respected psychological and physical rights* disagree 1 2 3 4 5 6 7 agree

        *Please explain any problems in space below or on questionnaire back.

    j. Asst. Coach supported (Organization) goals disagree 1 2 3 4 5 6 7 agree

    k. Overall evaluation of 1998 (Organization)

       (SPORT) EXPERIENCE WAS POSITIVE   disagree 1 2 3 4 5 6 7 agree

    l. Would you like your child to have this coach again?   NO   YES

Please COMMENT: Aspect(s) of your coach, team, or player experience you found to be particularly valuable or of concern: _____

_____

_____

Please use the back of this form for any additional comments or suggestions.

Questionnaire completed by: Male   Female   Couple

Years affiliated with (Organization) program: 1 2 3 4 5 6 7 8 9 10 or more

Thank you for your time. Signature (voluntary)_____(phone)_____

PLEASE SEND TO: Your Organization Office

© Sports Proactive Information Formative Feedback Inventory (SPIFFI) © 1996, 1997, 1998, 1999.
Shari Young Kuchenbecker, Ph.D., P.O. Box 49717, Los Angeles, California 90049
(310) 476-1745

APPENDIX C

National Sports Organizations:
Resources for Parents

Youth sports organizations are supported by an important volunteer force of parents and community members donating their time toward the future of our children. The following organizations have excellent programs in place and a commitment to improving youth through sports. Volunteers and donations are always welcome to help build quality programs through research and program improvements. Please share generously.

Amateur Athletic Foundation
2141 West Adams Boulevard
Los Angeles, California 90018
(323) 730-9600
http://www.aafla.org

American Youth Soccer Organization (AYSO)
National Headquarters
12501 South Isis Avenue
Hawthorne, California 90250
(800) USA-AYSO
FAX (310) 643-5310
http://www.soccer.org

Little League Baseball
National Headquarters
P.O. Box 3485
Williamsport, Pennsylvania 17701
(570) 326-1921
http://www.littleleague.org

Pop Warner Football
National Headquarters
586 Middletown Boulevard, Suite C 100
Langhorne, Pennsylvania 19047
(215) 752-2691
http://www.dickbutkus.com

Special Olympics
1325 G Street NW, Suite 500
Washington, D.C. 20004
(202) 628-3630
http://www.specialolympics.org

USA Youth Volleyball
715 South Circle Drive
Colorado Springs, Colorado 80910
(719) 228-6800
http://www.usavolleyball.org

Women's Sports Foundation
Eisenhower Park
East Meadow, New York 11554
(800) 227-3988
FAX (516) 542-4716
http://www.lifetimetv.com/WoSport

APPENDIX D

Four-Finger Whistling

(Thanks to Jani—Superstar mom to three nomads,
mermaid body-double in Walt Disney's movie *Thirteenth Year*,
and first-rate whistling coach)

Wash your hands. (Travel packs of antibacterial hand wipes are great for gyms, stadiums, and field events.)

Lick your lips all the way around and smile (very important).

Open your mouth about one inch.

Pull your lips over your teeth to cover them (modified toothless great-granny look).

Make "V" victory signs with your right and left hands. (Use your index and middle fingers.)

Make a teepee with your two middle fingers touching each other and your two pinkies touching, too.

Insert your fingers into your mouth at about a 45-degree angle.

Push the tip of your tongue gently in and back holding your tongue in a little "L."

Moisten and seal everything, leaving a little triangle hold between your fingers and pulled-tight lower lip.

Blow out—kind of like blowing through a straw—a thin stream of air should go out over your tongue, up over the "L," and down across your fingers and whistle as it passes over the moist teeth and mouth combo.

This is your instrument so . . . play with your combinations: angle of your fingers, tension in your tongue, tension in the "L" of the tongue, size of air stream, and the speed of air flow. Listen as you play around for the beginning of any whistling sounds. Once you get some noise, follow it and work it up. (You may find as many do that in the excitement of a real game, your tension will increase, as will available air, and you will get a lot louder! Bless adrenaline!)

Everyone's instrument is a little different, so it's up to you to find how to make it work for you. With a little motivation, perseverance, and fun, everyone can learn to play.

References

Anshel, Mark H. (2000). *Sport Psychology: From Theory to Practice*. 4th ed. Scottsdale, Ariz.: Gorsuch Scarisbrick, Publishers.

Bandura, Albert. *Self-Efficacy: The Exercise of Control*. New York: W. H. Freeman and Company, 1997.

Dement, William. *The Sleep Watchers*. Stanford, Calif.: Stanford University Press, 1992.

Kuchenbecker, Shari Young. "Coaches and AYSO Players: Children's Rights and Organizational Responsibilities." Report presented to AYSO National, September 28, 1997, rev. November 1, 1997.

————. "Positive Coaching through Formative Feedback: AYSO Year Two Results." Poster presented at the annual meeting of American Psychological Association. Boston, Massachusetts, 1999.

————. "Increasing Positive Coaching in Youth Athletics through Formative Feedback." Workshop for professionals presented at the annual meeting of American Psychological Association. Boston, Massachusetts, 1999.

————. "Increasing Positive Coaching through Formative Feedback in AYSO." Poster presented at the annual meeting of American Psychological Association. San Francisco, California, 1998.

————, C. Rigg, C. Weglarz, E. Alvarez, K. Fleming, S. Ribera, C. Ball, K. Rockenbach, N. Pohlot, A. Wisda, S. Stern, E. Fraines, D. Sahagun, J. L. Waltermeyer, C. Maher, C. Workman, D. Beauschesne, B. Goss, A. Webb, A. M. Froysaa, D. Sanchez, J. Schnell, C. Scott, and M. French. "Who's a Winner? Coaches' Views of Winning Young Athletes." Poster presented at the annual meeting of American Psychological Association. Boston, Massachusetts, 1999.

Maccoby, Eleanor E. *The Two Sexes: Growing Up Apart. Coming Together.* Cambridge, Mass.: Belknap Press, 1998.

Meyers, David G. *Psychology.* 5th ed. New York: Worth Publishers, 1997.

———. *Social Psychology.* 6th ed. Boston: McGraw-Hill College, 1999.

Nolen-Hoeksema, Susan. *Abnormal Psychology.* Boston: McGraw-Hill College, 1998.

Ross, Dorothea. *Childhood Bullying and Teasing: What School Personnel, Other Professionals, and Parents Can Do.* Alexandria, Va: American Counseling Association, 1996.

Santrock, John. *Life Span Development.* 7th ed. Madison, Wis.: Brown & Benchmark Publishers, 1997.

Seligman, Martin. *The Optimistic Child.* Boston: Houghton Mifflin, 1995.

Tamborlane, William V., ed. *The Yale Guide to Children's Nutrition.* New Haven: Yale University Press, 1997.

Women's Sports Foundation. *Gender Equality Report Card: A Survey of Athletic Opportunity in American Higher Education Then and Now.* East Meadow, N.Y.: The Women's Sports Foundation, 1999.

———. *Title IX: An Educational Resource Kit.* East Meadow, N.Y.: The Women's Sports Foundation, 1999.

Wooden, John W. *They Call Me Coach.* New York: Contemporary Books, 1998.

———. *Wooden: A Lifetime of Observations and Reflections On and Off the Court.* New York: Contemporary Books, 1997.

Zimbardo, Philip G., and Richard J. Gerrig. *Psychology and Life.* 15th ed. New York: Longman, 1999.

Index

Abdul-Jabbar, Kareem, xii, 77
abrasions, 180–81
abstractions, ability to deal with, 258
abuse:
    all-star athlete parents and, 84
    coaches and, 109, 111–15
    see also harassment; *specific types of*
        abuse
academics, 9–10, 218, 257–58
    balance and, 69, 72
    college scholarships and, 263,
        267–71, 281–84
    development and, 7
    emotions and, 144, 154, 159
    mental game and, 197
    nutrition and, 135
    and selecting right sport, 18
    spurts in, 32–33
    and turning girls and boys into great
        people, 241, 244, 252–55, 260
aches, 182
Achilles tendinitis, 171
acting as if technique, 101
action, actions:
    balance and, 64–65, 70–71
    too little emphasis on, 65
acute injuries, 54

aerobic exercise, 158–59, 162
age:
    all-star athlete parents and, 83
    coaches and, 106, 109, 111
    college scholarships and, 265
    injuries and, 165, 168
    nutrition and, 123–25, 130, 139
    and selecting right sport, 21–22
    self-efficacy and, 47–48, 57, 60
    sleep and, 137–38
    spurts and, 219, 221
    stalls and, 224–25
    and turning girls and boys into great
        people, 244
Alden, Betsy, 249
All-Sport Recruiting, 274
all-star athlete parents, 76–87
    becoming like, 80–84
    coaches and, 76–86, 114
    what they do, 80, 82
    what they don't do, 79
amenorrhea, 135–36
American Academy of Neurology, 172
American Association of Pastoral
    Counselors, 73
American Basketball League (ABL),
    xvi

American College of Sports Medicine, 136
American National Standards Institute (ANSI), 184
American Orthopaedic Association, 172
American Youth Soccer Organization (AYSO), 7, 9, 24, 34, 89–90, 109, 115, 142, 203, 245–47, 259, 290
amnesia, 174–75
Anderson, Ken, 162–63
ankle sprains, xi
anorexia nervosa, 132–33
Aristotle, 22
Associated Press, 188
Astin, Alexander, 250
athletes' foot, 181
athletic shoes, 5, 15
    motivation and, 94–95
    self-efficacy and, 44–45
attention abilities, 259
attitude, 157, 211
authoritarian parenting, 23
authoritative parenting, 23
awards, see rewards; trophies
Azusa Pacific University, 229

balance:
    actions and, 64–65, 70–71
    coaches and, 66–70, 75, 106, 115
    college scholarships and, 69, 283
    development and, 7
    emotions and, 63–68, 70–71, 75, 144–45, 156–57
    feedback mechanisms for, 122–23
    ideas for, 74–75
    in life of young athletes, 62–75
    maintenance of, 70–74
    mental game and, 191
    nutrition and, 122–23
    problems with, 71–74
    real winners and, 28
    and selecting right sport, 16, 18, 20, 22

    self-efficacy and, 48
    sleep and, 137–39
    stalls and, 227
    thinking and, 64–65, 68–71
Balelo, Nez, 273
Bandura, Albert, 37–38, 61, 143, 155, 191, 194–95, 237, 254
Barrett, Robert, 215
baseball, xiii, 8, 12, 15, 32, 217–18
    all-star athlete parents and, 77
    balance and, 69
    burnout in, 233–34
    college scholarships in, 273
    emotions in, 141, 144–45, 152, 162
    injuries in, 170–71
    mental game and, 189, 191–92
    motivation and, 93–94
    parental empathy and, 14
    in past, 4–5
    role models in, 207, 215
    and selecting right sport, 19, 21
    self-efficacy in, 49–50, 56–58
basketball, xii–xiii, 5, 9–10, 32, 284–85
    balance and, 65, 69–70, 74
    coaches in, 113
    college scholarships in, 272, 275–78, 280
    development through, 7
    emotions in, 145–46, 148–49, 160
    fun and, 287–88
    injuries in, 171
    mental game and, 192, 194
    motivation and, 90, 94
    perspective in, 294–95
    quitting and, 235
    role models in, 206–7
    and selecting right sport, 20–22
    self-efficacy in, 37, 41, 48–49
    stalls in, 222–23, 225, 228–29, 231
    in turning girls and boys into great people, 242
    women in, xvi, 49, 206–7, 252–53
Bauer, Josh, 288

Baumrind, Diana, 23
beach volleyball, 88, 207–8
beans, 128
behavior, 158, 161–62
    attitude led by, 211
    motor learning and, 212–14
    role models and, 211–14
    too much emphasis on, 66
behavioral contingency rewards, 92
Bergman, Abe, 184–85
Berkman, Justin, 233
Berra, Yogi, 189, 236
bias, self-serving, 198–99
bicycling, 183–85
binge eating disorder, 134
biofeedback, 158, 161–62
Blatherwick, Jack, 260
bleacher-related injuries, 53–54
bodybuilding, 135
body wisdom, 122–23, 138
Boston Globe, The, 133
bowling, 193, 213–14
boys:
    in future, 261–62
    turning them into great people,
        241–62
Boy Scouts of America, 111
Brain Injury Association, 172
breads, 128
Brentwood Flyer, 234
broken bones, 166–67, 178–79
Brownell, K. D., 133–35
bruises, 180
Bryant, Kobe, 228
bulimia nervosa, 132–34
bumps, 180
burnout, 155, 220, 233–34
buy, drive, supply, and monitor
        problems, 44–46, 50

calcium, 122–23
California, University of:
    at Berkeley, 23, 155

    at Davis, 272
    at Los Angeles (UCLA), xii–xiv, 122,
        145, 197, 208, 242, 250, 254, 272
calming self-talk, 195–96
Cantu, Norma, 279
Carolina Panthers, 235
Carpenter, Karen, 133
car pools, 118
Carson, Harry, 172
Carter, Don, 213
cereals, 128
Chambers, Marcia, 250
chaperones, 119
Chapman College, xiii–xiv
Chastain, Brandi, xvi
cheering rosters, 118
cheerleaders, parent, 100–101
cheese, 128
Chicken Soup for the Soul #3
        (Canfield), 296
Child Help USA, 151
Childhood Bullying and Teasing: What
        School Personnel, Other
        Professionals, and Parents Can Do
        (Ross), 61
circadian rhythms, 138
Citron, Rick, 291–92
classical conditioning, 148
clinical social workers, 73
clinical psychologists, 72–73
club programs, college scholarships
        and, 272–73
coaches, coaching, coachability,
        xiii–xiv, 10–12, 15–17, 33–34,
        105–20, 217–18
    abusiveness of, 109, 111–15
    all-star athlete parents and, 76–86,
        114
    awards for, 119
    balance and, 66–70, 75, 106, 115
    boot camp mentality of, 112–13
    calling, 84–85
    and changes in sports, 5–6

coaches, coaching, coachability (*cont'd*)
  college scholarships and, 263,
    265–67, 270–75, 282–83
  criticisms by, 5–6
  development and, 7, 105, 110, 112
  emotions and, 106, 141–42, 145–47,
    149–50, 152–54, 157–60
  and empathy with your child, 13
  expectations of, 33
  formative evaluation of, 110, 305–6
  fun and, 287–91
  gifts for, xi, 120
  injuries and, 112–13, 165, 168–69,
    172–75, 177–78, 180, 186
  limited resources for, 116
  limited time for, 116
  mental game and, 188–90, 194,
    196–97, 199
  motivation and, 88–92, 96–98,
    101–3, 105
  nutrition and, 129, 135
  offering to help, 97
  parental intrusion on, 114
  parents as child's first, 15–16
  and participating in sports, 3
  personal, 273–74
  perspective and, 291–95
  punishments used by, 149–50,
    152–53
  qualities of great, 107
  quitting and, 238–40
  real winners described by, 24–29
  respect for, 80–82, 84
  roasting of, 287
  role models and, xiii, 105, 108,
    201–4, 206, 209–10, 212–16
  saying thanks to, 117
  screening of, 110–11
  and selecting right sport, 16–17
  selection of, 105–7
  self-efficacy and, 41, 43, 45, 48,
    50–51, 53, 55–61, 112, 114
  sleep and, 138
  specific qualities valued most by,
    26–28
  spurts and, 220
  stalls and, 222–23, 226–28
  of successful athletes, 31
  support for, 116–20
  as tough job, 115–16, 120
  training and certification programs
    for, 6, 109–12, 115
  and turning girls and boys into great
    people, 241–42, 245, 249, 255–59
  two-adult policy in, 111
  on what damages young athletes'
    potential, 27–28
  what to do about terrible, 114–15
  who go above and beyond call of
    duty, 119–20
  winning and, 24–31, 107, 117
  yelling and, xiii, 107, 111–12
Coachman, Alice, 252
Cobb, Ty, 49
cognitive-behavioral appraisal, 158,
    161–62
cognitive development:
  balance and, 68–69
  and selecting right sport, 22
cognitive dissonance, 93
cognitive skills, 257–58
  spurts and, 219–20
  stalls and, 225–26
  see also mental game
colleges and universities, costs of
    attending, 264, 275
college scholarships, 263–85
  academics and, 263, 267–71, 281–84
  alternatives to, 283–85
  athletic skills for, 265–67
  balance and, 69, 283
  club programs and, 272–73
  for cream of the crop, 265–66
  for equivalency sports, 276–79
  for head count sports, 276–77, 279
  money in, 275–81

odds of getting, 264–65
personal coaching and, 273–74
personality and, 270–71
perspective and, 293–94
pros and cons of, 281–83
recruiting for, 271–75
renewability of, 282–83
sport camps and, 273
what it takes to get, 265–71
for women, 249–52, 274, 276–81
Collins, Kerry, 235
common sense, 3–4, 12, 111
communication:
   all-star athlete parents and, 84–85,
      87
   balance and, 64, 71
   coaches and, 51, 61, 85, 106, 114–15,
      118
   motivation and, 96
   player-player, 51, 61
   self-efficacy and, 41–44, 51, 54–55,
      57–61
   and turning girls and boys into great
      people, 242, 251
Community Action Program (CAP),
      260
community service, 75
competition, competitiveness, xiv–xvi,
      6–8, 11–12
   all-star athlete parents and, 81–82
   balance and, 68
   and changes in sports, 6
   college scholarships and, 265–67,
      272, 274, 282, 284
   development and, 7
   emotions and, 142, 157, 159
   and keeping winning and losing in
      perspective, 30
   mental game and, 189, 191
   motivation and, 88, 98, 101
   real winners and, 28–29
   and selecting right sport, 22
   self-efficacy and, 49

spurts and, 219–20
stalls and, 222, 225–26
and turning girls and boys into great
   people, 242, 244, 247–49, 253–54,
   256–57, 260
concussions, 172–76
Condé Nast Sports for Women, xv
Condensed Chicken Soup for the Soul
   (Canfield), 296
Congress, U.S., 249
Consumer Product Safety Commission,
   53
contrast effect, 151
contrast tense-relax exercise, 161
coolers and coolers on wheels, 129
Coopersmith, Seymour, 35
counselors, 73
cramps, 182
cross-training, 17, 22
curmudgeons, 102–3

David, Darin, 279
Deci, Ed, 93
Delaware, University of, 122
Dement, William, 138
Dempsey, Cedric W., 250
depression, 250–51
depressive realism, 198
development, 11, 34, 217–33
   all-star athlete parents and, 80–85
   coaches and, 7, 105, 110, 112
   cognitive, see cognitive development
   and empathy with your child, 13
   motivation and, 95
   nutrition and, 129–30
   quitting and, 236
   and selecting right sport, 16–19,
      22
   of self-efficacy, 39–40
   of skills and self-esteem, 7–8
   spurts in, 219–21, 234
   stalls in, 220–34, 236
   time needed for, 80, 83–84

difficult situations, handling of, 51
direct punishments, 149
discriminative modeling, 208–9
distant goals, immediate vs., 228
distant role models, 206–7
Doonesbury (Trudeau), 35–36
Douglas, Turhan, 211

eating disorders, 132–36
"Eating Disorders: The Most Lethal
    Psychiatric Disorder of Them All"
    (Huebner), 133
effort:
  coaches and, 106
  motivation and, 98, 101–2
  self-efficacy and, 37–38
eggs, 128
Ehrhart, Kevin, 169–70
elbow, Little League, 170
elbow guards, 186
electrolytes, 130–31
emotional conditioning, 147–56
  punishment and, 148–56
emotions, 140–63, 234
  all-star athlete parents and, 80–82
  balance and, 63–68, 70–71, 75,
    144–45, 156–57
  coaches and, 106, 141–42, 145–47,
    149–50, 152–54, 157–60
  experience and, 143
  fundamental attribution errors and,
    158
  instincts and, 142–47
  learning about, 145
  and needs of young athletes,
    12–14
  and not making the cut, 153–54
  and playing to the opposition,
    145–46
  positive affect and, 146–47, 150
  and power of optimism, 156–58
  and pride and happiness, 162–63
  role models and, 214

and selecting right sport, 16, 19,
    22–23
  self-efficacy and, 40–41, 43, 58–59,
    61, 142, 146–47, 150, 158
  stalls and, 222
  stress and, 154–56, 158–62
  temperament and, 143–45
  too little attention to, 67–68
  too much attention to, 66–67
  and turning girls and boys into great
    people, 242, 258
  winning and, 26, 140, 142, 147, 157,
    159, 166
  see also mental game
empathy, 295–96
  all-star athlete parents and, 80,
    82
  balance and, 74
  and turning girls and boys into great
    people, 254
  for your child, 12–14
encouragement, self-efficacy and,
    37–40, 43
equipment, 15
  and changes in sports, 4–6
  coaches and, 116
  motivation and, 94
  and selecting right sport, 17–18
  self-efficacy and, 44–46, 50,
    53–54
equivalency sports, 276–79
ESPN, 274
eustress, 221
executive abilities, 259
expectations, 33
  self-efficacy and, 49
  and turning girls and boys into great
    people, 243–44
experience, 16–18
  emotions and, 143
  learning from, 199–200
extended family, role models in, 205
extinction, 212–13

eye-hand coordination sports, leg
   sports vs., 21

failing, quitting vs., 237–38
families, family members:
  as role models, 203–5
  selecting right sport and, 18
fatigue, 47–48
feelings, *see* emotions
female athlete triad, 135–36
Ferguson, Bill, 25
Ferguson, Cathy, 77
Feshbach, Norma, 254
Feshbach, Sy, 254
Festinger, Leon, 93
Fields, Melissa, 237
fingers, jammed, 179
fish, 128
fluids:
  in injury prevention, 186
  nutrition and, 130–31
food, *see* nutrition; snacks
Food Guide Pyramid, 123–27, 130
football, xv, 10–11, 15–16, 32
  all-star athlete parents and, 78
  balance and, 65
  coaches in, 113
  college scholarships in, 275–76,
    279–80
  emotions and, 140–41, 143, 148, 152,
    154, 159–62
  injuries in, 164–65, 172, 176
  mental game and, 192
  quitting and, 235, 237–39
  role models in, 215
  and selecting right sport, 20–21
  self-efficacy in, 50, 53, 55–56
  stalls in, 222–23, 229–30
  and turning girls and boys into great
    people, 247, 257–59
foot-in-the-door technique, 211–12
Foreyt, J. P., 133–34
four-finger whistling, 309–10

French, Bob, 296
fruits, 127–28
fun, 286–91
  coaches and, 287–91
  playing for, 8, 93–94, 97
fundamental parental attribution
    errors (FPAEs), 158

Gahr High School, 76, 87
game, games:
  learning about, 80, 83
  love for, 89, 107
  schedules for, 118
  watching, 5, 118
Garden Grove Little League, 12
genetics:
  balance and, 63
  emotions and, 143, 158
  relation between athletic skill and,
    25–26, 31
  spurts and, 219
  stalls and, 221–22
Getting Better Every Day (Smith), 183
gifts, xi, 120
girls:
  advances in athletics for, xv–xvi,
    252–54
  college scholarships for, 249–52,
    274, 276–81
  female athlete triad and, 135–36
  in future, 259–62
  guy-superiority stereotype and, 251
  role models for, 252–54
  self-efficacy in, 38–39
  Title IX and, *see* Title IX
  turning them into great people,
    241–62
Glasgow Coma Scale, 177
goals, goal setting:
  distant vs. immediate, 228
  doable, 228–30
  stalls and, 227–30
Goldstein, Gabe, 233

golf:
    college scholarships in, 272, 277–78,
      280–81
    mental game and, 190, 193
    parental empathy and, 14
    and selecting right sport, 19, 21–22
    stalls in, 230
Granato, Cammi, 49
Grandma's Rule, 91–92, 99
Gregory, Gerry, 77, 229
Gretzky, Wayne, 49, 201–2, 239, 260
growth hormones, 20, 138
guy-superiority stereotype, 251
Gwinn, Tony, 49
gymnastics, 5, 9, 214
    balance and, 66
    college scholarships in, 276–78
    injuries in, 170, 178
    and selecting right sport, 20–22
    self-efficacy in, 50
    stalls in, 225
gymnast's wrist, 170

Hamm, Mia, 24, 89, 206–7
Handbook of Eating Disorders
    (Brownell and Foreyt), 133–34
happiness, 162–63
harassment:
    all-star athlete parents and, 84
    coaches and, 106–7, 109, 115
    complaint and review procedure for,
      302–3
    self-efficacy and, 54–61
    verbal, *see* verbal abuse, verbal
      harassment
    visual, 299–300
    youth athletic organization policy
      on, 299–303
Harry Potter and the Chamber of
    Secrets (Rowling), 34
harsh treatment, 3–4
Harvard University, 32, 63, 144
Harvard-Westlake School, 251, 293

hazing, 57–58
head, 161, 183–85
head count sports, 276–77, 279
Head Injury Prevention Community
    Action Program Plan, 185
Head Start, 75
height, xiv
    balance and, 65
    and selecting right sport, 20
    self-efficacy and, 50
    stalls and, 221–23, 225
    and turning girls and boys into great
      people, 245–46, 248–49
Held, Debbie, 129, 289–90
Held, Dick, 289–90
helmets, 183–85
Henrich, Christy, 133
hero worship, 202
herpes gladiatorum, 181
hockey, 5
    all-star athlete parents and, 78
    balance and, 66
    coaches in, 108, 113
    college scholarships in, 276–78,
      281
    development through, 7
    injuries in, 172, 176
    mental game and, 192
    nutrition and, 130
    role models in, 201–2
    and selecting right sport, 18, 21
    self-efficacy in, 40, 42–43, 49
    and turning girls and boys into great
      people, 259–60
Hoebel, Bart, 122
Hoggats, Eric, 176
Holmes, T., 155
home field advantage, 221
homeostasis, *see* balance
home snacks, 126–27
hormones:
    emotions and, 142, 145, 150–51
    growth, 20, 138

spurts and, 219
stalls and, 225
Horrigan, Joseph, 130
Hudnut, Thomas, 293
Huebner, Barbara, 133
hyperarousable temperaments,
    144

iatrogenic problems, 179–80
immediate goals, distant vs., 228
impetigo, 181
implement punishments, 149
indirect punishments, 149
individual sports, team sports vs.,
    21
infected wounds, 180–81
injuries, xi, xiv, 164–87
    all-star athlete parents and, 84
    balance and, 68, 71
    bleacher-related, 53–54
    and changes in sports, 5
    coaches and, 112–13, 165, 168–69,
        172–75, 177–78, 180, 186
    college scholarships and, 282–83
    emotions and, 156
    good technique and, 186
    lessons learned about, 165
    motivation and, 92, 94, 98, 102
    nutrition and, 135
    overtraining and, 167–70
    of parents, 12
    peculiar to young athletes, 170–72
    physical punishments and, 151
    prevention of, 182–87
    quitting and, 236–39
    real winners and, 27
    recognition and treatment of,
        166–82
    role models and, 214–16
    and selecting right sport, 17
    self-efficacy and, 44, 46, 48, 52–54
    statistics on, 53
    see also specific types of injuries

instant mental replays, 210–11
instincts, 142–47
intellectual competence, 257–58
Internet recruiting, 274
intramurals, 284
intrinsic rewards:
    emotions and, 146
    emphasizing, 99–100
    motivation and, 91–95, 97–100
    role models and, 213
    using highest level of, 99
irritability, 223–24
itching skin, 181

Jacobson, Leonore, 32–33
jammed fingers, 179
Jones, Charlie, 190, 193
Jordan, Michael, 235, 239
Jordan, Payton, 25
Journal of Psychosomatic Research,
    155
*Journal of the American Medical
    Association,* 184
judgmental thinking, 231–33
jumper's knee, 171

Kagan, Jerome, 63, 144
Kaiser Permanente, 172
Katona, Carly, 251
Kelly, Luke, 201
King, Billy Jean, 189
Klein, Bob, 77
knee, jumper's, 171
knee pads, 186
Kwan, Michelle, 24, 188–89, 195

lacrosse, 113, 196–97
language competence, 257
learning, xii, 80, 83
    about emotions, 145
    from experience, 199–200
    about injuries, 165
    motor, 212–14

learning (*cont'd*)
  and turning girls and boys into great
    people, 242–43
  see also academics
leg sports, eye-hand coordination
  sports vs., 21
Lemieux, Mario, 201
Let's Play Hockey (Blatherwick), 260
Life Span Development (Santrock), 24
Lindros, Brett, 172
Lipinski, Tara, 24
Little League, 5, 12, 24, 93, 141, 144,
  196, 217
Little League elbow, 170
Little League shoulder, 168, 170
Lobo, Rebecca, 49, 206–7
Lopiano, Donna, 249, 252
Los Angeles Times, 89, 152, 172, 176,
  235, 264, 272
lose, losers, losing, xiv–xv, 12
  all-star athlete parents and, 79, 83
  balance and, 63–64
  coaches and, 107
  emotions and, 140–41, 147, 159, 162
  keeping it in perspective, 29–31, 34,
    293
  knowing how to, 25
  mental game and, 191, 193, 196, 199
  motivation and, 90, 92, 101–3
  quitting and, 236
  real winners and, 25, 28–29
  and selecting right sport, 22
  stalls and, 223, 231–33
  and turning girls and boys into great
    people, 258
Love, Lisa, 272
Loyola High School, 30, 86, 169–70
Loyola Marymount University, xiv,
  65–70, 237
lumps, 180

Maccoby, Eleanor, 243, 246–47, 261
McFarland, Steve, 190

McGee, Chris, 25, 88
McGwire, Mark, 24, 202
Malone, Karl, 202
Maloney, Bryan, 273
Mandelbaum, Bert, 167, 170
Manning, Archie, 204
Manning, Peyton, 204, 206
Mano, Barry, 141
Mantle, Mickey, 24
marriage and family counselors, 73
Mary's Wager, 157
Maslach, Christina, 155
meat, 128
mental game, 188–200
  and learning from experience,
    199–200
  perfectionism and, 191–94
  role models and, 197, 214
  self-efficacy and, 191, 194–97
  stalls and, 233
  and success percentages among top
    competitors, 192–93
  and thinking like a winner, 190–91
mental mind games, 197–200
mental replays, instant, 210–11
metacognition, 189
Michigan, University of, 125, 250
milk, 128
Milwid, Beth, 253
momentum, 295
money, 5
  coaches and, 115, 120
  for college, 264, 275–81
  motivation and, 90–91, 93–94, 99
  and selecting right sport, 18
motivation, xiv, 8, 25–26, 31–32,
  88–105
  best, 93–94
  and changes in sports, 6
  coaches and, 88–92, 96–98, 101–3,
    105
  college scholarships and, 264
  mental game and, 196, 199

parent cheerleaders and, 100–101
quality moments and, 31
rewards and, 90–100
role models and, 100, 202
and selecting right sport, 17, 19–21
self-efficacy and, 40
spurts and, 220
stalls and, 226
successful athletes and, 32
and what not to say, 102–3
and what to say, 103–4
winning and, 26, 89–90, 96, 101–4
motor learning, 212–14
Mount St. Mary's College, xiv
mouth guards, 186
museums, 74–75

Naber, John, 229
Nash, Graham, xiv
Nash, Susan, xiv
Nater, Sven, xii
National Association of Collegiate
    Women Athletic Administrators,
    249
National Association of Intercollegiate
    Athletics (NAIA), college
    scholarships and, 264, 276,
    279–80
National Association of Social Workers,
    73
National Association of Sports Officials
    (NASO), 141
National Athletic Trainers' Association,
    172
National Collegiate Athletic Association
    (NCAA), xiv, 136, 194, 249–50,
    274–80
  college scholarships and, 263–64,
    266–70, 272, 274–79
National Council for Research on
    Women, 248
National Electronic Injury Surveillance
    System, 53

National Football League (NFL), 152
National Junior College Athletic
    Association (NJCAA), college
    scholarships and, 264, 276,
    280–81
national sports organizations, 307–8
Navratilova, Martina, 249
NCAA Eligibility Clearinghouse,
    267–68
neck, neck injuries, 161, 176–77
negatives:
  coaches and, 106, 117–18
  emotions and, 146–47, 150, 156
  mental game and, 195–96, 199
  motivation and, 95–98, 101–2
  quitting and, 239
  role models and, 203, 210–11
  stalls and, 227, 231
Newport Harbor High School, 176
New York Times, 250
Nichols, Chrystal, 152
Nike, 39, 70, 89, 250–51
Nolen-Hoeksema, Susan, 125, 250
Nomad, Jani, 204
Notre Dame University, 141
nutrition, 20
  balance and, 122–23
  developing healthy eating habits in,
    136–37
  eating disorders and, 132–36
  emotions and, 160
  fluids and electrolytes in, 130–31
  Food Guide Pyramid and, 123–27,
    130
  growing and, 129–30
  and making healthy choices easy,
    126–29
  motivation and, 91–92
  performance supplements and, 131
  to play well, 121–37, 139
  respect and, 125
  self-efficacy and, 44, 46, 137
  weight and, 131–36

nutrition (*cont'd*)
  worries about, 125
  see also snacks
nuts, 128

obesity rates, 65, 131–32
objectivity:
  all-star athlete parents and, 80,
    82–83
  and empathy for your child, 13
observation, role models and, 207–9,
    213
Office of Civil Rights, 250, 279
Olympics, xvi, 8, 25, 49, 77, 90, 117,
    133, 189, 196, 207, 214, 228–29,
    252, 260, 294–96
O'Neal, Shaquille, 206
On-line Scouting, 274
open gyms, 97, 284–85
optimism, 156–58
Optimistic Child, The (Seligman),
    156
Osgood-Schlatter disease, 171
osteoporosis, 135–36
overtraining, injuries due to, 167–70
overuse syndrome, 22

Pain In The Ass (PITA) parents, 292–95
Parcells, Bill, 190
parent cheerleaders, 100–101
parent intervention mandatory
    problems, 44, 52–61
parents:
  cautions for, 11
  coddling by, 67
  naïveté of, xii
  portrait of successful, 23–24
  pushy, 20
  roasting of, 286–87
  as role models, 204–5
  separating child's needs from, 11
  verbal and physical attacks
    exchanged by, 12

Pascal's Wager, 157
pastoral counselors, 73
past success, self-efficacy and, 37–38
patellar tendinitis, 171
peers, 11
  balance and, 63, 71–72
  development and, 7
  emotions and, 159
  quitting and, 237
  real winners and, 28
  and selecting right sport, 18–20
  self-efficacy and, 48–50, 56, 58
  spurts and, 219
  stalls and, 224
  and turning girls and boys into great
    people, 256–57
peer support programs, 73
Pelé, 24
Pennsylvania, University of, 135, 156
Pepperdine University, xiv
perfectionism, 191–94
performance supplements, 131
permanent retrograde amnesia, 174
permissive-indulgent parenting, 24
permissive-neglectful parenting, 23–24
personal coaching, 273–74
personality, college scholarships and,
    270–71
perspective, 291–95
  on winning and losing, 29–31, 34,
    293–95
Peterson, Marty, 101
photographs:
  coaches and, 116, 120
  and turning girls and boys into great
    people, 245–46
physical abuse:
  coaches and, 109, 112, 115
  punishments and, 151
  self-efficacy and, 44, 52, 54–55,
    57–58, 60
physical activities, health promoted by,
    8, 61

physical harassment, youth athletic organization policy on, 300
physical punishments, 148–51
  injury and pain from, 151
  reasons not to use, 149–51
physical restraint, 149
physiology, self-efficacy and, 37, 43
play, playing:
  for fun, 8, 93–94, 97
  loving to, 26–27, 29, 31–33, 70, 88, 90, 93, 147, 157, 239
  nutrition and, 121–37, 139
  to the opposition, 145–46
  to win, 101–4
playing time:
  all-star athlete parents and, 85
  coaches and, 108, 114
  self-efficacy and, 50
Pop Warner Football, 10, 24, 109, 172
positive affect, 146–47, 150
Positive Coaching Alliance, 110
positive listening, 96
positive rooting, 87
post-traumatic amnesia (anterograde), 174
potential, 27–28, 51
poultry, 128
practice, practices, 7, 25–26, 218, 294
  all-star athlete parents and, 84
  balance and, 66, 69
  and changes in sports, 4–5
  coaches and, 106–7, 111, 113–14, 118
  college scholarships and, 271
  emotions and, 142, 145, 148, 154, 156, 159
  fun at, 290–91
  injuries and, 166–69
  mental game and, 189, 191, 196
  motivation and, 90, 92, 95–97, 100–102
  quitting and, 236
  real winners and, 26

role models and, 211–12
schedules for, 118
and selecting right sport, 17
self-efficacy and, 42–43, 45–47, 50, 53, 56
spurts and, 220–21
stalls and, 223, 227–28, 233
and turning girls and boys into great people, 258–59
praise:
  coaches and, 106, 117
  motivation and, 91, 94, 100–101
  quitting and, 239–40
  role models and, 212–13
  spurts and, 220–21
  and turning girls and boys into great people, 257
Premack Principle, 91–92, 99
pride, 162–63
primary reinforcement, 91
Princeton University, 122
problems solving, self-efficacy and, 44–61
professional help:
  for abusive coaches, 112
  balance and, 71–74
  types of, 72–73
professional recruiting services, 274–75
progressive relaxation, 161
Prudential Healthcare and Troxel, 184
psychiatric social workers, 73
psychiatrists, 72
psychology, psychologists, xii–xiii, 250
  balance and, 63, 72–74
  and changes in sports, 6
  coaches and, 106–7, 112, 114, 119
  mental game and, 189, 194–95
  motivation and, 92
  nutrition and, 132
  real winners and, 27
  and selecting right sport, 23

psychology, psychologists (*cont'd*)
  self-efficacy and, 52, 55
  stalls and, 230
punishments:
  emotional conditioning and, 148–56
  role models and, 212–14

quality moments, quantity time and,
    31
quality parenting, 3–4
quickie head, neck, and shoulder
    relaxation, 161
quit, quitting, 235–40
  failing vs., 237–38
  how to, 239–40
  reasons to, 236–39
  when to, 236

Rahe, R., 155
Rassmussen, Bill, 274
reality, 7, 198, 264
  motivation and, 95–96
  and selecting right sport, 18, 20
reciprocal socialization, 85
record keeping, 230–32
recycling trash, 129
referees, xi, 15, 231
  all-star athlete parents and, 76, 79
  emotions and, 141–42, 152, 160
  fun and, 287
  motivation and, 102–3
  perspective and, 30–31, 291, 293
reinforced self-efficacy, 196–97
reinforcement, 91–92, 99
respect, 80–82, 84, 125
retrograde anmesia, 174
rewards, 234
  emotions and, 146, 150, 162–63
  hierarchy of, 91–92, 94–97
  intrinsic, *see* intrinsic rewards
  less is more with, 94–95
  motivation and, 90–100
  role models and, 212–14

setting up programs for, 98–100
  using least amount of, 99
Rigby, Cathy, 136, 225
Rivara, Dr., 184–85
Rochester, University of, 93
Rodin, Judith, 135
role models, role modeling, 12, 201–16
  all-star athlete parents and, 77,
      79–80, 87
  balance and, 74
  behavior and, 211–14
  coaches and, xiii, 105, 108, 201–4,
      206, 209–10, 212–16
  discriminative, 208–9
  distant, 206–7
  family members as, 203–5
  for girls, 252–54
  hero worship and, 202
  mental game and, 197, 214
  motivation and, 100, 202
  nutrition and, 136
  pain tolerance taught by, 214–16
  parental empathy and, 14
  parents as, 204–5
  physical skills and, 207–12
  power of, xiii–xiv
  and selecting right sport, 16
  self-efficacy and, 37, 39, 212, 215
  stalls and, 225, 228
  video playback and, 209
Rosenberg, Jay, 172
Rosenthal, Robert, 32–33
Ross, Dorothea, 61, 143
Ross, Sheila, 143
rosy lenses/cloudy lenses, 198
Rowling, J. K., 34
Royal, Darrell, 249
Runner's World, 135
Ryan, Bob, 93

safety:
  balance and, 63
  coaches and, 111

emotions and, 150
injuries and, 165, 183–87
motivation and, 94
and selecting right sport, 18
self-efficacy and, 52–54, 60
see also injuries
Safe Zone: A Kid's Guide to Personal Safety, The (Chaiet and Russell), 60
Salvation Army, 75
Santa Clara Swim Club, 224
Santrock, John, 24
Sapp, Warren, 235
Savage, Fred, xv
Sax, Linda J., 250
scaling skin, 181
Schmidgall, Jenny, 260
Schneider, Jack, 233–34
school counselors, 73
Science Bowl Competition, 253–54
Scott, Thomas, 122
season parties, 119–20
Seattle Special Olympics, 296
secondary reinforcement, 91
self-ameliorative efficacy, 195–96
self-efficacy, 11, 35–61, 283
  accepting, reflecting, and clarifying for, 41–43
  all-star athlete parents and, 85
  and buy, drive, supply, and monitor problems, 44–46, 50
  coaches and, 41, 43, 45, 48, 50–51, 53, 55–61, 112, 114
  definition of, 37
  development of, 39–40
  emotions and, 40–41, 43, 58–59, 61, 142, 146–47, 150, 158
  encouragement and, 37–40, 43
  as key to optimal performance, 191
  listening and watching for, 40–42
  mental game and, 191, 194–97
  nutrition and, 44, 46, 137

and parent intervention mandatory problems, 44, 52–61
physical fitness and lifelong health through, 61
quitting and, 236, 239
reinforced, 196–97
role models and, 37, 39, 212, 215
scaffold support for, 43–44
and selecting right sport, 19, 21
spurts and, 220–21
stalls and, 224–33
and take care of it yourself problems, 44, 50–52
and tough it out problems, 44, 47–49
trying and, 37–38
and turning girls and boys into great people, 242, 247–48, 251
Self-Efficacy: The Exercise of Control (Bandura), 37–38, 61, 191, 194–95
self-esteem:
  development of, 7–8
  and selecting right sport, 19
  self-efficacy and, 35–38, 61
self-fulfilling prophecy, 32–33
self-regulatory efficacy, 194–95
self-reinforcement, 91–92, 99
self-relaxation techniques, 158–62
self-serving bias, 198–99
self-talk, calming, 195–96
Seligman, Martin, 156
sexual abuse:
  nutrition and, 135
  self-efficacy and, 44, 52, 54–55, 58–60
  warning signs of, 59
sexual harassment, 106
  coaches and, 115
  youth athletic organization policy on, 300
shin splints, 171
shoulder, shoulders, 161
  Little League, 168, 170

siblings:
  as role models, 203–4
  self-efficacy and, 48, 56
Simers, T. J., 235
six-second quieting response, 160
skating, xvi
  development through, 7
  mental game in, 188–89
  parental empathy and, 14
skiing, xvi, 9, 24, 214
  self-efficacy in, 40
  stalls in, 222
skills, 265–67
  cognitive, *see* cognitive skills
  development of, 7–8
  genetics and, 25–26, 31
  role models and, 207–12
  self-ameliorative, 195–96
  self-evaluation of, 51
  self-regulatory, 194–95
  social competency, 255–59
skin, scaling or itching, 181
Skinner, B. F., 212
sleep, 137–39
Smith, Kathy, 182–83
Smoltz, John, 49
snacks:
  at home, 126–27
  nutrition and, 123, 126–29
  schedules for, 118
  for teams, 127–29
Snell Foundation, 184
soccer, xvi, 9–10, 239, 255
  all-star athlete parents and, 78
  balance and, 63, 68–69
  coaches and, 109, 115
  college scholarships in, 272, 277–78,
    280–81
  development through, 7
  emotions in, 142–43, 148
  injuries in, 169, 178
  motivation and, 88–90, 93, 95–96,
    98–100

  perspective in, 30–31, 292
  real winners in, 28
  role models in, 202–4, 206–7,
    212–13
  and selecting right sport, 20–22, 24
  self-efficacy in, 39–40, 48, 51
  sleep and, 138
  stalls in, 222–23
  and turning girls and boys into great
    people, 245–48, 259–60
social competence, 17
  future success predicted by, 254–59
  skills in, 255–59
  and turning girls and boys into great
    people, 242
socialization, reciprocal, 85
Social Readjustment Rating Scale, 155
social support:
  mental game and, 196
  for stress, 158–59, 162
social workers, 73
softball, 9, 252
  balance and, 64
  emotions in, 152–53
  self-efficacy in, 38
Southern California, University of
    (USC), 141, 211, 252
Spalding, Cary, 166
Special Olympics, 97, 296
Spelman, Cornelia, 60
Spitz, Mark, 8, 25, 77, 189, 224
sport camps, 97, 273
Sport Psychology (Wann), 232
sports:
  benefits offered by, 5, 11
  changes in, 4–6
  conditional rules of logic of, xii
  as double-edged sword, 11–12
  getting started in, 9–11
  hopping from one to another, 17
  professionalization of, 34
  reasons for participating in, 3–14
  selection of, 16–34

sports heroes, 206–7
Sports Illustrated for Women, xv, 260
Sports Illustrated 1999 Sports Almanac, 193
sportsmanship, 15, 32–33
all-star athlete parents and, 79–80
coaches and, 110
emotions and, 147, 162
motivation and, 100–101
real winners and, 26, 28
successful athletes and, 32
SportsPiks, 274
Sports Proactive Information Formative Feedback Inventory (SPIFFI), 110, 305–6
sprains, xi, 178–79
spurts:
in academics, 32–33
in development, 219–21, 234
secrets of, 219–20
self-efficacy and, 220–21
stalls:
in development, 220–34, 236
and frustration with performance, 223–24
goal setting and, 227–30
judgmental thinking and, 231–33
secrets of, 224–27
self-efficacy and, 224–33
short-circuiting of, 230–31
temporary, 222–23
Stanford University, xii–xiii, 25, 138, 155, 157, 205, 237, 243, 254
Steffes, Kent, 88, 207–8
Stern, Stacie, 237
Stevenson, Mary Piety Slaughter, 157
Stockton, John, 206
strains, 178–79
stress:
coping with, 158–62, 195–96
emotions and, 154–56, 158–62
mental game and, 195–96

positive appraisal of, 195
quitting and, 239
stress fractures, 166–67
stretching, 182–83
Strug, Kerri, 202, 214
success percentages, 192–93
Sundgot-Borgen, J., 134–35
superstitious behavior, 197
Supreme Court, U.S., xv–xvi
S-W-E-N head, 161
swimming, 8–10
balance for, 62–63
and selecting right sport, 21
stalls in, 224, 229
symbolic rewards, 91

take care of it yourself problems, 44, 50–52
Tamborland, William, 124
Tampa Bay Buccaneers, 235
Taufaasau, Adrien, 176
team managers, 118–19
team rosters, 118
teams, teammates, xiv, 218
all-star athlete parents and, 82, 86
balance and, 64, 67
burnout and, 233
and changes in sports, 4–6
coaches and, 105, 107–9, 113–14, 116–17, 119–20
college scholarships and, 271–73, 281–84
communication between, 51, 61
emotions and, 140–41, 143–46, 148, 153–54, 157, 162
fun and, 288–91
getting assigned to, 107–9
mental game and, 196–99
motivation and, 89, 96, 98, 100–104
perspective and, 291, 294–95
photographs of, 120
quitting and, 235–38
real winners and, 28–29

teams, teammates (*cont'd*)
  role models and, 206, 209, 211–12,
    216
  and selecting right sport, 17–18, 21
  self-efficacy and, 42–43, 50–52,
    55–58
  snacks for, 127–29
  social aspects of, 17
  spurts and, 219–20
  stalls and, 222–23, 225–27, 232–33
  successful athletes and, 32
  and turning girls and boys into great
    people, 241–42, 245–48, 251–54,
    256–58, 260
team sports, individual vs., 21
T-ball, 85–87, 231–32
temperament, 143–45
tennis, xiii–xiv, xvi, 11, 13, 214
  balance and, 67
  college scholarships in, 272, 276–78,
    280–81
  mental game and, 189, 192
  motivation and, 101
  and selecting right sport, 21
  stalls in, 222
  and turning girls and boys into great
    people, 241
Texas, University of, 249
They Call Me Coach (Wooden), xiv
thinking:
  balance and, 64–65, 68–71
  judgmental, 231–33
  too little attention to, 68–69
  too much emphasis on, 70
Title IX, xv–xvi, 242
  college scholarships and, 274, 279
  and women in sports, 248–52, 260,
    262
Toppel, Curt, 30–31
Toppel, Haldis, 30
tough it out problems, 44, 47–49
toys, 91–92, 94
track, 22, 87, 166, 252

training, 17
  and changes in sports, 6
  injuries and, 167–70
  and participating in sports, 3–4
  and selecting right sport, 22
  self-efficacy and, 48
traveling, 118
  in author's van, 297–98
  and changes in sports, 5–6
  and selecting right sport, 18
  self-efficacy and, 44–45
Trevino, Lee, 193
trophies, xi, 119
  emotions and, 162–63
  motivation and, 91–92
  spurts and, 220
  and turning girls and boys into great
    people, 245–46
Trudeau, Garry, 35–36
*Two Sexes: Growing Up Apart, Coming
  Together* (Maccoby), 247, 261

umpires, *see* referees
United States Youth Volleyball League
  (USYVL), 109
USA Beach Volleyball, 88
USA Hockey, 172
USA Youth Volleyball Association
  (USAYVA), 24
use-overuse injuries, 54

vegetables, 127
verbal abuse, verbal harassment:
  coaches and, 109, 112
  emotions and, 141
  self-efficacy and, 44, 54–57, 60–61
  youth athletic organization policy
    on, 300
  see also yelling
verbal punishment, 149
Victims of Crime Resource Center, 60
video playback, 209
visual harassment, 299–300

visualization, 195–96
volleyball, xiv–xvi, 9, 10, 253, 285
    all-star athlete parents and, 76, 87
    coaches and, 109, 116
    college scholarships in, 272, 276–81
    emotions and, 144–45
    motivation and, 88
    nutrition and, 121–22, 129, 135
    real winners in, 28–29
    role models in, 202, 205, 207–8,
        210–11
    and selecting right sport, 19, 21
    self-efficacy in, 37, 39, 51
    stalls in, 229
    and turning girls and boys into great
        people, 242, 247–48, 256

Walker, Pam, 272
walking on, 284
Walton, Bill, xii
Wann, Daniel, 232, 238–39
Washington Medical School, University
    of, 184
water:
    in injury prevention, 186
    to play well, 130–31
    self-efficacy and, 44–46
water skiing, 214
Weglarz, Cindy, 237
weight:
    balance and, 65
    emotions and, 144
    nutrition and, 131–36
    stalls and, 225
weight training, 168
West Coast Baseball School, 273
What Makes Winners Win: Thoughts
    and Reflections from Successful
    Athletes (Jones), 190, 193
whistling, four-finger, 309–10
White, Burton, 271
Whittredge, Matthew, 215
Williams, Natalie, 242

Wilstein, Steve, 188
win, winners, winning, xiv–xv, 11–12,
    15, 293–96
    all-star athlete parents and, 80, 85
    balance and, 63–64
    being winners and, xii
    coaches and, 24–31, 107, 117
    college scholarships and, 282
    early success shown by, 31–32
    emotions and, 26, 140, 142, 147, 157,
        159, 166
    in every game, 29
    as made, not born, 33–34
    mental game and, 190–91
    motivation and, 26, 89–90, 96, 101–4
    and participating in sports, 3
    perils of playing to, 101–4
    perspective and, 29–31, 34, 293–95
    quitting and, 236
    and selecting right sport, 22, 24–34
    stalls and, 223–24, 231–33
    and turning girls and boys into great
        people, 253, 257–58
Windham, Rhonda, 252
Wisconsin, University of, 101
withholding punishments, 149
women, see girls
Women's National Basketball
    Association (WNBA), xvi, 10, 49,
        206, 281
Women's Professional Volleyball
    Association, 167
Women's Sports & Fitness, xv, 260
Women's Sports Foundation, 38–39,
    249, 260, 275, 279
Wooden, John, xiii–xiv, 197, 208–9
Woods, R., 254
Woods, Tiger, 21–22, 190
Working with Men: Professional
    Women Talk About Power,
    Sexuality and Ethics (Milwid), 253
Workman, Carla, 237
workout facilities, 284–85

wounds, infected, 180–81
wrestling, 181
wrist, gymnast's, 170
wrist guards, 186

Yager, Eileen, 122
Yale Guide to Children's Nutrition, The (Tamborlane), 124
yelling:
  all-star athlete parents and, 76–77, 79
  coaches and, xiii, 107, 111–12
  emotions and, 141–42, 149–53
  motivation and, 102–3
  at referees, xi
  see also verbal abuse, verbal harassment
yogurt, 128
young athletes:
  focusing your energy to help, 16–17, 85–87
  goals for, 19
  portrait of successful, 24
  types of problems for, 44–61
Your Body Belongs to You (Spelman), 60